Learning and the Development

of Cognition

Learning and the Development of Cognition

By Bärbel Inhelder, Hermine Sinclair, and Magali Bovet

TRANSLATED BY SUSAN WEDGWOOD

Harvard University Press, Cambridge, Massachusetts, 1974

Originally published in French as
Apprentissage et Structures de la Connaissance
(Paris: Presses Universitaires de France).

© 1974 Presses Universitaires de France.

Acknowledgments

Collaborators (former Assistants at the University of Geneva, École de Psychologie et des Sciences de l'Éducation) :

Monique Anthonioz, licenciée en psychologie
Odile Baggio, licenciée en psychologie
Tuat Bang, licenciée en psychologie
Christiane Challandes, licenciée en psychologie
Monique Chollet-Levret, licenciée en psychologie
Catherine Darbellay-Fot, licenciée en psychologie
Robert Maier, docteur en psychologie
Pierre Mounoud, docteur en psychologie
Ioanna Papandropoulou, licenciée en psychologie
Marie-Paule Prot, licenciée en psychologie
Madelon Robert, licenciée en psychologie
Adina Sella, licenciée en psychologie
Colette Simonet-Rossel, licenciée en psychologie
Henriette Stoll-Jeanrichard, licenciée en psychologie

    The authors wish to express their thanks to Professor François Bresson, Directeur à l'École Pratique des Hautes Études (Paris), for his critical reading of the manuscript. The precious collaboration of Mrs. M.-L. Ravex-Nicolas, who typed and edited the French text, is gratefully acknowledged. Thanks are also due to Géo Romy, who made the drawings.

    The research described in this book and the English translation were made possible through the generous financial support of the Ford Foundation. The authors also wish to express their gratitude to the Fonds National Suisse de la Recherche scientifique for its continuing support of research in cognition.

Contents

Foreword

BY JEAN PIAGET

I am most pleased to introduce a book that concerns a topic so near to my heart. The novelty of the findings, the clarity of the theoretical interpretation, and the sometimes even excessive caution of the conclusions enable the reader to separate clearly the experimental results from the authors' theoretical tenets. Thus the importance of the detailed experimental descriptions can be appreciated even by those who, unlike myself, do not share the epistemological point of view which oriented the authors' research.

The authors' first intention was to add to our knowledge of the cognitive development of the child by investigating not simply the already well-established structural characteristics of each stage, but the mechanisms which assure the transition from one level to the next. In this respect, the most important conclusion that appears to follow from the findings reported in this book is that there exist very few cases where a primitive structure becomes directly differentiated into substructures (resembling the way in which natural numbers dissociate into negative and rational numbers). On the contrary, the different subsystems, which at first develop in a relatively independent but partially parallel way, interact in a complex manner, resulting in further elaboration, principally of the structural features common to the substructures in question.

For example, development of the concept of measurement does not stem from a simple application of the number concept to that of continuous quantity, but, just as the number concept is derived from a synthesis of class inclusion and seriation, the concept of measurement is derived from a synthesis of displacement and additive partitioning. These two developments were already known to be parallel, but partially independent. The new findings reported here indicate that the structurations bearing on discontinuous quantities (which lead to logico-arithmetical operations) are far more independent from those bearing on continuous quantities (which lead to infralogical or spatio-temporal operations) than was previously supposed. But the independence of these two subsystems (of which the discontinuous subsystem is always slightly more advanced than the continuous) does not exclude the possibility of applying constructive strategies from one to the other: certain methods of repeated one-to-one correspondences, strategies based on transitivity and possibly on commutativity operations can apparently become common to both subsystems when genuine interactions take place between the two types of thought-structures. The authors' results suggest that the interactions between substructures give rise to the elaboration of common forms of equilibrium rather than to simple transfers or direct derivations. The learning experiments made it possible to study such interactions in detail from two points of view: sometimes (and far more frequently than one would have predicted) the provoked interactions between the two types of subsystems result in disequilibria, since a factor particular to one of the subsystems acts as a disturbing, not a facilitating, element on the other; at other times, the provoked interaction has a favorable effect in that certain assimilations, which may be partly reciprocal or partly one-way, influence thought processes that can become common to both substructures and thus play the role of logical intermediaries.

The examples of disturbances are numerous and they are of exceptional interest to me because they show the ubiquity of the equilibration processes, whose necessity derives from the various accommodations implied in each new application of a conceptual scheme. These disturbances give rise to two different types of compensation. First, the subject can try to accommodate two schemes one to the other, even though their applications may appear incompatible (several chapters describe the conflicts which arise between ordinal and numerical correspondences). Second, these compensatory accommodations may generate the idea of possible compensations between different properties of the same objects, as happens when children predict that, when put into identical containers of water, a small heavy object will make the water rise to the same level as a large light object—the children imagine a possible compensation between weight and volume.

I am most interested in the different ways in which the subjects react to disturbances that elicit feelings of contradiction (in other words a disturbance of which the subject has become aware), but that do not lead to complete compensations. Such disturbances give rise to compromise solutions: for example, when asked to construct with matches a straight line of the same length as a zigzag model, the child who still feels that equality of length has to correspond both to equality of number and coincidence of the end points of the lines may break some matches into bits so as to eliminate what he sees as a contradiction. Interestingly, such compromise solutions seem to appear only in infralogical problems or in situations where there arises a conflict between what is continuous and what is discontinuous, i.e., where several heterogenous dimensions have to be taken into account. In problems of logic or number, the subject either allows contradictions, because he is not yet sufficiently aware of them, or overcomes them immediately because he apprehends them clearly.

Different types of transition mechanisms occur in those situations where the interactions do not lead to disturbances, but where the logical mediators referred to above allow gradual progress. The most interesting example is that given in Chapter 7, where class inclusion training has an effect on conservation concepts (and vice versa, but less noticeably). In this case, it is not the class inclusion concept as such which influences notions of conservations, but the quantificatory aspect of the inclusion operations ($A < B$ if $B = A + A'$) which acts as a logical mediator facilitating the quantification necessary for conservation. Since conservation concepts require a quantification accompanied by bidimensional or tridimensional compensations which are almost metrical (although genuine measurement is not involved), whereas the quantification inherent to the class inclusion concept implies only the notion of equal or unequal cardinality, it is possible that the favorable influence of class inclusion training on conservation is also due to another logical mediator which might be called "commutability" in the sense of a very general form of commutativity.* This commutability accompanies the inclusion concept and must play a role in the quantification inherent in conservation concepts (the simple displacement of two parts, one with regard to the other, does not change the total).

The findings pertinent to the mechanisms of development are thus highly informative as are, in my opinion, those more directly concerned with questions of learning—despite the authors' extreme caution when trying to interpret these with regard to the learning process. Certainly, their training procedures were designed within the framework of a specific theory of cognitive development. However, in spite of this introduction of experimental aspects derived from studies with a certain epistemological interpretation (no experimental procedure can be free of such aspects), the findings provide new information since three different effects of training were obtained: a total absence of progress; an acceleration of what would have been the acquisition process with the experimenter's intervention; or a momentary regressive effect, i.e., the arousal of conflicts which may be resolved at varying rates. No learning occurs when the subjects are too young for there to be a possibility of extending the zone of assimilations to the new factors introduced in the training and then linking it to that of the concept to be acquired. A positive effect is obtained when the aspects introduced by the training constitute an assimilatory instrument (a logical mediator), but this is also dependent on the subject's developmental level, i.e., his competence (in the almost embryological and psychogenetical sense that Waddington gives to this term). Finally, there is the case where the new factor gives rise to a disturbance and necessitates a compensatory accommodation between conceptual schemes which are still heterogenous; this regulation is possible only if the subject is competent to effect the new construction.

These different effects of the training have a direct bearing on

* The $AB = BA$ commutativity is a reciprocal substitution concerning the conservation of the whole, insofar as the whole is independent of the order. In "commutability" A changes its position only as regards B, but when the subject understands that he is dealing with a simple displacement he concludes that therefore $A + B$ is conserved: in this sense, "commutability" constitutes a possible commutativity.

theories of cognitive development, but they are also important for theories of learning, since experimental factors have been introduced with a view to modifying development. What in fact is learning? According to Hull and his school, it is the unique source of development. For others it constitutes a modification of development. The results described in this book raise a fundamental objection to the first conception of learning in that, under identical experimental conditions, the introduction of new factors has different effects according to the individual developmental level of the subjects. In most cases, the training procedures resulted in the transition from one level, or sublevel, to the next and such transitions were noted most frequently with subjects who at the pre-test were slightly more advanced than the others. Regressions were rare and not one of importance was observed. Evidently, development cannot be reduced to a series of bits of learning and the notion of competence has to be introduced as a precondition for any learning to take place. As regards the second conception of learning, the conclusions that can be drawn from the findings are more limited and the authors' caution more justified. The importance of their results lies in the discovery that all the observed modifications of thought patterns consist either in developmental accelerations or in conflicts. The latter first play a disturbing role (with just a few momentary regressions) and then a constructive role leading to new acquisitions which continue to conform to the known developmental trends. Moreover, these accelerations result in stable acquisitions, mostly confirmed by the second post-test. However, the authors are right in refusing to draw general conclusions concerning the value of other training methods. Some of these could well lead to behavior modifications which do not conform to the usual reaction norms (to use another biological term). Others may lead to developmental effects similar to those described in this book, although, unlike the latter, they do not incorporate training factors whose constructive character was inferred from earlier cognitive experimentation.

The authors had no intention, in this volume, of analyzing and comparing the different types of training methods. In my opinion, three questions remain open as regards the theoretical implications of the various results of these different training methods. First—and it is surprising that this problem has been so rarely discussed—one must ask whether the progress obtained is stable or whether, like many things learned in school, it disappears with time. Second, one must determine whether the observed accelerations are accompanied by deviations from the general development trend. Certain educational experiments concerning didactic methods of teaching the quantification of class inclusion have been repeated by psychologists, who have shown that such training may result in a disturbance of the subject's understanding of the relationship between the complementary classes A and A'. The final and most important question concerns the necessity of checking whether progress obtained independently from natural development can serve as a basis for new spontaneous constructions or whether the subject who passively receives information from the adult will no longer learn anything without such help, as was so often the case with traditional methods of education. The importance of the training methods described in this book lies in the fact that the subject's creative capacities are encouraged rather than suppressed.

Briefly, I think that B. Inhelder, H. Sinclair, and M. Bovet have discovered and proved more than they themselves are willing to admit, and I am convinced that their readers will share my delight with their often surprising and always informative studies, which constitute a distinct advance in our knowledge of both learning and cognitive development in general.

Learning and the Development of Cognition

Introduction / Cognitive Development and Learning Theory

It may be surprising that Genevan developmental psychologists have seen fit to add yet another book on learning to the large number already published, particularly since Jean Piaget and his colleagues have frequently emphasized the subject's own activity rather than his reactions to environmental stimuli as being important for the acquisition of knowledge. Within the conceptual framework of developmental psychology and genetic epistemology, the role played by external factors in the acquisition of knowledge remains secondary. In his article "Apprentissage et connaissance" Piaget (1959) clarified his position on the subject of learning by introducing a distinction between learning *sensu lato* and learning *sensu stricto*, the former embracing cognitive development as a whole and including the latter, which is always subordinate.

The question arises whether experiments on learning have a place within the psychological and epistemological framework. The authors believe that work on learning is not only compatible with developmental psychology, but that it may help to overcome some of the difficulties encountered in cognitive learning theories. All theories of learning are constructed from postulates about the nature of knowledge and hypotheses on cognitive development. There have been many recent attempts to adapt what are basically stimulus-response theories of learning to the increasing complexity of experimental findings, but they may in fact be impossible if the difficulties turn out to be inherent in the fundamental epistemological tenets of such theories.

The postulates and hypotheses that Piaget has elaborated in his later theoretical work may not be diametrically opposed to the stimulus-response learning theories, but they are nonetheless very different from empiricist views on learning. A brief theoretical description of the epistemological background of the Genevan learning studies is thus necessary to explain our choice of problems and our experimental procedures.

For Piaget, scientific epistemology is concerned with the way knowledge has grown during mankind's history and increases ontogenetically. The task of developmental psychology is to study the constructive process in the child and to formulate hypotheses about the laws of development. Here we will discuss Piaget's theory under three headings, which highlight the main features of his epistemological position.

PIAGET'S EPISTEMOLOGY

THE BIOLOGICAL APPROACH TO THE STUDY OF
COGNITIVE DEVELOPMENT

Piaget qualifies his developmental epistemology as "naturalistic, but not positivist" and regards cognitive acts as the prerogatives of organisms equipped with structures which can both assimilate and accommodate, i.e., which enable the organism to deal with its environment in certain ways. This basic biological principle cannot be reconciled with theories in which mental development is regarded as being perpetually modifiable, such as the learning theories which maintain that, given the right conditions and correct training methods, developmental rate can be accelerated at will, and "errors of growth" avoided.

Ever since his first work on the *Limnaea stagnalis*—research that coincided with his first observations of nascent intelligent behavior in his own children—Piaget (1936) has regarded the adaptation of an organism to its environment from a point of view as far removed from Lamarckian empiricism as from Darwinism. He believes in a third possibility, intermediate between the theory of characteristics acquired under pressure of the environment and the theory of mutations. His observations and experiments concerning the morpho-

2

genesis of a type of snail, the *Limnaea stagnalis*, confirmed this possibility. This snail is transported at birth, or during its period of growth, from still to disturbed waters, and its development undergoes hereditarily stable modifications resulting in forms found only in certain turbulent regions of big lakes. This variation cannot be explained solely by the pressure of the environment, but depends on what Piaget has called kinetogenesis: during growth (approximately six months) the snail's foot displays an increasing motor activity so as not to be washed off the rocks by the waves; this activity (traction of the columellar muscle) results in a widening and shortening of the shell.

According to Piaget, a similar mechanism must account for the first cognitively adaptive behaviors of the child. Adaptive behavior results from functional assimilation of pre-existing biological structures. The first signs of mental activity are those behaviors through which new elements are incorporated (i.e., assimilated) into genetically preprogrammed structures, such as sucking objects other than the nipple. This assimilatory behavior is repeated and extended to a variety of objects, and, since it has to be slightly modified (i.e., accommodated) to each different object, it leads to sensorimotor recognition of objects and events. Herein lies the origin of the first "knowing" activities of the subject. The different exploratory activities such as sucking, looking at, touching, become coordinated. An object can be assimilated to several such knowing activities (which Piaget calls schemes) at the same time: for example, it can be looked at, touched, and shaken. Schemes thus assimilate each other and from their integration stem new activities which were not, as such, part of the hereditary organic equipment.

This biological interpretation, in terms of action schemes, assimilation, and accommodation, is radically different from theories which account for development by associative or conditioning mechanisms. The latter are essentially based on links between events and objects, imposed on the subject by his external environment, whereas Piaget regards the subject as interacting with his environment, integrating new elements into already existing structures and gradually elaborating new structures.

Using the same biological approach, Piaget has studied the development of reasoning. Before the onset of the first coherent thought-systems (around the age of seven) there is a period of "intuitive" thought (the preoperatory period) during which the mechanisms that assimilate new material into already existing structures have a distorting effect on the child's apprehension of reality. At that time, cognitive schemes are only partially coordinated, and frequently lead to contradictory judgments. The development of conservation concepts is characterized by behavior that seems to show that young children are sometimes impervious to experience. One of the many examples is the way children base a quantity judgment on only one dimension, e.g., on the length of the "sausage" made by rolling out a ball of modeling clay, totally ignoring its width (or vice versa). Such behavior can hardly be explained by empiricist or associationist theories, which account for the learning of new behavior by the impact of external cues. Genevan research on memory (Piaget and Inhelder, 1968) showed that cognitive schemes remain active over a period of time without external stimulation and that they may be altered through their own functioning during development. There has to be a reason for the retention of certain cues and not of others when all of them are easily perceptible and, as can be shown experimentally, are in fact perceived. It is more than probable that organizational processes are at work favoring the assimilation of certain elements.

This organizing activity is difficult to understand in behaviorist-empiricist terms. Admittedly, modern behavior theorists accept the existence of unobservable factors intervening between the stimuli and the responses and acknowledge that this intervention is the contribution of the organism itself. But curiously, many authors limit this intervention of the organism to the dynamics of needs and their reduction, and refuse to invoke an organizational competence to account for new behavior.

Many modern learning theorists appear to ignore the recent discoveries of biologists and continue to interpret behavior as if there were a distinct separation between the genotype on the one hand and the various phenotypes on the other; when accounting for new behavior acquired through learning, they refer only to phenotypes.

By contrast, Piaget's work (his explanatory hypotheses in zoology as well as in psychology) shows a striking concordance with modern trends in biology (e.g., Dobzhansky's work) and embryology (e.g., Waddington's work). His important work *Biologie et connaissance* deals with this convergence.

Modern biologists no longer make a clear distinction between genotypical and phenotypical mechanisms, recognizing that they interact. The genome appears to have its own laws of organization (or regulatory mechanisms): it adapts to the environment by innovations in response to the stimulations or tensions produced by changes in its environment. Embryological research has shown that the organism must have reached a certain level of "competence," or sensitivity, to specific environmental stimuli before it can respond to them. This new approach no longer stresses the role of external stimuli, but concentrates on the internal competence or sensitivity of the organism: stages of embryonic development are characterized by changes in competence.

This correspondence between biological and psychological findings and theories can hardly be coincidental; if it indicates more than a superficial resemblance, then the existence of a continuity between basic biological mechanisms and cognitive competence must be accepted. This is in fact Piaget's position (1967): "It is not possible to understand psychological development without considering its organic roots."

Though such statements have been interpreted as a return to "innate" ideas, this is not Piaget's intention. On the contrary, he emphasizes the subject's interaction with his environment and the gradual elaboration of cognitive schemes which follow this interaction. The transitions from one stage of knowledge to the following stage can thus be seen as phenotypical transformations which account for modifications in the subject's cognitive competence. Cross-sectional studies have revealed the existence of a succession of different stages of sensitivity to certain stimuli in the course of intellectual development. In the learning studies, the children are presented with situations designed to activate their cognitive scheme and their search for new combinations. Encounters with such deliberately enriched situations may incite the children to invent novel ways of assimilating

5

their informational content and may thus result in a higher level of competence.

From the interactionist point of view, the relation between the knowing subject and the object to be known is one of interdependence; it is impossible to dissociate the "knowing subject" from the "knowable object."

Piaget holds that objects can only be known by a series of successive approximations constructed by the subject through his various activities. In a way, the object constitutes an ultimate frontier which the subject seeks to approach but never completely reaches. Furthermore, the subject's instruments of knowledge are biological in origin and thus come within the scope of the physical world. However, they extend beyond biology in that they lead to the construction of systems of relationships which in turn enrich both the cognitive and physical realities that are to be known.

From this point of view, it becomes impossible to hold that objectivity can be reached spontaneously and immediately. On the contrary, in order to be objective the knower must be constantly active in elaborating structures and in decentering or changing his focus of attention. From the very beginning this elaboration takes place in two complementary but interdependent directions: one leading to the development of logical and mathematical forms of knowledge and the other to the knowledge of objects and their spatial, temporal, and causal relationships. Between these two poles there exists a whole range of intermediate types of knowledge.

Experience plays an important part in cognitive development, but this part varies according to what is being learned. For example, understanding that equivalent numerical quantities can be arrived at by the repeated establishment of one-to-one correspondences is not the same as relating the displacement of water to the volume of an immersed object. A number of misunderstandings and controversies regarding the contribution of learning *sensu stricto* to the acquisition of knowledge and its possible acceleration are due to a lack of understanding of Piaget's distinction between "simple" and "reflective" abstraction (1950). In the case of simple abstraction, on the one hand, the person extracts from the object only those properties that are relevant to a specific bit of knowledge; in this case the information comes from the object itself, even though what a subject notices in the object depends on how he can relate the various factors through his own logical activities. In the case of reflective abstraction, on the other hand, the person derives the information from a coordination of the mental actions that he carries out on the object. Neither these actions nor their coordination originates in the object, whose role is simply that of a support. This distinction between the two types of abstraction is important for any theory concerned with learning, and the role of simple abstraction should not be confused with that of reflective abstraction.

In the experiments dealing with concepts of physical quantities (Piaget and Inhelder, 1941) which are referred to in this book, it is necessary to make a distinction between what the subject learns from the point of view of the form, or the logical-mathematical framework of the concepts (reflective abstraction), and what he learns from the point of view of the content of the concepts (simple abstraction). For the very young child there is almost no distinction between form and content in this sense, and it is impossible for an observer to separate the two in the child's behavior; with development, however, the distinction becomes clearer. Even in the inclusion problems whose solution seems to require only pure logic, the child's reactions at the elementary stages clearly depend to a large extent on the contentive aspects of the different experimental situations in which the formal aspects of the problems are presented.

In the learning experiments the training techniques are essentially aimed at the acquisition of the formal aspects of knowledge; they emphasize the role of reflective abstraction and bear on operations. However, they are always related to the acquisition of specific concepts, whose content varies with each experiment.

DEVELOPMENTAL CONSTRUCTIVISM

One of the main problems dealt with in this book is the study of the transition from one stage of cognitive development to the next through investigations into the mechanisms that promote the growth of knowledge. This problem has its natural place within the framework of constructivist epistemology. Previous Genevan research has already clarified the concept of developmental stages; it has revealed the constant order of their succession and the hierarchy of the under-lying structures that become integrated with development according to certain laws. The major concern of the present work is to discover the processes of integration that result in novel types of behavior; these will be studied by means of a method based on learning.

The basic hypothesis of developmental constructivism (Piaget, 1960) postulates that no human knowledge, with the obvious excep-tion of the very elementary hereditary forms, is preformed in the structures of either the subject or the object. This runs counter to the neonativist trend among psychologists and particularly rationalist psycho-linguists who maintain that linguistic competence and, by extension, cognitive structure are not only present at an extremely early age, but hereditary. Furthermore, a child's cognitive perform-ance is supposed to be affected by various factors which may produce deformations, depending upon the perceptive strategies adopted by the child (Mehler and Bever, 1967). While it is difficult to refute a nativist position when one is dealing with nonobservable structures, we would agree with Piaget (1968) that such an interpretation does not help to solve any problem; all it does is to transfer the question from the psychological to the biological level by formulating it in terms of biological development. Classically, the behaviorists, from their epistemological point of view, believe knowledge to be either a functional copy or else a direct reflection of reality. They are not particularly interested in the mechanisms involved in the construc-tion of intelligence. If these mechanisms are referred to at all, they are regarded as an extension of those mechanisms which are supposed to determine the more elementary types of behavior, such as condi-tioning or associative connections. The more advanced functions are thus reduced to those of a lower order of development. In the con-structivist view, by contrast, no such reduction is intended; the con-tinuity between the functions of the lower levels and those of a more advanced one is maintained. Piaget proposes a single explanatory principle to account for the transformations that lead to novel types of behavior that characterize each successively more complex stage of development. This principle is based on regulatory or autoregulatory mechanisms which account for both the structure of the different cognitive stages at various levels of complexity and their mode of construction.

The operatory structures studied in the learning experiments are those that underlie the child's capacity to compensate for or to cancel out disturbing factors, both those which result from changes in the environment and those which are the indirect product of the child's own growth. The operatory systems constitute a particular case of more general regulations at the psychological levels and at organic levels. They represent an extreme or ideal case since their reversible character allows for perfect compensation or cancellation. All actions can be annulled by corresponding inverse actions; mentally, even physical modifications can be compensated for by a reciprocal transformation.

The particular interest of such a constructivist conception for learning theory lies in the suggestion of a complete continuity between the psychological regulatory mechanisms that have a temporal dimension and the systems of atemporal logical operations.

Study of two types of psychological phenomena can throw light on this continuity. First, much information can be gained from the study of the structural characteristics of those levels of cognitive development that occur in between the major stages, in particular during the preoperatory period that marks the transition between sensorimotor and operatory intelligence. Second, detailed analysis of the moments of access to higher level knowledge (wherever they occur) may provide insight into the regulatory mechanisms themselves.

Some important information on the preoperatory period has recently been obtained by Piaget and his collaborators, who have taken an interest in not only the negative, but also the positive aspects of these modes of thinking. A certain semilogic is present in the child of four to five, culminating in the acquisition of concepts of qualitative identity and functional dependency (Piaget et al., 1968a and 1968b). Both these concepts result from the transposition on a representational plane of sensorimotor action schemes, which are the source of all subsequent cognitive acquisitions, logical operations as well as knowledge of the physical world.

It is much more difficult to obtain insight into the regulatory mechanisms themselves. All regulations that take place during biological growth and psychological development are constructive processes and not just a means of preserving an already attained equilibrium; and all constructive processes imply compensating activities that counteract disturbances in equilibrium.

In the constructivist approach, great importance is given to the functional similarity between biological and psychological regulatory processes. Waddington compares embryological development, which he views as the product of an epigenesis, to a mathematical construction. According to Waddington, a state of equilibrium or homeostasis results from a process of equilibration or homeorhesis. If, during embryological development, external factors bring about a deviation of normal growth, regulatory mechanisms guide the interaction between organism and environment in such a way that the disturbance is compensated for and the original direction of growth is resumed. These adjustments also have a temporal dimension, a "time talley," ensuring optimal speeds of epigenetic assimilation and organization.

Such biological constructivist ideas are very similar to psychological constructivism. The stages of psychological development are also considered to be regulated by endogenous equilibrating mechanisms whose contents and resulting structures are not preprogrammed by hereditary factors.

Starting from such premises, we could study the dynamic processes of learning through the observation of cognitive construction when it takes place in conditions that, within the limits of our knowledge and real life restrictions, provide the child with optimal possibilities of interaction with the environment.

RESEARCH ON LEARNING AND LOGIC FROM THE PERSPECTIVE OF THE CONTROVERSY BETWEEN EMPIRICISM AND CONSTRUCTIONISM

During the first few years of its existence the Center of Genetic Epistemology—the combination of studies on child development and epistemology—took up a somewhat polemical position as regards logical empiricism. Empiricists have substantially modified their theories since the work of the Vienna Circle. As has been stressed by one of their representatives, Apostel (1965), a careful distinction must be made between empiricist methodology, which is heuristically useful, and its postulates, which in many respects do not seem to stand up to critical analysis.

A great deal of current learning research in the United States is based on an empiricist type of epistemology. Surprisingly enough, some extensions of this theory are also found in contemporary French psychology (Le Ny, 1967).

Some members of the Center of Genetic Epistemology (Jonckheere, Mandelbrot, and Piaget, 1958) have studied children's readings of experimental situations at various levels of cognitive competence, and found that at all levels (perceptual, sensorimotor, or conceptual) children never simply record the facts, but always make inferences from the situations presented to them. These subjective inferences go beyond the directly observable phenomena and are based on systems of coordinated actions, which Piaget believes are at the origin of prelogical and logical thought.

Members of the Center (e.g., Smedslund and Morf, 1959) have also studied the relations between logic and learning, and raised the question whether it is possible to acquire knowledge without an active process of structuration. In other words, can learning occur independently of the learner's logic, or on the contrary, is his logic always involved in any sort of learning?

Apostel (1959) attempted to give a theoretical definition of the various types of learning by contrasting their common characteristics with other types of behavior. His axiomatization of learning is based on a point of view similar to that of Harlow, who adopts the idea of "learning sets," and maintains that the basic process of all learning is that the subject "learns to learn." Apostel also believes that every learning situation is facilitated by previous ones. During his successive learning experiences, the child elaborates methods of learning, and it is in these methods that Apostel finds an implicit logic, whose origins he, like Piaget, believes are to be found in the infant's sensorimotor activity.

Matalon (1959), in an experiment dealing with the above problem, shows that success at learning random and alternating sequences depends upon the age of the subject. The younger children first focus their attention on their own successive actions and manage only very progressively to take into account the sequences that were actually presented. These results cast doubt on the empiricist postulate as expressed by Le Ny (1967): "Psychological activity becomes incorporated into lasting structures, i.e., relationships of contiguity and frequency that are observable manifestations of the essential objective relationships which govern the environment." Whatever the degree of regularity of the objectively observable phenomena, they are always organized by the human learner, and his constructive activity is governed by a sort of logic inherent in the actions through which his observations are assimilated, and therefore interpreted.

A number of learning experiments were also carried out in the Center. These consisted in presenting the subjects with typically empiricist learning situations, in which predictions could be checked against the actual outcome of some experimental action.

Certain Genevan cross-sectional studies on conservation and class inclusion can be presented in the form of empiricist learning situations.

In the conservation of weight experiments (a concept that has both a logical and a physical aspect) Smedslund (1959) asked children to make predictions about the weight of one of several initial balls of clay after it had been made into a sausage or divided into smaller pieces. As soon as they had given their answer, it was checked by putting the quantities of clay on the scales, so that the children could see whether the weights were equal or unequal.

The very nature of the quantification of inclusion problem made it more difficult to devise a learning experiment based on the principle of checking predictions against experimental facts. In one of the versions designed by Morf (1959) a certain quantity of liquid was poured into small plastic beakers (some green, some yellow) and the children were asked whether there was more liquid in the green beakers or more liquid in the plastic beakers. After giving their opinion they were asked to check it, using large measuring glasses. In this way, the logical problem of the greater extension of a class B compared to either of its subclasses A and A' is translated into physical terms.

These two experiments gave clear results: while it was possible to help the children acquire some knowledge of physical conservation by having them repeatedly weigh the object after each change in shape, it was not possible, or only partially so, to get them to understand a corresponding logical composition, i.e., transitivity of weight. Outside the experimental situation, however, children generally either succeeded or failed at both problems. This suggests that both problems require operatory structures of the same level of complexity. Smedslund's later work (1961) has shown that knowledge acquired by means of the above experimental technique is lost more rapidly than when it has been learned by techniques which require more active participation on the part of the child.

The results of the learning experiment on logical inclusion are even clearer: the "checking method" had practically no effect on the acquisition of the relevant logical structure. On the other hand, a rapid try-out of another procedure suggested that if the child were given certain exercises bearing on class intersection, the results were slightly better.

Such experiments (see also Gréco, 1959, and Wohlwill, 1959) clearly showed that while readings of experimental situations can to a certain extent facilitate the understanding by means of a simple abstraction of some of the physical properties of objects, such readings do not ipso facto lead to the formation of operatory structures. As Piaget hypothesized, these structures, particularly in the case of logical and mathematical operations, appear to be the product of the subject's own coordination of actions, which is carried out by means of a process of reflective abstraction.

These experiments were not designed to throw light on the possible existence of prestructures from which the operatory systems derive, nor on the processes through which coordinations are formed. Nevertheless, it is only through the observation, or reconstitution, of the learning process that it will be possible to decide whether it is an operatory (or semioperatory) structuration or a stocking of information (Gréco, 1959). The psychological, rather than the epistemological, issues involved in learning concern the dynamic processes, and the experiments discussed in this volume were designed to elucidate two different problems:

What are the psychological mechanisms that are necessary and sufficient for a complete structuration of operatory systems?

Furthermore, what are the laws of learning that at each developmental level account for the acquisition and modification of knowledge?

UNSOLVED PROBLEMS

Piaget's creation of genetic epistemology has resulted in many important psychological discoveries. An interdisciplinary approach is of inestimable value, since it helps to decide which questions to ask, both about the history of human knowledge and about cognitive development. Moreover, it can suggest ways to formalize psychological constructs. The study of different geometries ranging from, e.g., intuitive forms of topology to Euclidian structures, can lead to a study of how these concepts are constructed by the child. The convergence between Bourbaki structures and Piaget's descriptions of the child's cognitive structures in terms of algebraic logic has oriented our study of certain concepts of conservation, and more generally, of the development of natural thought. The parallel study of epistemology and of child development enriches both disciplines, and the relationship is never one-sided. There is no question of simply posing mathematical or logical problems in psychological terms: often it is only a psychological investigation that suggests a convergence and the possible use of a formal model. Piaget's approach to problems of development has resulted in many new findings, but mainly it opens up new ways of studying many still unsolved problems, such as those mentioned below.

The findings of developmental psychology have shown the existence of a succession of stages in cognitive development, but little is as yet known about the mechanisms of transition from one major stage to the next and about the passage between two successive substages. In order to account for the transition mechanisms, structural and dynamic models have to be combined.

14

DEVELOPMENTAL LINKS BETWEEN CONCEPTS

The problem of the developmental links between the various concepts is evident in the "décalages," i.e., nonsynchronous acquisitions of concepts which are based on the same operatory structures. The various conservations provide the most striking and well-known example of such "décalages." Learning experiments may provide a satisfactory method of analyzing the reasons for "décalages," since the presentation of situations that highlight the similarities between the various conservation concepts can lead to the observation of conflicts between the child's organizing activity and his incapacity to adapt this activity to particular objects.

CONNECTIONS BETWEEN DIFFERENT TYPES OF COGNITIVE CONSTRUCTIONS

It seems heuristically useful and theoretically legitimate to make a distinction between the various types of knowledge, such as logical-mathematical, spatial-temporal, and kinetic, or physical knowledge. The developmental and psychological links between these different types of knowledge have not yet been sufficiently explored and the use of methods involving learning is one way of studying the problem.

Concepts do not develop in closed systems but are in constant interaction with each other—even though for methodological reasons they are studied separately—and it is this interaction that accounts for the child's progress during learning experiences. Consequently, the "décalages" between the various arithmetical, geometrical, and physical concepts of conservation are of particular interest for the study of learning, as are the relationships between logical structures, such as class inclusion, and the types of structures that underlie the concepts of geometrical and physical conservation. One of the basic problems of all research into learning is to discover how knowledge in one field is extended to other closely related fields. Traditionally, this is the problem of transfer. From our point of view, it is preferable to think in terms of the extension of fields of operativity; and this implies a careful analysis of the differences and similarities between the various types of cognitive constructs.

THE DYNAMIC FACTORS OF DEVELOPMENT

Logical analysis of cognitive structures and of their order of appearance has shown that intellectual development proceeds in a certain direction. This analysis, however, is not sufficient to explain the dynamic processes that are responsible for mental development. Although the dynamics of development can never be observed directly, it is conceivable that learning studies can contribute to the understanding of these processes.

The main stages of cognitive development have been revealed by cross-sectional studies. Attempts to express this order by means of formal models (Apostel, Grize, and recently Wermus) have resulted in a number of hypotheses about the developmental links between these structures. But cognitive development, which is one expression of biological growth, is essentially a temporal and causal process. A logical and structural system of reference can provide an explanation for the orderly succession of the phenomena, but not for their gradual change, and even less for the dynamic and causal factors of progress. Biologically speaking, the causal factor is found in the regulatory mechanisms that govern the rate of development; are similar mechanisms at work in the establishment of cognitive structures?

These considerations raise several questions for research into cognitive learning: can appropriate learning conditions help to shorten the intervals between successive stages in cognitive development? If so, will this type of learning accelerate development in a uniform manner? In other words, are the different systems of operative schemes that characterize a given moment in cognitive development equally sensitive to environmental pressure, or to experimental training techniques? Or do the same exercises have different effects at the various stages and substages of development?

These questions have both theoretical and practical importance, particularly for education. Unfortunately, they cannot be answered conclusively without submitting children to a substantial number of experiments, which might well affect development. We decided upon a far more restricted, but more positive approach. From our knowledge of the course of development and from a number of preliminary studies, we established experimental conditions which appeared most favorable for cognitive development. The processes of cognitive change and integration that are expressed in the child's responses during the actual training lend themselves to a detailed qualitative analysis, rather than to a quantification of results.

INTERACTION OF DEVELOPMENTAL FACTORS

The importance of autoregulatory or equilibration mechanisms for biological development has already been mentioned. According to Piaget, these mechanisms also intervene in cognitive development, not as a third element to be added to maturation and learning, but as an equilibrating factor that governs the interactions between the others.

It is difficult to apprehend the essentially dynamic mechanisms of equilibration by means of cross-sectional studies of children of different age groups. In learning studies, a child's successive cognitive acquisitions in a given experimental setting can be followed over a certain period of time, and transition processes can therefore be observed more closely. Environment—sociocultural and linguistic—is another factor in development, and its interaction with maturation and learning may also be governed by equilibrating mechanisms. Although this was not our main interest, two studies relevant to this topic will be discussed. An intercultural study compares the ways in which children of very different environments elaborate the cognitive structures as they are expressed in various task performances. In addition to the demonstration of different speeds in the acquisition of concepts, such studies can throw light on the question whether the same cognitive structures can be acquired in different ways or whether, even in cases where there appear to be certain deviations in development, basically the operatory system is always constructed in the same way.

One of the ways in which environment influences cognitive development is through language. A number of investigators subscribe to the view that nonconservation judgments are simply due to language difficulties and explain the acquisition of conservation by the fact that the child grasps conservation once he has mastered the language sufficiently to be able to understand the instructions and explain his reasoning. This problem can also be approached through learning experiments. The extensive modifications of the child's reasoning processes that characterize his acquisition of conservation concepts were shown to be accompanied by a change in his use of quantifying terms. By training nonconserving children to use higher level quantifiers, the influence of language in this particular area can be investigated.

THE METHOD OF CRITICAL EXPLORATION

Experimental methods have been devised by empiricists to study learning. From their point of view, the basic mechanisms of learning are to be found in the laws of contiguity and frequency. The subject is supposed to establish associative links between certain events. The nature of these associations is explained by the spatial or temporal contiguity of the situations, whereas their force stems mainly from the frequency. Essentially, the subject's "internal" activity is limited to a capacity to generalize (which has yet to be adequately explained), and this capacity presupposes the ability (again only partly explained) to distinguish objects and events that are different from those that are equivalent. The subject also intervenes insofar as his needs and their reduction influence the strength of the association. These laws are thought to be very general and to underlie all types of acquisition (motor, cognitive, etc.) both in man and in animals. Many learning theorists abide by the empiricist principle of studying only observable behavior and have tried to develop a methodology which can reveal the associative mechanisms in their pure form. To ensure that all subjects start the experiment from the same "baseline," the proposed tasks are usually of a type not encountered in real life. However, in any but the simplest tasks, phenomena appear which cannot be explained solely by the basic laws, and for which complementary mechanisms (such as mediation) have to be invoked.

The Genevan epistemological position leads, in a sense, to a reversal of values. Mechanisms that are considered complementary by associationists are our main concern. We tend to regard the basic associationist laws as constituting special cases of more general laws of biological and psychological functioning. This totally different emphasis calls for a different methodological approach.

Since Piaget's "clinical method" (now known as "the method of critical exploration") has proved to be most appropriate for the study of cognitive development in general, this was the technique employed (with certain modifications) in our learning studies.

This method has undergone a number of changes in the course of the investigations carried out by Piaget and his collaborators. Initially, Piaget conceived of the interaction which occurs in the acquisition of knowledge in terms of interindividual relationships and viewed intellectual growth in terms of progressive decentrations of the child's point of view. In order to explore their reasoning, he talked with children and tried to follow the often intricate patterns of their thoughts, taking as a model the "clinical method" in which the psychiatrist tries to discover the roots of a patient's beliefs and to explore the nature of his pathological imagination. At this time (1927), Piaget was interested in studying the child's conception of phenomena which were not directly accessible to experimentation, in the strict sense of the term, such as the movements of the stars and the clouds, and the origin of names and dreams. The authenticity and psychological coherence of the children's beliefs could only be checked in the course of a conversation guided so as to reveal the reasons for their interpretations of reality and for the changes in their thinking.

Later, Piaget (1936, 1937) studied his own children in their early years, combining naturalistic observation with the observation of their behavior in specially contrived situations. These observations revealed a different aspect of the interactionist principle: the first cognitive conquests, e.g., object permanency, appeared as the product of a relationship between the subject's activity and the physical world.

Finally, Piaget combined the "clinical method" with experimentation. In the study of the different concepts of conservation and in that of the problems of classes and relationships, the children were invited to give their judgments about phenomena they could produce themselves with objects they were allowed to handle. The experimental method has to be varied according to the specific problems to be investigated. The type of interrogation is therefore not quite the same for problems of a logical nature as for those dealing with physical phenomena. In studies on the conservation of weight and volume (Piaget and Inhelder, 1941), for example, the child is given the opportunity of comparing what he has predicted will happen with what actually happens in certain situations. By contrast, for the first concepts of conservation of mass (Piaget and Inhelder, 1959) and for logical quantifications, the correctness of a judgment cannot be checked experimentally but becomes self-evident if the reasoning process is consistent. To elaborate such concepts, the subject must, on the one hand, adjust his judgments to the reality of observable phenomena and, on the other, ensure that they are not contradictory. From the age of four, this coordination is greatly facilitated when the children find that their own judgments are contradicted by others. In the experimental situation, such contradictions are introduced by the experimenter.

The learning studies reported in this book deal mainly with the acquisition of the different conservation concepts. Some of these are closer to physical concepts, whose adequacy can be experimentally checked; others are of a more logical nature. However, all conservation concepts depend on the prior acquisition of object permanency.

In order to understand that an object continues to exist, even though it has partially or completely disappeared from the field of vision, it is sufficient for a child to be able to recapitulate its displacements. By contrast, in order to understand that a given quantity remains the same despite a series of changes in the shape or position of the objects, the child must realize that such changes are reversible, i.e., that these transformations can be annulled.

To make sure that a child has really grasped the notion of the conservation of a given quantity under certain transformations, it is necessary to choose experimental situations where the changes in shape or position represent problems that cannot be solved by perceptual evaluation alone, but require logical reasoning in the broad sense of the term. Indeed, studies of the role of perceptual evaluation in conservation of length problems have shown that many five-year-old children are able to make a correct visual estimation of the respective lengths of two parallel sticks with their ends unaligned; many of these children, however, cannot make correct judgments of lengths in a situation where two identical sticks are first laid out immediately above each other in exact alignment, and then one of them is pushed slightly to one side so that it protrudes at one end. In this latter situation, the children have difficulty in understanding that the displacement has not modified the respective lengths of the sticks. Similarly, these children do not understand that a class B is larger than one of its subclasses A or A', since they have not yet grasped the principle of logical inclusion. However, once again, the experimental situation has to be constructed carefully to avoid apparently correct solutions based on lower-order strategies or perceptual mechanisms.

Genevan research into the development of concrete operations has been designed not only to study how the judgments vary according to the subject's age or level of cognitive development, but also to discover the arguments which accompany such judgments. In fact, it is often these arguments that reveal the nature of the intrinsic obstacles the child's thought encounters. In the case of conservation concepts, quantitative invariance can be justified by several well-known arguments (identity, reversibility by cancellation, and compensation); but the mention of only one of them is not a sufficient indication of the existence of conservation since it may express only a partial coordination of operative schemes. Consequently, different situations must be presented for each concept. The child is also encouraged to give several arguments so that the experimenter can assess their consistency and stability in order to determine the degree of completion of the child's operatory structures.

It has often been objected that such a method of investigation allows the individual experimenter too much freedom. It is certainly true that this method yields reliable data only if the experimenter has acquired a very thorough theoretical background and mastery of the interviewing technique. It is essential that he be fully aware of the various hypotheses which can be formulated about the child's reasoning and of the different techniques that can be used to test these hypotheses. He must know how to observe and listen to the child and how to react to responses, which will frequently surprise him. In fact, the more unexpected the child's responses, the more productive we consider the experiment to have been. It is only when an inventory has been made of as many types of responses as possible for the different developmental levels that a selection can be made from among the situations, types of questions, and counter-arguments which seem to be the most relevant and instructive. The analysis and interpretation of responses relies partly on what is called "vérification sur le vif." This fundamental feature of the critical exploration method requires that the experimenter constantly formulate hypotheses about the children's reactions from the cognitive point of view, and then devise ways of immediately checking these suppositions in the experimental situation.

It is not easy to explain in detail how the various experimental situations were designed. Each time research was started in a new area, it was necessary to proceed by trial and error, aided somewhat by intuition. Rather than programming our research in detail beforehand, we always allowed ourselves a more or less lengthy period of exploration during which it was essentially the responses of the children that guided us. No adult is able to reconstruct his own cognitive development. Development is an unknown territory that can only be charted by studying children, whose actions and ideas will continue to surprise us.

Each new study in cognitive development brings its own discoveries, and they frequently point to gaps in our previous knowledge. To take but one example, the first studies of the preoperatory period mainly revealed the negative features of this stage. The recent work of Piaget and his collaborators (1968), however, highlights some of the positive features of this period. These can be formulated in terms of a "semilogic" resembling a system of one-way mappings. Since our initial learning techniques were set up before these discoveries, it is evident that they present some shortcomings in this respect. Research in cognitive development is constantly evolving and forms a whole; it cannot be divided into separate sectors. Since the methods of studying intellectual growth depend on our overall knowledge of cognitive development, they are also subject to modifications, although the main characteristics outlined above remain the same.

The present work on learning is based on a number of prior studies, each of which provided results calling for a particular method of analysis.

Initially, Piaget was primarily concerned with the developmental factors that characterize the changes in the child's explanations of the world around him (Piaget, 1926, 1927). These explanations were categorized according to their common characteristics and particular attention was paid to transitional types of responses. The early research showed up three parallel lines of development: (1) from an initial adualism, i.e., a confusion of the result of the subject's own activity with objective changes in reality, to a differentiation between subject and object; (2) from a magical and phenomenological interpretation of the world to one which is based on objective causality; (3) from an unconscious focusing on one's own point of view to a decentration which allocates the subject a place in the world alongside other persons and objects. These three lines of development were interpreted in functional terms: as assimilation and accommodation in reference to the child's interaction with the physical world, or as socialization when applied to his interaction with other people.

Later, in the study of the operations that underlie the system of scientific concepts related to number (Piaget and Szeminska, 1941), measurement (Piaget, Inhelder, and Szeminska, 1941), physical quantities (Piaget and Inhelder, 1941), and logical classes and relations (Piaget and Inhelder, 1940), the need was felt for structural models to explain the processes involved in the formation of these concepts. In Piaget's view (1949, new edition in press) the most suitable of these models is that of the algebraic "grouping," which he defines by analogy with mathematical groups, although the former have certain constraints when compared with the latter. The "groupings" of classes and relations, together with their infralogical equivalents, help to specify the necessary and sufficient conditions for the existence of a particular structure of reasoning. Moreover, they serve to describe the characteristics of the end product of a process of growth as a particular system of mental operations. Such systems form levels of equilibrium, and provide the foundations for further cognitive development. The logical and infralogical systems of concrete thought prolong the action structures of the sensorimotor period, but since they are subsystems of a more extensive higher-order structure, they also pave the way for the mathematical group structures of the period of formal thought.

The experimental work on operatory structures and the theoretical attempts to express the findings in terms of formal models were carried out simultaneously. The search for formalizations was heuristically important for the experiments, and the theoretical constructs constantly benefited from the experimental data. The children's remarks provided us, for example, with explicit expressions of reasoning based on reversibility: "I know I've still got the same clay, I've only got to make the sausage again in my head and it'll make exactly the same ball as before," etc. The "grouping" and "group" models bear a close resemblance to the process of natural thought.

This insight into the course of mental development and the successive structures must be supplemented by a better understanding of the modes of transition between one stage and the next, and of the mechanisms which govern the connections and developmental links between specific structures. The clinical method had proved appropriate for following the course of the child's reasoning; the above problems, however, called for a more directive experimental method. Training procedures appear particularly suitable for this purpose since they provide the child with optimal opportunities for interaction, both with the physical environment and with the experimenter.

CONSTRUCTION OF TRAINING PROCEDURES

Although our learning experiments vary considerably, they nevertheless all have certain characteristics in common, which will be described briefly below.

We started with the idea that under certain conditions an acceleration of cognitive development would be possible, but that this could only occur if the training procedures in some way resembled the kind of situations in which progress takes place outside an experimental set-up. If such training procedures could be constructed, it would then be possible to analyze both the favorable conditions and the children's reactions and thereby to observe in some detail the different transitions and the dynamics of progress. Since no pre-established training methodology was available, we let ourselves be guided by what was already known about very general trends in development and about the types of difficulties young children encounter when they try to reason about the problems presented in earlier cross-sectional research.

Cognitive development results essentially from an *interaction* between the subject and his environment. In terms of successful training procedures, this means that the more active a subject is, the more successful his learning is likely to be. However, being cognitively active does not mean that the child merely manipulates a given type of material; he can be mentally active without physical manipulation, just as he can be mentally passive while actually manipulating objects. Intellectual activity is stimulated if the opportunities for acting on objects or observing other people's actions or for discussions correspond to the subject's level of development.

The design of training procedures should also take into account the fact that new structures are formed through the integration and coordination of already existing schemes. Such uncoordinated schemes are not at all comparable to incorrect pieces of information; they should not be regarded as errors which need to be eliminated by suitable training. For example, the young child's idea that a given quantity of liquid increases when poured into a narrower glass is based on a preoperatory, ordinal type of reasoning (a difference in level is always taken to indicate a difference in quantity). Such reasoning cannot, and for that matter should not, be eliminated by coercion. The information that a child selects as the basis for a deduction may be inadequate for the correct solution of a specific problem, but the choice effected is characteristic of a certain stage in development which cannot be omitted. Consequently, in the training procedures disturbing factors of a situation should not be masked and faulty judgments should not simply be refuted; rather, the inadequate schemes should be used as a foundation for further constructions.

This idea that schemes, or preconcepts, should be coordinated and integrated to new structures links up with another point, which is that of the existence of *necessary stages* of development. This hypothesis implies the existence of certain major paths leading to the acquisition of knowledge. Training procedures should steer the subject in the right direction, even if this results temporarily in incorrect reasoning. Variations are, however, possible, and it is certainly not true that for each acquisition there is only one predetermined construction process.

The typical responses for each age group and the general order of acquisition of the various concepts studied in the learning experiments were already known. Moreover, the time interval between the acquisition of one concept and that of another could be estimated. However, both the ages of acquisition of the concepts and the intervals between them were influenced by sociocultural and, more especially, educational factors.

Previous research had revealed some of the intrinsic characteristics of young children's reasoning which hinder the acquisition of specific concepts; other such characteristics became apparent in the course of the preliminary investigations which preceded the learning experiments.

On the basis of the above findings and hypotheses, experimental situations were designed in order to elicit the use of the different modes of reasoning presumed to play a part in the concept under study. By presenting the child with a range of problems, each calling for a different scheme, we hoped to arouse a conflict in the child's mind between these schemes that would lead to new types of coordination between them. In experimental situations it is possible to control the introduction of various problems, whereas in everyday life the same problems are encountered in a more random and less coherent manner. However, the training procedures do not resemble "programmed learning." On the contrary, experimental situations that might almost automatically elicit the correct answers were avoided. "Programmed learning" runs counter to the idea that for true learning to occur the child must be intellectually active.

Although strict programming of the learning situations was avoided, the training procedures still concerned particular concepts and remained inside their field of application. In real life, concept formation occurs in a less ordered way, and the different notions influence, contradict, or support one another. Little is known about these relationships, and an attempt was made to investigate the links between, for example, physical and logical qualifications.

In every learning study the selection of the subjects is important and varies according to the objectives of the research. Sometimes it is sufficient to choose children who have not yet acquired the relevant concept. This may even be done by selecting children of a particular age at which previous research has shown the concept is not yet acquired. For our purpose, stricter requirements were necessary, and the selection tests were sufficiently elaborate to allow the elimination of subjects who were on the verge of acquiring the concept.

On the other hand, our selection criteria did not take into account differences in the socioeconomic status of our subjects, in the degree of schooling, or in IQ. All learning experiments were carried out in the Genevan state nursery and primary schools, attended by children from a fairly wide range of sociocultural environments. The younger subjects, however, tended to come from the less privileged classes, since in Geneva children from well-to-do families often attend private nursery schools. All the children were considered of average or superior intelligence by their teachers. Since our aim was not to carry out a differential study, but rather to gain a better understanding of the general processes involved in the development of a child's reasoning, variations in socioeconomic status or in IQ were not taken into account.

The selection tests also served as part of the pre-tests. Since it was felt necessary to determine as precisely as possible the level of each subject, i.e., how far he was from acquiring the relevant concept, the pre-tests became gradually more elaborate and included: (1) detailed questioning allowing the division of the subjects into several groups according to their level; and (2) at least one task dealing with a closely related notion, generally one acquired at the same age.

Evaluation of progress in the fundamental notions after training involves a comparison with acquisitions outside the experimental situations. Once a truly operatory acquisition has taken place, there is no regression (except in pathological cases). In the task situation the stability of the notion is apparent from the subject's behavior when the experimenter attempts to make him change his mind, and from the validity of his arguments.

The fundamental concepts derive from coherent systems of mental operations; consequently, they cannot be separate entities. Grasping one of them implies the understanding of others. Acquisition of these concepts takes place very gradually and opens the way to new discoveries.

In order to assess the operatory value of the progress obtained after training, the post-tests have to satisfy certain requirements.

1. At least two post-tests are necessary, the second of which serves to check the stability of the progress. On the other hand, they should not be conducted too far apart because the age groups studied have a very rapid rate of development. A compromise had to be found, based on the general data on the order of substages and time intervals between the acquisitions of notions. An interval of several weeks appeared suitable.

2. The post-tests should include a more stringent replication of the pre-tests. The objective of the latter is to determine the potentiality of a subject's reasoning, an objective which requires a certain flexibility in the method of questioning. Since in the post-tests the aim was to assess the stability of the acquisitions, greater use was made of counter-arguments.

3. The post-tests should also include at least one problem involving material different from that used in the pre-tests and training procedures: for example, a class inclusion pre-test with different subclasses of flowers was followed by training with subclasses of fruit and then completed by a test with subclasses of animals.

4. As far as possible the post-test should include a question that requires a type of answer different from those called for by the situations of the pre-test and the training procedure. For example, if during training repeated one-to-one correspondence has been used to suggest judgments of equivalence, then the post-test should deal with the constitution of equal or unequal quantities of liquid. However, it is essential to make sure that the post-test problems are of the same level of difficulty as the concept dealt with in the training procedure. In some cases, this was checked by interviewing a group of children who had already acquired the concept but who had not been given training.

5. The post-test—again as far as possible—also should include a problem whose solution requires a notion related, but not identical to that treated during the training. For example, in the conservation post-tests, questions about transitivity were asked (Smedslund, 1959),

and in class inclusion post-tests questions about intersection were added.

ANALYSIS OF RESULTS

Analysis of results, like training technique and selection and testing of subjects, has to correspond to the objective of an experimental study. Cognitive learning research directed toward measuring the progress of certain groups of subjects or toward comparing different training methods requires systems of scoring and statistical elaboration of the data. Such analyses are not suitable for apprehending the dynamics of the developmental processes. Consequently, we devoted much time and space to a qualitative analysis of the progress of individuals, and to a detailed comparison of the different substages observed in the pre-tests with those obtained in the post-tests. Nevertheless, tables are presented to show the global proportions of success and failure, and the individual's responses to the various tasks.

A close examination of everything that occurs during the training sessions is essential for our purpose. Lengthy extracts from protocols* are therefore included to illustrate the different types of responses. From those it appears that the learning situations often suggest different strategies to different children—a reassuring finding, since we did not want to enforce one particular type of learning. It is always possible that such enforced strategies are foreign to a child's way of thinking and therefore quite unsuitable for the study of the dynamic processes of natural thought.

A detailed comparison of the results of the two post-tests is also important. Rapid and stable acquisitions, regressions, and delayed progress are interesting phenomena that become even more meaningful when they are compared, for each individual, to pre-test results and behavior during training.

Finally, as our studies progressed and results were obtained, both the training procedures and the tests were improved, since each new experiment profited from the experience gained. Unfortunately, this type of learning experiment is costly; it is a lengthy undertaking, the

* *Translator's note.* The word "protocol" is used throughout in the sense of "interview record" or "interview sequence," depending on context.

selection of subjects is often laborious, and subjects sometimes do not complete the full number of training sessions.

Despite the difficulties inherent in this type of learning study, the results may point the way to an application of developmental theory in the field of education. Piaget's theory and the extensive experimentation attached to it can be applied to educational practice only in a very indirect way, as many educators have been forced to admit. Although learning studies certainly do not close the gap between cognitive psychology and classroom practice, they constitute a link in the chain that may eventually unite the two.

1 / Concepts of Conservation of Continuous Quantities: From Observation to Inference

INTRODUCTION

Our first learning experiments dealt with the acquisition of concepts of conservation of physical quantities. The cross-sectional studies had already clarified some of the epistemological and structural aspects of concepts of conservation in general and of conservation of physical quantities in particular. A grasp of these concepts indicates the presence of an underlying system of mental operations that is characterized essentially by two forms of reversibility, inversion or cancellation on the one hand, and compensation of reciprocal relationships on the other. The particular psychological interest of conservation tasks lies in the fact that they elicit judgments and arguments expressing these two forms of reversibility.

From the logical point of view, an operation changes state A into state B, leaving at least one property invariable and allowing for a return from B to A which cancels the original change by means of an inversion. Psychological investigation shows that children support their correct conservation judgments by the following three types of arguments: reversibility by inversion, e.g., "You've only got to pour the liquid back into the first glass and you'd see there's still the same amount to drink"; reversibility by compensation of reciprocal relationships, e.g., "The liquid is higher but the glass is thinner, it amounts to the same thing"; and additive identity, e.g., "We haven't added or taken anything away." It is legitimate to hypothesize that concepts of conservation of physical quantity are generated

31

by logical systems of mental operations which, as Piaget has already shown, are isomorphic with the structures of logical "groupings."

The epistemological interest of the development of conservation concepts is evident. These concepts are neither preformed in the child nor acquired by means of simple observation of real events, but are the product of a process of elaboration which Piaget seeks to explain in terms of equilibration and autoregulation. Conservation concepts are also of special interest to psychologists, because their growth is governed by very regular laws of development. Finally, psychopathological studies of retardation or deviation of normal development highlight the importance of conservation concepts from a different perspective.

Research into the development of concepts of conservation of quantity has been followed with considerable interest by both child psychologists and developmental psychologists and a number of replication studies have been carried out. In the original conservation studies a given quantity of liquid was poured into glasses of different sizes (Piaget and Szeminska, 1941) or a ball of modeling clay was first changed in shape and then broken into several smaller pieces (Piaget and Inhelder, 1941). These studies revealed that the child's initial understanding of conservation is based on a general undifferentiated concept of invariance which provides the basis for subsequent, more specific quantifications and measurements (e.g., of height and length). This first notion of conservation of continuous (or physical) quantity is developed before any actual physical quantification of mass, volume, or weight is possible. Differentiation between, on the one hand, the underlying synchronic operation structures and, on the other, the continuous and causal action is only partial (Piaget and Garcia, 1971).

Three stages have been found in the development of the concept of conservation of continuous quantities: the first is characterized by a number of answers and arguments indicating an absence of conservation; the second is characterized by responses of an intermediate type; and the third is characterized by the acquisition of conservation.

The common characteristic of the first stage, in which the children do not have the concept of conservation of quantity (either in the case of solids or in that of liquids), is that the children focus either on the action carried out (pouring of the liquid, flattening out of the modeling clay, etc.) or on the resulting appearance of the material. They neglect the fact that the final appearance of the material is determined by the action which brought about the change in shape of the modeling clay or in the level of the liquid. More detailed analyses show that there are several sublevels within this elementary stage. It is only at a certain point in development that the child begins to establish relationships between some of the features of the experimental material, and, initially, these relationships are partial and are restricted to a few features only. For instance, if a child thinks that there is more liquid to drink when it is poured into a thinner glass "because the liquid comes up higher," he has apparently compared the initial equality of height of the liquid in the two glasses with the subsequent rising ("going beyond") of one level above the other. A number of studies of spatial representation and concepts of speed and movement in the child have shown that such ordinal comparisons based on "going beyond," "overtaking," etc., are fundamental for the elaboration of the elementary systems of space and movement which eventually lead to systems of measurement.

At another substage the child becomes capable of mentally returning to the starting point of the experimental situation and predicting that there will once again "be the same to drink" or "just as much to eat," although he judges that at present the quantity (of liquid or modeling clay) has increased or diminished as a result of the change in shape. In one of our first publications (Piaget and Inhelder, 1941), this type of judgment was called "empirical reversibility," i.e., the possibility of an effective return to the initial state, to distinguish it from logical reversibility. The main difference between this reversal and logical reversibility is that in the first instance, although the return action is the inverse of the transforming action, it neither cancels out this transformation nor compensates for it; it is merely a second action which, for the child, is completely independent of the first.

A subsequent series of studies carried out at the Center of Genetic Epistemology on notions of functional dependency and identity showed that this idea of a possible inverse action is subsumed by a system of one-way mappings whose semilogical nature has been shown by Piaget (1970). The child establishes a series of one-way relationships of the type $y_1 = f(x_1)$, where x_1 is the action of lengthening the clay ball and y_1 is the decrease in thickness and $f =$ the relationship of dependency of y' on x'. He then establishes $y_2 = f(x_2)$, where x_2 is the inverse action of "fattening" the sausage into a ball and y_2 is the reduction in length. At this level, however, these two covariations, or functions, are still envisaged successively and are not yet coordinated into a single system which will transform the covariations of dimensions into compensations between dimensions.

The semilogical system of one-way dependencies does not yet comprise quantitative invariants, but only an idea of qualitative identity. At this point, the child is unable to distinguish between certain invariant properties of an object and others that change. He will reply, for instance, that "it's always the same liquid," "the same clay," even though he judges that the quantity has increased or diminished. For the child of this level the permanent properties of objects are qualitative in nature and are observed directly, whereas for the child of the operatory level, quantity is conserved; this is possible only if a coherent system of thought operations has been constructed.

The responses of the intermediate type are generally characterized by vacillations between nonconservation and conservation judgments. A child might keep changing his mind in one situation; or he might answer correctly in one situation and wrongly in another equally difficult situation—it is impossible to predict which questions or experimental situations will elicit correct or wrong answers. It is, however, often possible to order the answers of a group of subjects on a post hoc basis.

At the third level, the child maintains conservation of quantity and justifies it by arguments based on logical identity, reversibility by cancellation of the change, and compensation between dimensions, based on an understanding of the reciprocity of the relationships (e.g., every increase in length implies a corresponding decrease in thickness).

There is undoubtedly a continuity from the semilogical and qualitative identities to logical operations and conservation of quantities, but it is also clear that this development is based on a process of integration and complete restructuring. This will become even more evident from the results of the present learning studies. Piaget (1970) notes that logical, quantitative identity is not merely an extension of qualitative identity. This is shown in three ways: (1) quantitative identity results from the product of a direct operation and its inverse; (2) within the framework of a closed, coherent system it is felt as necessary; and, finally, (3) it is only one of the components of this coherent system, and it cannot account for its other components, such as the two forms of reversibility.

Quantitative identity, based on a system of operations, should not be confused with the sort of responses found by Piaget and Taponier (Piaget and Inhelder, 1963, 1966) in situations where the child is asked to show (by pointing, or putting a spot of paint on a glass) where the level of a liquid will be when it is poured into glasses of different shapes, and also to say whether there will be more, less, or the same amount of liquid in the glasses. Some children predict that neither the level nor the quantity will change—here there is clearly no question of "logical" conservation since they do not foresee any transformation at all.

Generally speaking, elementary number conservation is acquired earlier than concepts of conservation of physical, continuous quantities, although the developmental process is similar. In situations where the child is asked to accept the initial equality of a number of beads which have been placed in two identical glasses by means of a process of repeated one-to-one correspondence (see Appendix), and then is asked what happens when the beads are poured into glasses of different sizes, we note not only the same sequence of responses as for the tasks of conservation of liquid or modeling clay, but also the same types of arguments. One notable difference, however, between discontinuous and continuous quantities is that in the former case the children usually say: "There isn't one bead more (in either of the glasses), we always put one with one." In terms of the grouping structure, this remark refers to the "identity operation," since the method of forming equivalent quantities by a process of one-to-one correspondence highlights the action of adding.

In a study (Inhelder and Piaget, 1963) of the child's understanding of the principle of recurrence, the importance of repeated actions of one-to-one correspondence for the development of concepts of conservation of continuous quantities became very clear. In this study, the child was asked to place two beads simultaneously into two glasses ("a red one with a blue one," as the children say), and to repeat this action a number of times, first using pairs of identical glasses and then different ones. In the first experimental situations the child could see the result of this repeated action because transparent glasses were used. Then opaque glasses were substituted and the result was no longer visible. The purpose of this study was to have the child predict the outcome of an action that was repeated a great many times ("if we continued to do this all afternoon," etc.). Another version of the experiment started with unequal quantities. In yet another, a one-to-two correspondence was used, in order to see whether the child conserved both equal and unequal quantities. The results showed that at a relatively early age the child can make inferences from these "recurrences" which lead to the concept of conservation of numerical equality (or inequality), often justified by the following argument: "Once I know it's the same, I know it forever." At this stage, however, numerical conservation is still incomplete and cannot immediately be generalized to all situations involving a change in appearance of collections of elements.

The well-known experiments on "spontaneous" and "provoked" correspondence and on the concept of numerical equivalence (Piaget and Szeminska, 1941) provide specific details on the primitive methods whereby the child estimates discontinuous quantities in terms of "numerosity" (i.e., the quality of being numerous) and not yet in terms of the number of elements. At first, the child fails to differentiate between the evaluation of quantity based on numerical criteria and that based on spatial criteria. If children of four to five years are asked to make up a collection of elements which is equal in number to that of the experimenter's collection, which is presented in a certain way (e.g., "choose as many eggs as there are egg-cups lined up on the table"), there is a tendency for them to construct their collections so that the starting and end points of the rows of objects coincide. However, when they are asked for an evaluation, a different reaction is sometimes noted: they consider the line where the elements are closer together to contain more elements than the longer one in which the elements spread out. Even though the child of the preoperatory level may be able to establish a one-to-one correspondence (facilitated by the use of educational toys), this does not mean that he will consider the equivalence as lasting when the visual correspondence is destroyed. For instance, he might say that there are more eggs when these have been spread out, or that there are more eggs when they have been packed closely together. This early notion of numerosity, strongly influenced by configurational features, will eventually result in the concept of conservation of number based on a system of operations having properties resembling those of mathematical groups.

A particularly interesting notion whose development is immediately prior to that of conservation of number is that which P. Gréco (1962), following Cournot's terminology, has called "quotity," to distinguish it from numerical "quantity." The child of the level of "quotity" is quite capable of giving the correct answer when asked how many objects there are in one collection after he has counted those in the other, but he still thinks that there are more objects in one of the collections: "there are six there, and six there, the same numbers of counters when you count them, but it's not the same, there are more counters there." Furthermore, children sometimes affirm the invariance of the correspondence between the elements of the two collections—"there's one red for each blue"—but continue to maintain that all the same "there's more there than here."

These findings lead to certain hypotheses about the reasons why the child acquires conservation of discontinuous quantities before that of continuous quantities. Well before acquiring the operatory concept of number (which, according to Piaget, results from a synthesis of class inclusion and serial order), the child can often count, if only to three or four, or label the objects in another way. This knowledge allows him to attribute a certain measure of individuality to the elements and to preserve their qualitative identity despite a change in their position. Enumeration also facilitates his understanding of the serial aspect of the natural number system. Finally, individualization of the elements not only allows him to establish the initial correspondence between elements of the two collections, but helps him return to this correspondence by means of an "empirical return," i.e., the anticipation of a possible inverse action.

The individualization of the elements by means of reasoning based on qualitative identity and the establishment of relationships based on serial order and one-to-one correspondence are operative schemes which lead to the numerical evaluation of collections of objects. Research carried out by Piaget and his coworkers has shown that these schemes do not by themselves form the fully operatory concept of number, but have to be coordinated with class inclusion schemes.

Practice with the preliminary action-schemes in a variety of situations may prepare the child for further acquisitions in conservation problems of different types. In particular, it may further his understanding of the covariation of dimensions. Specific difficulties may arise according to the nature of the property conserved (number, quantity, length, etc.). Learning studies appear particularly suited for testing such hypotheses.

PRELIMINARY INVESTIGATIONS

As a result of the discussions of the well-known Woods Hole Symposium (1959), which were summarized by J. Bruner in a lively and original report (1961), we decided to study for the first time the mechanisms of cognitive development through studies of learning. Some prominent physicists who were involved in the establishment of school programs had taken an interest in our work on the development of scientific concepts in the child. The biologists who took part in the symposium shared our doubts as to the degree of malleability of developmental processes. Psychologist members of the group, by contrast, believed that it was possible through the use of suitable methods to correct what they called "errors of growth" in child thought.

Until that time, our approach had been similar to that of the naturalist who makes controlled observations on animal behavior in its natural, or at least usual, environment, without attempting to modify the animals' development. However, an eventual application of our psychological findings to education, and in particular to the teaching of scientific concepts, implies a search for the type of situation that is particularly favorable for progress.

A first attempt was made at Harvard University two years later when we had the privilege of being invited to join the Center for Cognitive Studies. Initially, the aims of our experiments, carried out together with Bruner and his collaborators, were to clarify the problems of conservation of quantities, to provide details of our method of investigation, and to compare our approach to the study of learning with approaches of other schools of thought.

Some of the techniques that were drawn up jointly for the preliminary studies were subsequently used by both the Harvard and the Geneva teams as a basis for more appropriate training procedures. Since each team had its own epistemological and developmental perspective, it is not surprising that the resulting separate research programs show two rather different approaches.

The initial joint project dealt with the acquisition of conservation of quantity in situations where liquid is poured into glasses of different shapes and sizes. Three techniques, either separately or combined, were applied to the same experimental display (see Fig. 1.1; cf. Bruner et al., 1966).

The first technique explored the possible effects of appropriate

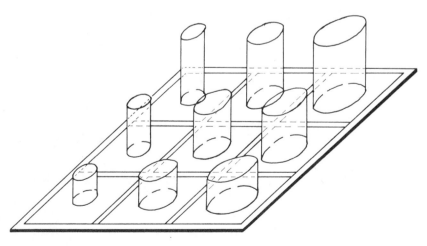

Fig. 1.1

verbal descriptions of the dimensions of the glasses. We first studied the language that children use spontaneously to describe glasses of different heights or diameters, or both, as well as their understanding of instructions given by the experimenter when he asked them to choose certain glasses (e.g., "choose a thinner and taller glass than this one").

In the second technique, the children were asked to predict the level of a given quantity of liquid if it were poured successively into a number of different glasses. At first, we used glasses of different diameters, then glasses of different heights, and finally glasses differing in both diameter and height. After each prediction, the liquid was actually poured and the children were encouraged to check whether their predictions were correct. The experimenter also asked them to explain the correspondence or discrepancy between prediction and outcome.

In the third technique, the emphasis was on pouring the liquid from one glass to another and back again. The contents of one glass was poured into several others, and each time the liquid was poured back into the original glass, and the child was asked if the quantity of liquid had remained the same or changed. Children of the non-conserving level, who usually judged that the glass where the liquid reached the higher level had more, were then asked what would happen if the liquid were poured back into the original glass ("Will the glass be completely full, only a little bit full, or will it overflow?").

Some of the more interesting findings of these first investigations can be summed up as follows.

1. It was evident from these preliminary investigations that the effects of teaching techniques are governed by the child's initial level of cognitive development, as measured by a pre-test.

2. No differences were noted between the results of the three techniques. None of the three methods—verbal training, conflict due to a discrepancy between prediction and outcome, and the pouring of the liquid back into the original glass—was particularly effective when used alone.

3. Even the cumulative effect of the three techniques used together was less predictive of the result of the post-test than the

child's initial level of reasoning. Apparently, the child's capacity to integrate the information drawn from the exercise is the factor that mainly determines progress. It seems therefore that the benefit a child is likely to gain from the three techniques depends more on his level of cognitive competence than on the specific type of teaching technique used.

4. Finally, there remains the question of comparing the progress of the subjects of this experiment with that of children who are given no such training. This question later became one of our major concerns and was constantly borne in mind when we tried to improve our training techniques and the design of our pre-tests and post-tests in order to evaluate the progress accomplished by the subjects in the course of the experiments.

Bruner and his colleagues designed a series of original techniques on the basis of these preliminary investigations, the results and interpretations of which are incorporated in *Studies in Cognitive Growth* (1966). Our own studies, reported in the present publication, gradually took a rather different direction from those of the Harvard group.

The basic problem which oriented our research planning is that of the relationship between development and learning. We adopted the hypothesis that any increase in knowledge is the result of contact between a person's already-established schemes and reality, and we postulated that the systems into which schemes are organized change with development. In this context, appropriate pre-tests have to be used to select subjects who can be classed according to the degree of organization of their schemes. These subjects should then all be given the same opportunity of contact with specific observable realities, so that the effect of these observable features on schemes of different levels can be shown. Therefore, for this first study we selected two groups of children: one group of nonconserving children and another of children who were mostly situated at the intermediate level. In this second group we even included some children who were on the verge of acquiring conservation.

If, as we hypothesized, a cognitive learning situation is one which favors contact between a person's organized system of schemes and certain features of the real world, then the experimental situation should be designed so as to allow the subjects to observe the pertinent aspects of the situations, and, in particular, those which they would normally tend to neglect when seeking a solution to a problem.

A FIRST EXPERIMENT: COMPARISON OF LIQUID LEVELS AND QUANTITIES

In this first experiment, concerning the flow of liquids, several situations were presented to the child in an attempt to facilitate the contact between the subject and the observable environmental factors (see Fig. 1.2). The children did not passively watch the experimenter carry out various demonstrations with the apparatus; they were asked to open and shut the taps themselves, to let the liquid flow into the different jars. They were asked to make predictions as to what would happen and then to compare these predictions with what actually did happen when they performed the actions. Evidently, the

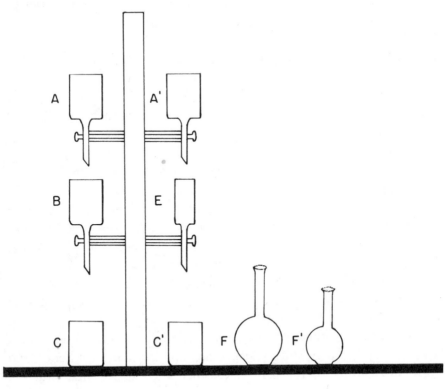

Fig. 1.2

conservation of quantities, which is acquired before the understanding of measurement, can be neither confirmed nor refuted by direct observation. We presumed, however, that if a child were able to correct his predictions of the outcome of his actions by observing what actually happens, he would sooner or later begin to make inferences about the relationship between the level and the quantity of liquid and become capable of solving the problem first by trial and error and later immediately. A child's gaining of confidence from proving himself right is less important, in the context of this research, than his being led to make inferences as a result of comparing predictions and observations.

We also tried to help the child by trying to shift his attention away from the static result, i.e., the level of the liquid, as this is an inherent characteristic of nonconservation reasoning. Therefore, we directed his attention toward the continuity of the filling and emptying of a series of jars in a virtually closed system,* where the liquid flowed from a first jar to a second and then a third jar, placed one above the other. In this way, the child was provided with the opportunity of witnessing the causal aspects of a continuous physical process (the initial and final states are the same) as well as the kinetic aspects (the rate of rise of the level of the liquid depends on the diameter of the jar). Obviously, observing the physical reality does not, in itself, lead the child to understand that the different steps of a physical transformation are mentally reversible. However, under certain conditions, which we shall discuss in this chapter, this point can be made more salient by the use of certain experimental procedures.

TRAINING PROCEDURE AND SELECTION OF SUBJECTS

Materials. Three pairs of cylindrical jars are fixed to a frame made of two vertical columns (see Fig. 1.2). The jars are 7 cm high and their diameter is 5 cm. Both the top jars (A and A′) and the middle ones (B and B′) have an outlet tap at the bottom which the child can

---

* Virtually closed because the liquid flows from one container to the next, and is repeatedly poured from the last jar back into the first.

43

easily handle. The top pair of jars (A and A') and the bottom pair (C and C') remain unchanged during the experiment; the middle pair (B and B') are sometimes replaced by other jars of different shape and size, either narrower (N: height 7 cm, diameter 3 cm) or wider (W: height 7 cm, diameter 7 cm). Two small flasks of different sizes (F and F', see Fig. 1.2) are used to pour equal or unequal quantities of liquid into the top jars.

TRAINING SESSIONS

There are four phases in the experiment, presented in two training sessions. Each session lasts about 20 to 30 minutes. There was an interval of a week between the two sessions.

First Session

Phase 1. The first phase is mainly intended to allow the child to become familiar with the apparatus and to draw his attention to the fact that the liquid flows from A to B and then to C. The child is asked to fill the larger of the two flasks (F) with liquid ("so that the ball of the flask is completely full but there's nothing in the neck") and to pour the liquid from F into A, and then to open the tap and let it flow into B. He is then asked to describe what happened and to predict the quantity of liquid he would find in F if F were put in the place of C: "When the liquid has run down into the flask (F), will it fill up the ball of the flask completely or not? Or will the liquid come up into the neck of the flask?" The child then lets the liquid flow into F and so is able to see whether his prediction was correct.

The same procedure is followed for the second column: the child is asked to pour from F into A', and to let the liquid flow into B'. When the experimenter has replaced C' with F, he is asked to predict the amount of liquid there will be in F, and to check his prediction as before.

Phase 2. The purpose of the second phase is to focus the child's attention on the fact that equal quantities of liquid at the beginning and the end of the process (the liquid flows from F to F, passing through A and B or A' and N/W) rise to different levels in the middle pair of jars when these are not the same shape or size. The child is asked to compare the amounts of liquid flowing down the two columns. This means that at any point in the procedure he can compare the level of the liquid in a pair of jars (top, bottom, or middle pair).

The child fills A and A′ using the same flask F for each. He checks that the two jars contain the same amount of liquid and that the levels are equal. He lets the liquid in A flow into B and is then asked to let the same amount of liquid flow into N: "enough liquid so that there's the same amount to drink in B and N." The levels of the liquid in B′ and N are carefully marked (with rubber bands or tape), and the child is asked to predict the quantities of liquid there will be in C and C′ if he lets the liquid run through: "Will there be the same amount of liquid in both jars, or more in one?" The child then lets the liquid flow down: from B into C and from N into C′. He can either make the levels in B and N equal, so that, objectively, the quantities are not equal—in this case, when the liquid has run into C and C′ he sees that the quantity and the levels are unequal and that some liquid is left in A′—or he can let all the liquid run into B and N, accept the inequality of the levels, and end up with equal quantities and levels in C and C′. The same procedure is repeated using W instead of N.

The experimenter notes the child's reactions to these problems and tries to find out the reasons for his actions. When the quantities of liquid in C and C′ are not equal, the experimenter notes whether the child has taken into account the liquid left in A′, and if so, if this has any effect on his method of evaluating a quantity of liquid. In the nonconservation stage, when the child is faced with jars of different shapes and sizes, he usually evaluates the quantity of liquid by considering only its level.

Second Session

Phase 3. The third phase is based on a previous experiment (Piaget and Inhelder, 1963, 1966) where children had to predict the level of a quantity of liquid in several glasses of different sizes which were partially hidden by a screen.* In that experiment some non-

* Research carried out in collaboration with S. Taponier.

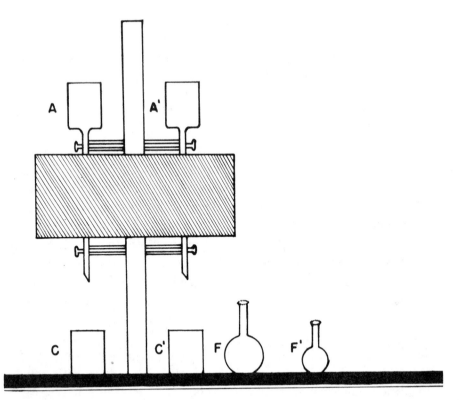

Fig. 1.3

conserving children gave correct answers, although these were not of an operatory level.

In the third phase, the child is asked once again to compare the liquid flowing down one column with the liquid flowing down the other. The middle pair of jars are now hidden by a screen (see Fig. 1.3). The child fills A and A' with the same quantity of liquid (using the same flask F). He then sees that when the liquid has run through the middle pair of jars, the bottom ones, C and C', contain equal quantities of liquid. When the liquid runs through once more, he is asked to predict the quantities of liquid in the hidden middle pair of jars. The screen is removed and the child's reactions to the difference in the liquid levels are noted. He is then asked to predict the quantities in C and C'. All his reactions when he sees what actually happens to the liquid and when he compares this with his own predictions are noted for each problem.

Phase 4. The purpose of the fourth phase is to study the conservation of unequal quantities. The procedure of this part of the experiment is the same as that used in the second phase, except that the child fills A and A′ with unequal quantities of liquid. A is filled from flask F (full) and A′ from a smaller flask, F″. The difference in quantities is such that, when the liquid is in the middle pair of jars, B and N, the levels are equal. At each level (A, B, and C) the child is asked to compare the quantities.

The training procedure allows the child considerable freedom of action. Each phase is presented once, but if during one phase a child seems to hesitate between several possible solutions then this phase is repeated.

In the first situations of the second phase, the child always uses the same flask both to fill A and A′ and to collect the liquid after it has run through the middle pair. This phase is likely to lead the child to discover by means of empirical evidence that the quantities of liquid are equal. If in the final part of phase two and/or in phase four the child makes the levels in the middle pair of jars equal, and later, when the liquid has run through to the bottom pair, is surprised that they are no longer equal, the experimenter draws his attention to the liquid left in A′. This can help the child to realize what happens when he divides up the liquid, and to think about the complementary relationship between two parts of a whole.

In phases two, three, and four, the child's attention is drawn to the covariation of the dimensions in two different ways. In phases two and three, equal quantities of liquid imply a compensation between the diameter of the jar and the level of the liquid; in phase four, the equal levels imply a compensation between the quantity of liquid and the diameter of the jar.

In phase one, the apparatus used, a closed circuit where the liquid flows from F to A to B and back to F again, strongly suggests a possible return to the starting point. This actually happens.

We tried to organize the problems put to the child in such a way that he was encouraged to make quantitative evaluations as he was carrying out the various instructions. It is clear that the experimental situation cannot instill the necessary mental operations in the child, nor can it modify the operations he possesses; it can only suggest the operations involved. The experimental procedure can only present unexpected situations that awaken the child's curiosity and lead him to query his naive conceptions, or even to interpret reality in a new and different way.

SELECTION OF SUBJECTS

Thirty-four subjects aged from 5;1 to 7;0 were selected on the basis of their reactions to two physical-quantities conservation tasks (liquid and modeling clay; see Appendix). The same tasks formed the post-tests, the first of which was presented after the training procedure and the second three weeks later.

Fifteen children were clearly at the preconservation level (type I, NC). These subjects never made a conservation judgment. They can be classed according to the arguments they used. At the lowest levels, they did not even consider the argument of a return to the starting point and focused their attention on one factor: either one of the dimensions, or the action of pouring the liquid. At the more advanced levels, they gave arguments based on an empirical return and on the covariation of the dimensions.

When we began this study, our knowledge of the nature of partial coordinations was somewhat scant. Since then, however, Piaget has discussed their characteristics, which are that they consist of a sort of semilogic and are organized into functionally dependent systems. Our present knowledge of the development of these systems allows us to improve the classification of preconservation responses and to understand more clearly the possibilities and difficulties of cognitive learning.

Nineteen children reacted in a way which is typical of an intermediate stage. Within this group, it was possible to distinguish three developmental subgroups. Six children belonged to the first subgroup (type II, NC-Int); they gave only incorrect answers for one task, and a few correct answers in the other. The second subgroup (type III, Int-Int), was made up of nine children who gave some correct and some incorrect answers in both tasks. The third subgroup (type IV,

Int-C)—four children—gave correct answers for the modeling clay conservation task, but gave some incorrect answers for the liquid conservation task.

A control group (eight children) provided us with confirmation that once conservation has been acquired, the problems presented during the training sessions are solved immediately. A second control group (again, eight children) showed that children at an intermediate level who do not take part in the training sessions make no progress.

RESULTS

COMPARISON OF PRE-TEST AND POST-TESTS

The first and most striking finding was the existence of a close relationship between the child's initial level of development (pre-test) and the types of reasoning he used in the training sessions (see Table 1.1). Not only did none of the 15 type I, NC, children acquire conservation, but only two of them reached the intermediate level. On the other hand, 16 of the 19 children who were at an intermediate level in the pre-test used more advanced types of reasoning in one of the two post-tests; 10 of them even acquired conservation (type V). One should note, however, that 4 of these subjects started off with an understanding of conservation for the modeling clay conservation task. The progress they made seems to result from the extension of certain structures to different contents rather than from the construction of new structures.

From an analysis of the curves that indicate the relationship between the results of the pre-test and post-tests, it appears that the order of the types of responses remained constant. As far as most of the children were concerned, the training sessions did not have much effect on their relative position in the total sample, although at the beginning the children were fairly close to one another and in the post-test they were much farther apart. This was particularly the case in this experiment because the type I children made hardly any progress.

Another finding, also of a general nature, concerns the dynamics

TABLE 1.1

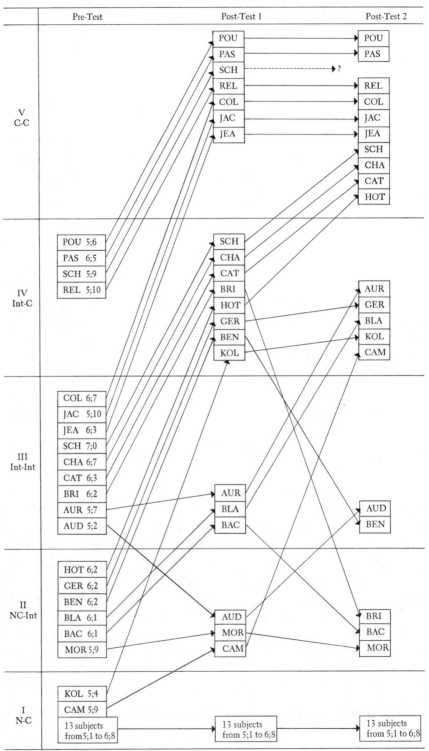

Note: Although the same initials appear in several tables, it must be emphasized that no child took part in more than one training procedure.

of the transition mechanisms: the intermediate-level reactions were relatively unstable. Some of the children who reached the intermediate level during the training sessions made further progress between the first and second post-tests, while others regressed. This difference in reaction patterns seems to confirm the hypothesis of the existence of stages. While the instability of the intermediate-level reactions appears to be due to the lack of coordination between the different schemes, the stability of the more advanced reactions seems to depend on the coherence of the system of schemes. This coherence is an essential characteristic of a developmental stage.

It is clear that the curves representing the relationship between the results in the pre-test and post-tests show only the transition from one stage or substage to another. They do not indicate the progress or regressions that might have occurred during the actual training sessions; nor do they show if a child has only been able to make finer distinctions in his reasoning in the post-test. These points become clearer in the section on verbal learning.

Of the 15 children who were at the preconservation level before the training sessions, only CAM (5;9) and KOL (5;4) made substantial progress and arrived at level IV in the second post-test. Their developmental curves are very different: CAM was at level II in the first post-test and then progressed to level IV in the second. KOL, on the other hand, reached level IV immediately.

In the subgroup whose initial level was II, NC-Int, only one child, MOR (5;9), made no progress at all. However, the progress of BAC (6;1) and BEN (6;2) was not stable, as BAC reached level III at the first post-test only to return to level II at the second, and BEN reached level IV at the first post-test, but was only at level III at the second. GER (6;2), having progressed from II to IV, remained at this level, while two other children made further progress after the first post-test: BLA (6;1) progressed from II to III and then to IV and HOT (6;2) from II to IV and then to V.

In the subgroup whose initial level was III, Int-Int, one child, AUD (5;2), seemed to regress slightly in the first post-test, but returned to his initial level in the second. Another child, BRI (6;2), reached level IV at the first post-test, but regressed to II at the second. The 7 other children progressed as follows: AUR (5;7) reached a higher level (IV) only at the second post-test; CAT (6;3), CHA (6;7), and SCH (7;0) reached level IV at the first post-test and then V at the second; JEA (6;3), JAC (5;10), and COL (6;7) reached level V at the first post-test.

All the children in subgroup IV reached level V in the first post-test; those we were able to retest (second post-test) remained there.

These results raise two general questions. First of all, why did the training sessions that helped the intermediate-level children to progress (sometimes to the extent that they acquired conservation) have virtually no effect on children at the nonconservation level? Second, why did the more advanced children make real progress in cognitive development, while the less advanced children did not, despite the fact that the experimental conditions were the same? What are the psychological mechanisms that account for this?

The purpose of the training sessions in this first experiment was to help the child to become aware of the observable features of the situation pertinent to the solution of the problem and, above all, to highlight the observable features that the child at the nonconservation level tends to neglect. What is the exact role of these observable features at different levels of the construction of concepts dealing with the conservation of physical quantities? Do these observable features disturb the child's primitive conceptions, inciting him to make new coordinations? Or are they ineffective until the child can make certain inferences from them? In the latter case, can these inferences be activated by continual confrontations between the child's predictions and what actually happens in the experiment? To answer this question fully, one would have to go far beyond the scope of this experiment. We think, however, that the following examples of types of responses given during the training sessions may provide some useful information on the subject.

ANALYSIS OF THE RESPONSES DURING TRAINING SESSIONS

A brief analysis will be made of the children's reactions during the training sessions. The first example concerns a child whose level in the pre-test was I and who made no clear progress during the training sessions.

Most of the level I children who made no progress were nevertheless perfectly capable of apprehending all the relevant observable features of the situation that the more advanced child seemed to use for solving the problem. The level I children noted the difference in the levels of the liquid in C and C', an observation that contradicted their predictions (phase 2). They were also capable of noticing the liquid left in A' when they had made the levels equal (and the quantity unequal) in B and N (or W). However, these observations did not seem even momentarily to influence their reasoning. These children did not know how to use the observations. The level I children who gave slightly more advanced arguments in the pre-test sometimes corrected their previous answers. But none of these children applied what they had seen to other situations.

EXCERPTS FROM PROTOCOLS

BAB (5;6) is at the preconservation stage: his reasoning is based on the changes of one dimension or on the actual act of pouring the liquid or changing the shape of the modeling clay.

In the first phase of the experiment he thinks that the quantity of liquid increases when it is poured into N and then diminishes when it is poured back into F. He is amazed to find that F contains the same amount of liquid at the end of the experiment as at the beginning.

In the second phase, he begins to notice the covariation of the dimensions, but without realizing that his successive judgments contradict one another: "If you look at it from the side there's more here (N); if you look at it from the top, there's more here (B)."

During the third phase, BAB seems a little unsure of himself. At first he stops the flow of liquid into B and N at the same level, but when he is asked, "Is it the same or different when you drink it and when you look at it?" he says nothing and his expression betrays his confusion. He finally opts for a compromise solution, and lets a few more drops of liquid flow into N (so that the level of N is higher than the level of B, but there is still some liquid left in A'). But, and this is striking, he expects that the levels in C and C' will be equal and that C and C' will contain the same quantity of liquid. It is only later that he notices the liquid left in A', and when questioned again on the quantities in B and N, he admits that there was less in N. This retroactive correction seems isolated, in the sense that it has no effect on his other judgments; when the procedure is repeated (using W instead of N), he once again makes the levels in B and W equal, and does not notice the liquid left behind in A until later.

In the fourth phase, BAB thinks that the quantities are equal as long as the middle jars are hidden by the screen. When the screen is removed, he seems very intrigued, and spontaneously says, "There's nothing left at the top"; but when he sees that the levels are not equal, he goes on saying that the quantities are not equal.

Each judgment is restricted to its own particular context, and it is interesting to see how difficult it is to change the preconservation child's judgments, despite the compelling observations made during the experiment. Apparently, the only benefit gained from the training sessions is that the child can now evaluate the two dimensions, but without coordinating them: "more lemonade seen from the top (larger diameter), less seen from the side (smaller diameter)." In order to demonstrate that there is more modeling clay in the little pieces than in the ball, the child piles up the little pieces vertically.

Two other level I children who are slightly more advanced, but not capable of progressing to a higher level, have more lively reactions to the, to them, unexpected inequality of liquids in C and C′. BEL (5;11) is very surprised, and cries out: "You have to take that (liquid left in A′) too; you have to take it all." BAL (5;7) says: "We should have put it all in there." Afterward, they both admit that they put unequal quantities in B and N, but this does not help them correct their mistakes or give right answers to the questions that follow.

The reactions of the level I children seem to confirm the hypothesis that as long as the child does not incorporate the observable features of the situation into a system of inference allowing him to link the various observations made in the successive phases of the experiment, he cannot make any progress. The observable features themselves cannot alone lead to change in the thought processes.

The retroactive corrections are a first step forward, even though they do not lead to correct predictions in the other situations. The discrepancy between observation and prediction does create a certain unease in the child's mind, but at this developmental level he is not yet capable of organizing the successive observations into a coherent system of schemes. Consequently, he is not aware of the contradictions between his predictions and observations and he cannot make the correct inferences that would lead to correct predictions. One could suppose that it is only when the child has a certain capacity to assimilate and coordinate the observable features that he becomes capable of making the correct chain of inferences.

The children who begin the experiment at levels II (NC-Int) and III (Int-Int) and thereafter progress to the more advanced types of reasoning clearly show us how they use the unexpected observable features of the situation. Here is a typical example.

GER (6;2) starts off at level II and reaches level IV after the training sessions.

During the pre-test, the only difference between GER and the level I children is that she gives a correct conservation answer for the situation where liquid is poured into several small glasses. The argument she gives is that of primitive identity: "because in there (original glass) and in there (glass from which the liquid was poured into the smaller ones) there was also the same." However, she does not use this reasoning in any of the other situations (liquid conservation task and modeling clay conservation task).

During the training sessions she begins by reasoning in the same way as the level I children, except that during phase 2 she correctly predicts the inequality of the liquid in C and C′: "more here (C) and less here (C′) because there's still some left at the top." This is the beginning of an inferential process. However, her progress is minimal, because when she lets all the liquid run into N she is bothered by the fact that the levels in B and N are unequal. She does not try to explain how equal quantities in A and A′ can come to different levels when they are in B and N. Only in the following phase does real conflict occur: GER continually changes her mind: "There's more lemonade in N because it's thinner, and there (B) it's fatter," she says; then immediately afterward: "No, it's the same" —"How do you know?"—"Because I can see it"—"How can you see it?"— "I just know." She does not yet attempt an explanation based on compensation of the dimensions.

At the beginning of the fourth phase of the experiment she seems to understand that unequal quantities of liquid in A and A′ can come to the same levels when they are poured into B and N. However, she abandons the idea of conservation of inequality by predicting that the levels in C and C′ will be equal. But she later explains the inequality between C and C′ by referring to the middle jars: "(not the same) because one's thinner (N) and the other's fatter (B), that still makes more lemonade (despite the equal levels)."

Whenever GER corrects her answers, she encounters new obstacles; she does not grasp the crux of the problem and makes no attempt to overcome the conflicts, as do the more advanced children.

In the post-test, GER gives some correct answers in the modeling clay conservation task. She wavers between conservation and nonconservation answers, and the only arguments she gives are primitive identity arguments which are closely tied to the training situations. Her arguments never give us the impression of logical necessity.

JAC (5;10) begins the experiment at level III and reaches the conservation level in the post-test. The progress he makes is rapid and marked; he is capable of linking his predictions, and is aware of the contradictions and tries to resolve them. The experimenter intervenes very little, so that JAC's reactions will be completely spontaneous.

During the pre-test JAC continually switches between conservation judgments and preconservation judgments (Int-Int). He takes a lively interest in the problem and is able to think both in terms of an empirical return and in terms of the covariation of the dimensions.

In the first phase, he correctly predicts that the levels and quantities in C and C′ will be equal. When the liquid flows from A′ to N and then to C′, he says: "Gosh, it's coming up very high (in N), but I've poured with the same flask (F), I poured it all."

In the second phase, he expresses a conflict: "How can I do it? If I stop at the same place (equal levels in B and N) I won't have enough to drink at the end (C′), look, I left a bit up there (A′). To have the same at the end, I've got to put it all in, but then it comes up to a different place." He lets all the liquid flow into B and N and spontaneously says: "That looks like too much, doesn't it?" When the liquid flows into W and N he is very perplexed: "It's even funnier, if I don't leave this little bit at the top I don't get the same (pointing to the levels) in that one, it's so wide (W), and in that thin one . . . Well, it must still be the same amount of lemonade, it's all there . . . I know, it just looks as if there's more . . . in the thin glass the lemonade is all squashed up, it has to go up; in the wide one it's spread out."

During the third phase, once the screen is removed, he is delighted to find that his predictions are confirmed: "Ah, I know, it's like last time (previous session), there's always the same amount of lemonade to drink, it just looks as if there's more, the lemonade is in different places in the glasses."

During the fourth phase, he is at first perplexed by the equal levels in B and N: "How come? I poured into there (A′) with the little bottle (F′), and now it's equal . . . Ah! I know, it's still less, we'll see at the end; wait a minute, wait . . . I know, there's always less in this line (column), we haven't added any in the middle so it must be right."

In the post-tests JAC clearly understands the conservation of the liquid and the modeling clay; he gives arguments based not only on compensation and identity, but also on reversibility: "It's when I make it into a ball again, when I think about that, I'm quite sure."

This example shows how children who have started off by at least considering the possibility of conservation—even if, influenced by the striking changes in shape of the modeling clay, they give preconservation answers—can later modify their judgments because of their own inferences. The observable features of the situation, although they are not the direct source of knowledge, force the child into comparing his successive judgments. In this way he can become aware of the contradiction between them.

Finally, we shall describe some of the reactions of a subject from level IV who solves all the problems immediately, without needing to observe what actually happens.

Pou (5;6) in the pre-test gives conservation answers based on reversibility for the modeling clay conservation task: "If we make a ball again, it's the same." But he is still unsure of himself in the liquid conservation task, and after some hesitation returns to his original preconservation judgment: "More in the thin glass because it's narrower than this (original glass)."

During the training sessions, his reasoning becomes more explicit and at one point he refers to the compensation of the dimensions. In the second phase, he thinks: "There (N) it's longer, and there (W) it's wider, so it should come lower." He also uses a transitivity argument: "If you want to have the same here (C) and the same as there was in the beginning, there must be the same here (middle pair of jars) . . . when it runs down into the bottom glasses, it's as if we put it back into the top ones."

In the fourth phase, he triumphantly exclaims: "There I poured from the big bottle (F) and there from the little one (F'). Everything ran out, so in the end you have to have a little lemonade here and a lot there." When questioned about the equality of levels in the middle pair of jars, he says: "You can make a mistake when you look at it like that, but there can't be the same to drink."

In the post-tests he gives conservation answers for all the situations.

In this case, the observable features of the situation allow the child to make predictions and some explicit inferences based on a chain of causal implications of the "if . . . then" type, which in the child's language is expressed by "if you want to have . . . there must be."

CONCLUDING REMARKS

The results of this first exploratory learning experiment raise a certain number of questions; they will be partially answered in other chapters. Let us summarize these questions here.

The role that the observable features of the situation play in the formation of conservation concepts seems to differ greatly depending on the initial level of organization of the child's schemes. Our training sessions were designed to simulate the conditions necessary for the development of the logical system which underlies the conservation of physical quantity. Indeed, covariation, an empirical return, and qualitative identity were suggested by our experimental situations. These operations, from the point of view of reasoning, correspond to the subsystem of relations which Piaget calls "functions" (in the mathematical sense); their essential characteristics are qualitative identity and a semilogical structure. It seems that the child at the preconservation level is not yet able to benefit from the training sessions. We can hypothesize that the children who do not make any progress are unable to establish the necessary relationships between the different observable features of the situation. In other words, the observable features are assimilated only if the child is able to incorporate them into the schemes he already has.

This is a curious state of affairs, which, as far as we know, has only been observed in learning experiments. The level I children are not completely impervious to experience, as they would be if they did not even notice the observable features of the situation; nor do they seem to ignore them as did the subjects in the Center of Genetic Epistemology's study on the "awakening of awareness," where, for example, the child often succeeds in performing a quite complex action without being aware of how he does it—he is, for instance, capable of letting go of a slingshot at the right point in its trajectory to hit a target, but when asked questions, he will maintain that he let go when the stone was straight in line with the target. Our subjects, on the contrary, notice the unexpected observable features, but simply do not put them to use. The lack of assimilation is not due to shortcomings in the subject's powers of observation, but to the fact that the observable features are not integrated into inferential mechanisms.

The way in which the intermediate-level subjects integrate the observable features into inferential mechanisms and the increasingly rapid progress made during substage II provide further support for our general hypothesis that sensitivity to environmental cues and progress during the training sessions depend on the child's initial level of development, rather than being independent of it, as in the case of a stimulus-response type of learning theory.

Clearly, the transition between the level where the child does not use the new observable features and that where he can integrate them within a system of inferences is not abrupt. In fact, the transition is made very gradually by means of an increase in the retroactive corrections and accurate predictions, which become interdependent. Such predictions are possible only when they are related to prior inferences. In this particular case, it is interesting to note that the inferences are closely dependent on the corrections which the child is able to make, retroactively, to his earlier solutions.*

* This first experiment has certain similarities with those of Bruner and his colleagues (Bruner et al., 1966). Like the Genevan group, Bruner wants to go beyond the simple study of responses to conservation problems in order to learn more about the underlying mechanisms responsible for cognitive progress and to analyze the part played by the subject's awareness of conflicts between different ways of apprehending reality. However, from here, our paths begin to diverge: for the Harvard team, these conflicts occur essentially with regard to the ways of representing reality, which can be either iconic or symbolic; the symbolic representations (mainly verbal descriptors) are considered of a higher level than the former and conflicts arise between them which lead to a cognitive reorganization. For the Geneva team, it is not a question of conflicts between the ways of apprehending reality, which (as Piaget and Inhelder have already shown, 1966) are themselves dependent on operatory development, but of conflicts between different assimilatory schemes. Our first experiment, in our view, shows that awareness of a contradiction between schemes and observables or between different schemes is a function of the inferential processes, which are themselves dependent on the subject's level of competence.

2 / From One-to-One
Correspondence to the Conservation
of Physical Quantities

Cross-sectional studies have shown that children acquire the concept of conservation of discontinuous quantities (when the experimental material consists of small collections of objects) between six months to one year earlier than that of continuous quantities. This raises the question, which in fact constitutes one of the major concerns of the learning studies, of the relationships between the two concepts. Does one concept stem directly from the other? Or are they both products of the same process of elaboration applied to a different content? How does the child progress from one concept to the other?

In a number of experiments on the development of the concept of recurrence in the child (Inhelder and Piaget, 1963), it was found that children gave correct answers to problems of equality or disparity of collections of elements when these were constituted by a repeated one-to-one correspondence well before they were able to give correct answers to the task where the experimenter changed the lay-out of one of two collections, each containing the same number of objects. In these experiments of recurrence, both the child and the experimenter simultaneously added a number of objects, one at a time, to two collections laid out in front of them. Sometimes the initial collections had the same number of objects, sometimes they did not. The two collections obtained by this repeated action of adding objects one by one were laid out in different ways, and when the children were asked questions about the number of objects in them, even some subjects younger than five years were able to give correct answers. Although it was often difficult to evaluate the logical nature of these answers, the very fact that such young children gave them in a situation where a repetitive process was involved gave us the idea of using a similar procedure for the acquisition of the concept of conservation of quantity of matter.

We hoped to facilitate the possible transition from the conservation of discontinuous quantities to that of continuous quantities by using, as our experimental material, first individual objects such as counters and then small wooden beads. Subsequently, small seeds were used. In this way the material progressively took on the aspect of a continuous quantity. By means of the process of "iteration," i.e., by simultaneously adding one element at a time to each of the original quantities, this material was first placed into identical opaque glasses, then into transparent glasses of different sizes, and, finally, the contents of the initial glasses were poured into different ones. The iteration process maintained the one-to-one correspondence between the objects of the two collections throughout the experiment, and it was this numerical equivalence that the child was called upon to assess. The actual appearance of the material after the objects had been progressively added, however, was less and less suggestive of the one-to-one correspondence which resulted from the iterative process. At a given point in cognitive development two types of evaluation, one resulting in a judgment of equivalence between the quantities, based on the repeated process of simultaneously adding the same number of objects to the two collections, and the other leading to a judgment of nonequivalence, based on the different appearance of the two collections, are likely to induce conflicts in the child's mind. We therefore felt that if the child were made aware of the contradiction between these two types of reasoning, this might lead him to apply the appropriate mental processes for solving the problem.

TRAINING PROCEDURE, TESTS, AND SELECTION OF SUBJECTS

In the training procedure three types of situations were presented.

1. DIFFERENT LAY-OUTS OF NUMERICALLY EQUAL COLLECTIONS, CONSTRUCTED BY THE CHILD ACCORDING TO A MODEL

a. The experimenter lays out 7 or 8 counters on the table in three different patterns (line, right angle, circle) and asks the child to make

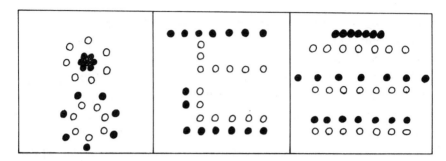

Fig. 2.1

up a set which has the same number of counters (see Fig. 2.1). "Put as many of your counters as I have of mine, the same number, amount . . . no more, no less, etc." The experimenter notes the child's spontaneous responses (random lay-out, rough copy of the general shape of the model, one-to-one correspondence, or counting), and then experimenter and child proceed to check whether the two collections do in fact have the same number of counters by arranging them so that one counter of one collection is directly underneath one of the other (visual one-to-one correspondence).

b. The experimenter then alters the shape of one of the collections, either by spacing out the elements in a long line or by putting them all closely together and asks conservation questions, requesting reasons for the child's answers and putting forward objections.

2. REPEATED ONE-TO-ONE CORRESPONDENCE, WITH CONTAINERS OF DIFFERENT SHAPES

a. The experimenter and the child simultaneously drop 8 or 10 balls, one at a time, into two identical opaque glasses, A and B (see Fig. 2.2): "Each time I put a ball into my glass you put one into yours." The experimenter then asks questions concerning the number of balls in the two collections: "Are there the same number of balls in each glass, or more in one than the other?" "How can we tell since we can't see?" "Do we have to check?" and so on. If necessary, the experimenter checks the child's answers by laying out the two collections on the table in one-to-one correspondence.

b. The same procedure is followed as for the above situation, but this time two transparent glasses of different diameter and height

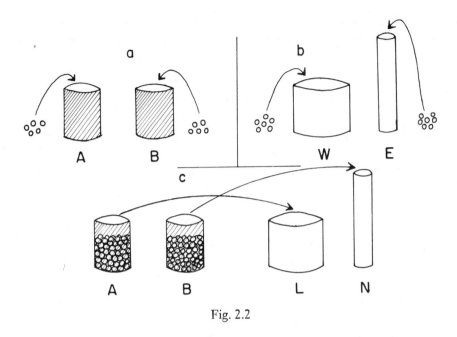

Fig. 2.2

(W and N) are used so that the child may actually see the differences in height and width between the two collections. The experimenter then asks the same questions about the number of objects in the collection as in situation a. The appearance of the result of the iterated addition can help the child make the correct multiplicative connections between the dimensions ("higher but thinner").

c. When, despite reminders of the repeated one-to-one correspondence, the subject continues to affirm that the quantities are not equal, the experimenter shows their equality (by taking the balls out of the glasses). Then the experimenter goes back to the opaque glasses A and B and pours their contents into two transparent glasses of different diameter and height (N and W), and asks conservation questions, insisting on justifications and using counter-arguments (see Fig. 2.2).

3. QUASI-CONTINUOUS QUANTITIES

The same procedure is followed as in situation 2, except that two small identical glasses, filled with seeds, are used in three different ways.

a. The experimenter and the child simultaneously pour seeds five or six times in succession from the small glasses into two opaque identical glasses, A and B.

b. They both simultaneously pour seeds several times from the small glasses into two transparent glasses, W and N.

c. Finally, the two collections of seeds in A and B are poured into two other transparent glasses W and N.

The whole procedure takes three sessions, each lasting from 15 to 20 minutes. The different problems were not always presented in exactly the same way, but were slightly modified depending upon each child's particular difficulties.

In problem 1, if the child spontaneously based his solutions to the first two situations on either a one-to-one correspondence or on counting, and gave correct conservation answers, the third situation was omitted.

In problem 2, situations a and b were always given to the children, but not necessarily situation c.

In problem 3, if a was not solved correctly, the rest was omitted.

Subjects and selection criteria. Fourteen children aged from 4;9 to 6;3 years were selected. Thirteen were in nursery school, one was in primary school (first grade). The subjects selected for training had given nonconservation responses in at least one of the above tasks. The mental structure necessary for the acquisition of conservation of continuous quantities had not yet been, or was only partially, acquired.

Pre-test. The pre-test consisted of two conservation tasks: liquid and modeling clay conservation (see Appendix).

Post-tests. Post-tests 1 and 2 were the same as the pre-test.

Duration. The first post-test was given from one to three days after the first training session. This was followed by a second post-test some four to six weeks later.

RESULTS

COMPARISON OF PRE-TEST AND POST-TESTS

A comparison of the results of the pre-test and post-tests (see Table 2.1) shows the progress that was accomplished.

TABLE 2.1

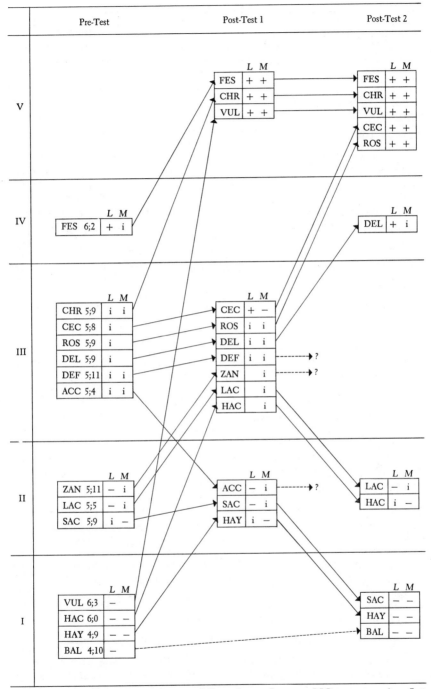

Note: L = liquids task; M = modeling clay task; − = NC response; i = Int response; + = C response.

1. For a first global analysis, the subjects were classified into three major categories according to their answers in the liquid and clay modeling conservation tasks.

Nonconservation (NC) category. All answers are incorrect, despite the help given by the experimenter. The subjects say, for instance, that "there is more to drink in one of the glasses" or "more to eat in the sausage."

Intermediate (Int) category. Some correct answers are given to the conservation questions. This category includes both children whose reasoning is still fairly close to nonconservation—children who hesitate between correct and wrong answers for only one of the tasks or for one of the situations of either task—and those whose reasoning is clearly more advanced—those who give correct answers to every part of either task.

Conservation (C) category. All answers are correct for both tasks.

General results. The pattern of results of the pre-test and two post-tests given in Table 2.1 indicates two important findings.

The results of post-test 1 show that the subjects who initially give clear nonconservation responses progress toward the intermediate stage (Int) and even to the C stage. Of the four children who are initially NC, two become Int and one becomes C (one child was not given the post-tests), while of the ten subjects who are initially in the Int category, eight remain at this level and two attain conservation.

The second post-test shows, on the one hand, a regression for the initial NC group (one subject reverts from Int to NC) and, on the other, some progress for the initial Int group (two more subjects acquired conservation). Three children who were initially Int were not given the second post-test. Quite possibly these subjects might have made the same progress as the others of their group.

There seem, therefore, to be two types of changes in responses, which depend upon the child's initial level of reasoning.

Children who start from a clear nonconservation level progress slightly (the details of this progress are most instructive and will be discussed further) but may return to a lower level a few weeks later.

Children who start off with some idea of conservation (as indicated by a few correct answers to the conservation questions) seem to gain no immediate benefit from the training sessions, but do, however, make some progress subsequently in post-test 2 (i.e., they give evidence of "delayed progress").

2. For a qualitative analysis of the children's responses in order to characterize their individual progress five categories were used instead of three.

I. The children give wrong answers to all the conservation questions for both liquids and modeling clay tasks.

II. The children give some correct answers for one of the tasks and completely fail the other.

III. The children give some correct answers for both tasks.

IV. The children give correct answers for all the situations of one of the tasks and fail, or else give only some correct answers, for the other.

V. The children are completely successful at both tasks.

Using these five categories, we get the following results.

a. One child (BAL) remained in category I throughout the experiment, i.e., his reasoning level neither regressed nor progressed; three children did not take the final post-test, so it was difficult to make a complete assessment of their progress. In the first post-test, however, two of these children, ZAN and DEF, remained at their initial level (categories III and II), whereas ACC regressed from III to II. This unusual regression was also noted in the control group.

b. Three children reverted to a lower level at the second post-test after having made some progress at the first: HAY progressed from I to II and then reverted to I; LAC progressed from II to III and then reverted to II; HAL progressed from I to III and reverted to II.

c. Some subjects made delayed progress, since their progress became apparent only at the second post-test or their responses improved between the first and the second. DEL started off in III and remained at this level at the first post-test, but then attained IV at the second; Ros and CEC also started at III and made no progress until the second post-test, when they reached category V. Thus two of these three children were completely successful in the final post-test.

d. Other children were successful immediately after the training sessions and did not regress: Vul, initially in category I, reached V in the first post-test, as did Chr (initial level, III) and Fes (initial level, IV).

The developmental patterns of groups b and c seem to be the most interesting ones. The subjects in group b seem to have acquired a type of reasoning which is not really operatory, or is only partially so, since they later regressed to a lower level. Those in group c are interesting because of the time taken for their progress to manifest itself, which would suggest the occurrence of an internal, unobservable process of structuration that is activated by the training sessions.

As for the children in group a, one explanation of their results might be that there was too great a gap between their initial level and the training problems.

The results of the children in group d are of no special interest, except that they helped us to realize that the pre-tests used in this experiment were probably inadequate and did not permit a true evaluation of the child's initial level, since they consisted only of two conservation tasks (liquids and modeling clay). In fact the initial situations of the training sessions (1.a and b) were more suitable than the pre-tests for assessing the true level of the subjects. *All* the children who reached category V in the second post-test gave correct judgments based on the concept of quotity and even some correct conservation responses, whereas three of the five subjects who ended up in categories I and II could not even solve the problems involving quotity and all five gave incorrect answers to problems dealing with elementary numerical conservation.

The types of justifications used for correct answers during the tests also show the differences between the children who regressed, those who progressed in post-test 2, and those who progressed immediately.

Children who regressed either provided no reasons for their correct answers, or mentioned only the initial quantities ("We had the same thing," i.e., the same amount of modeling clay or liquid).

Children who made gradual or delayed progress also referred to the initial equality to justify a conservation answer. At the first post-test, given immediately after the training sessions, they gave no reasons at all for their responses to the problems dealing with the differences in appearance, although the questioning sometimes led them to alter their judgments. Only at the second post-test did they give arguments referring to the actions carried out and to the compensatory relationship between the dimensions.

Children who made immediate progress, however, gave the various correct arguments as early as the first post-test.

ANALYSIS OF THE RESPONSES DURING THE TRAINING SESSIONS

An analysis of the response patterns of the different groups during the training sessions reveals that all the children showed some improvement and gave at least a few more correct answers than they had given at the pre-test. Several children who did not show any progress at the post-test showed some improvement during the training sessions and gave responses of an intermediate level for the easier situations, although they faltered when faced with the more complicated ones (e.g., DEF). Others who finally (at the post-tests) showed that they understood the concept of conservation had trouble with fairly elementary problems such as situation 2.b when the difference between the appearance of the two collections gradually became more obvious. In fact, two children had so much difficulty with these situations that it did not seem worthwhile going on to those where the contents of one glass are poured into another (situation 2.c). Surprisingly, however, one of these two children (CHA) was immediately successful at the first post-test and the other (CEC), after having given only a few correct answers at the first post-test, was completely successful at the second.

These contrasting types of response patterns suggest the existence of two distinct ways of approaching the problems of the training sessions. It seems as if, at an elementary level, the child initially grasps the repeated adding action in the experimental situation by means of an isolated scheme. He apparently conceives of this action of putting the balls into a glass one by one as a particular action that always results in a specific situation, but does not understand the action in terms of a logical process of addition.

The more advanced subjects, on the other hand, who already possess a number of logical schemes, seem much less sensitive to this purely repetitive aspect and sometimes do not refer to it at all. Consequently, their answers are at first incorrect, since their level of reasoning directs their attention toward the various obstacles to conservation, such as the difference between the appearances of the contents of the two glasses. Though they can dissociate height from width they cannot yet completely coordinate these dimensions, and though they have some idea of a possible return to the initial state, their reasoning still lacks reversibility.

The types of arguments used by the children to justify their answers during the training sessions seem to confirm this interpretation. It is generally subjects who make no progress, or who regress in the post-test, who use as their sole argument the process of iteration, i.e., the fact that the balls are repeatedly added in a one-to-one correspondence. By contrast, although the children who make progress also sometimes use this argument, they use others as well, such as the compensation of the dimensions of the contents of the glasses, or the reversibility in the case of the pouring. This points to the possibility that correct answers based on repetitive addition actions may be of low operative status.

EXCERPTS FROM PROTOCOLS

The following abstracts of three protocols will serve to illustrate the different types of responses noted during the training sessions and the pre-tests and post-tests.

DEF (5;11): *No Progress*
Pre-Test

Liquids. DEF gives the wrong answer when A is poured into the narrow glass (N), then begins to waver and spontaneously suggests that B be poured into a narrow glass to see if the liquid will come up to the same height as A did in N. He agrees that the quantities are the same when the experimenter stresses the "amount to drink," but is perplexed when the latter points out differences in level and diameter. When A is poured into a wide glass (W), he first answers incorrectly—"It's me who takes longest to drink (B)"—but then says that the amounts are equal, before again changing his mind and reverting to nonconservation when the experimenter puts forward objections or insists on the differences in the dimensions.

Modeling clay. When the clay ball is changed into a flat "pancake" and then into a "sausage," DEF's responses clearly indicate nonconservation: (more in the pancake) "Yours is bigger, I'm eating that (ball); (more in the sausage) "Now it's me who's eating longer . . . more."

Category: Int.

Training Sessions

In the situations involving a correspondence between discrete elements (Fig. 1.2), DEF either uses one-to-one correspondence or counts the elements in the model (but makes a mistake!), or else he makes a rough evaluation without using either of the above methods, again making a mistake, which he realizes as soon as the experimenter makes a one-to-one correspondence to check the answer.

When it comes to the conservation questions, DEF gives incorrect answers as soon as the appearance of the two collections is changed. However, some slight progress is noted in the final situation when the experimenter, after DEF has given a nonconservation answer, puts the two collections in a one-to-one correspondence and then again alters the lay-out of one of them. DEF maintains that the two collections are no longer equal in number, but nevertheless predicts that they could become the same if arranged "properly," and refuses to add any elements to the one he considers to have fewer objects. However, he wants to make sure his answer is correct by counting and, having done this for one collection, correctly predicts the number of elements in the other ("Six in A"—"Then how many in B?"—"Six"). He then states that both collections have the same number for all the situations.

DEF thus makes progress, but this is based on his realizing, when the one-to-one correspondence is demonstrated again, that he has made a mistake. Moreover, this is only possible because he can make use of counting, which for him is a kind of "strategy" or "method." DEF does not yet understand that conservation is a necessary state of affairs, although he is beginning to grasp the idea of invariance based on quotity.

In the situation where the child has to construct collections of elements, DEF immediately gives the correct answer to the conservation question concerning the contents of two identical opaque glasses in which he and the experimenter have dropped little balls (situation 2.a) and bases his answer on the action of iteration: "I know, we both put one in at the same time—that's why!" Similarly, when it comes to the transparent glasses of different shapes (situation 2.b), he maintains that the contents are equal, again basing his answer on iteration, but when the experimenter draws his attention to the appearance of the contents, he is incapable of giving an argument concerning the different shapes of the glasses, even though he repeats his correct answer. He is perplexed only when asked a question relating to the number of objects, which he does not know how to answer ("If I have ten in N, can you tell how many you have in W?"—"A very little . . ."). He maintains the equality of the collections when the contents of A and B are poured into N and W, but gives no explanation.

Quasi-continuous quantities: DEF judges correctly in the situations with the glasses of different shapes (situation 3.b), again basing his answer on iteration—"We both put in at the same time, we both put in the same thing"—and does not yield to counter-arguments.

When all the contents of one glass are poured into another (situation 3.c), he begins to hesitate; he says that the amounts are equal, but does not even justify his answer by referring to the action of pouring and changes his mind as soon as the experimenter points out the differences in appearance.

Post-Test 1

Modeling clay. This problem produces a variety of responses, with the child giving a few correct conservation answers, for which he either cannot give a reason at all, or else gives a very elementary one.

Liquids. He answers some of the pouring questions correctly, but his reasons, when he gives them at all, are irrelevant and he yields to counter-arguments. As a whole, however, the results are slightly more advanced than for the pre-test, without justifying a change of category.

Category: Int.

Post-Test 2

DEF gives nonconservation responses for both tasks. Furthermore, he incorrectly predicts the levels in the liquids situation, i.e., he predicts that when A is poured into W, the liquid will rise to the same level as in B.

Category: NC.

The responses throughout the actual training sessions seem to be fairly advanced and indicate clear progress when compared with the incorrect answers to the questions of the pre-test, and also when compared with his first reactions to the problems involving one-to-one correspondence. However, his frequent use of the iteration argument is striking and DEF gives no reasons for his correct answers, referring neither to compensation of dimensions nor to reversibility.

The child's responses to the two post-tests are instructive in this respect. In fact, his partial progress at the modeling clay and liquids tasks in the first post-test (i.e., a few correct answers, but no explanations), followed by a regression to complete nonconservation six weeks later, would suggest that there was no truly operatory progress and that the changes noted were closely linked to the actual context of the training sessions. In other words, as mentioned previously, DEF was applying an as yet nonoperatory scheme of iteration as a limited strategy for answering a specific question, without having grasped the additive nature of this action. We shall return to this case when discussing the value and shortcomings of this training procedure.

DEL (5;9): *Partial Progress*

Pre-Test

Liquids. When faced with the first situation, where the contents of one glass are poured into another, DEL asserts that the quantity has not changed, but can give no justification. His answers to the following situations are incorrect, based on the levels of the liquids.

Category: Int.

Training Sessions

In the first situations (different lay-outs of numerically equal collections), DEL answers correctly for a series of changes in the lay-out of the collections and refuses all counter-arguments, although he is unable to give reasons.

In the problems involving glasses of different shapes and repeated one-to-one correspondence, DEL starts off by declaring incorrectly that the amounts are different. It is only when he is asked the conservation questions in terms of number ("If you counted first all your balls and then all mine, how would it be, would there be the same number or a different number?") that he agrees that the amounts are equal, basing his judgment on the iterative actions: "We put balls in at the same time and stopped." When the contents of glasses A and B are poured into others of a different shape (N and W) he agrees that the amounts remain the same, but bases his answer solely on the iterative action and is unable to answer the questions concerning the different levels.

He has no trouble giving correct answers to the problems involving quasi-continuous quantities (situation 3) and, what is important, in situation 3.b not only does he refer to the iterative actions but, for the first time, he also becomes aware of the relationship between the dimensions, albeit fleetingly.

Post-Test 1

Modeling clay. DEL is at an intermediate level for the modeling clay problems: after one of the changes in shape (clay rolled out into a sausage), he gives a conservation answer backed up by arguments of reversibility: "If he (another child) made it (the sausage) back into a ball, he'd have the same thing"; but for the next change (into a "pancake"), he denies that the amounts are the same, correcting his judgment only when the experimenter insists on the quantitative aspect of "the amount to eat."

Liquids. DEL also makes mistakes in the liquids task. He correctly answers the conservation questions after the contents of one glass have been poured into another, referring to the initial quantities—"We both had the same height in our jars"—but has difficulty with another question, and even when he hesitatingly gives a correct answer, he cannot provide an explanation. Finally he reverts to nonconservation answers. The result is thus more or less the same as for the pre-test, the only difference being that when DEL does manage to give justifications for his answers, these seem to indicate a slightly greater flexibility of reasoning.

Category: Int.

Post-Test 2

Modeling clay. Three weeks later, when once again faced with the modeling clay problems, DEL unhesitatingly and immediately answers correctly and gives appropriate reasons showing that the change in shape has been noted, even though it is not very clearly explained (in the experimenter's opinion at least): "They both have the same thing, but because you've squashed one, you can't see what it's really like." However, he still wavers when the experimenter deliberately tries to raise doubts in his mind.

Liquids: When it comes to the liquids task, DEL immediately answers all the conservation questions correctly and refers to the initial quantities and the compensatory relationship between the dimensions: "There you can see it (the level) is smaller because the circle's a bit bigger (B); here the circle's a bit smaller, but it's higher (N)."

Category: Int-C.

DEL seems to show delayed progress: progress is scarcely noticeable at the first post-test, but seems well entrenched three weeks later. It is interesting that DEL based his solutions to the first problems of the training sessions (situations 1 and 2) solely on the iterative actions, and only in the final situation (3) began to relate the dimensions.

Unlike DEF, discussed above, this child progressed beyond a limited use of the repetition of a one-to-one correspondence. It seems, in fact, as if the learning context enabled DEL, who started off by basing his judgments of equality on a system of additive actions, finally to acquire the complementary operations of multiplication that are needed to solve the problem.

VUL (6;3): *Acquisition of Conservation*
Pre-Test

Liquids. In the liquids task VUL gives nonconservation responses, basing his answers on the levels of the liquids, although he explains the covariation of the levels by relating the dimensions of the two glasses: "This glass is rounder (W), the other one's small (N)"—"What happens when the circle is small?"—"There's more (liquid)."

Category: NC.

Training Sessions

In the first situations (different lay-outs) VUL makes up the second collection by means of one-to-one correspondence, then after the lay-out has been changed, he gives a conservation response with the following reason: "I looked at the numbers and that makes nothing." He presumably means that he visually established the equivalence by one-to-one correspondence and saw that no element was left unpaired.

In the problems where he and the experimenter drop balls into transparent glasses of different shapes (situation 2), and the contents are poured from one glass to another, he answers all the conservation questions correctly and refuses to yield to the experimenter's counter-arguments. However, despite the experimenter's insistence, he can give no reason for his judgment of equal quantities, not even the iterative argument. In an attempt to get the child to give some reasons, the experimenter repeats situations 2.b and c, whereupon VUL clearly invokes the covariation of the dimensions: "This one's thinner (N) and that one's bigger (W)."

VUL answers all the questions for the problems concerning quasi-continuous quantities correctly and once again refers to the covariation of the dimensions. He is not swayed by the experimenter's counter-arguments.

Post-Test

Liquids. He is absolutely certain of his correct answers to the two situations of the liquids task and in explanation expresses the idea of compensation even more clearly than before: "You'd think there was more in N than in W, look where it comes up to!" "No, the same (amount), the circle's much smaller than that one (W) . . . because the circle is smaller, it fills up more quickly."

Modeling clay. He has no difficulty with the clay task. His explanations reveal reasoning based on identity—"There's just as much, because before it (the "pancake") was round, now he's squashed it"—and show that he has made a clear distinction between the quantity (unchanged) and the shape (changed): "No (neither more nor less); it's the circle which is bigger."

Two aspects of VUL's results are of particular interest. First, the completely correct and confident answers he gave right from the beginning of the training sessions provided a striking contrast to his performance in the pre-test. It is possible that he already possessed the necessary underlying mental structures but was not able to apply them to the situations of the pre-test, which was unusually short (no modeling clay task). Second, it is striking to note that, in contrast to DEF and DEL, he made no reference whatsoever during the training sessions to the iterative actions. It seems that the child's mental structure was clearly at an advanced level and this allowed him to progress beyond the actual context of the learning situations by means of an immediate (but unobservable) process of assimilation, or of integration of the schemes which he already possessed with those elicited by the training procedure, the latter being slightly different from, but complementary to, the former.

These three cases seem to exemplify different ways whereby the subject relates his schemes to the experimental situations.

DEF seemed to focus all his attention immediately on the iterative actions, but this scheme remained isolated and did not lead to an understanding of the complementary relationships between the dimensions. His focus on this single scheme may even have masked the other aspects of the situation, so that he simply decided to ignore them.

DEL also concentrated his attention on the iterative actions, but since he was more advanced initially he progressed beyond the use of this single scheme, and even rejected it in favor of others. Unlike DEF, he assigned a meaning to the iterative actions, which seems to indicate the beginnings of a logical understanding of the situation. An internal process of coordination of the various schemes appears to have occurred during the interval between the two post-tests. However, it cannot be decided whether this emphasis on the additive aspect of the actions—through the selection of the specific situations presented and the questions asked—did in fact actuate the child's awareness of the multiplicative relationships, or whether the exercises of the training sessions acted in a very general way by promoting a progress in coordination.

Finally, in the case of VUL, all the aspects of the problems were apprehended logically and systematically interrelated.

GENERAL DISCUSSION

The above findings led to a distinction between, on the one hand, responses which consist solely of a focusing on the iterative actions and, on the other, those which are based on a general system of coordinations.

In the first two examples (DEF and DEL), the scheme of a repeated one-to-one correspondence apparently led to a simple focusing on the initial equality which prevented these children from being completely absorbed by the actual appearance of the collections, and thus resulted in some conservation answers. These subjects did not, however, understand that the changes in appearance were in fact the result of a transformation which leaves quantity invariant. The focus of their attention was limited to the immediate context of the experimental training situation and did not correspond to a real progress in the development of their reasoning. By contrast, it seems that the emphasis placed on the numerical equivalence of the collections formed by the iterative method helped the children who made delayed progress to understand the transformations carried out on the collections and the ensuing differences in their appearance. At first these children mentioned only the iterative argument, but subsequently, at the second post-test, they not only made use of the argument of numerical equivalence in situations outside the context of the training sessions, but could also apprehend other aspects of various problems.

Finally, in the case of the subjects who consistently answered correctly as early as the first post-test, we can hypothesize that their rapid progress during the training sessions was due to a more advanced initial level and that their results at the first post-test were symptoms of a process of reorganization that for other subjects took a much longer time.

In this respect, it is worthwhile describing the responses of CHR (5;9), who seems to have had more difficulty during the training sessions than was expected from the results of his pre-test (category Int-Int). Furthermore, at first sight these difficulties appeared to be greater than those of DEF, which led us to predict that CHR's final results would not be very advanced, whereas in fact he displayed an operatory understanding of the problem as early as the first post-test.

In the training sessions, when faced with the first changes in lay-out of a collection of objects (situation 1), CHR incorrectly answers: "There are too many blue counters (widely spread out)." When the experimenter suggests that he remove some from the row that he considers to have the greater number of counters, he merely rearranges the collection into a one-to-one correspondence, thus implicitly refusing to take any away. After another change in lay-out, he answers correctly—"They're both the same; there you've stuck the counters (red) together and that's why the line's shorter"—and refuses to be swayed by any of the experimenter's subsequent counter-arguments.

CHR seems, therefore, to have benefited from the training situations, since he can now differentiate between changes in lay-out or shape and changes in number.

When it comes to comparing numbers of objects in glasses of different shapes (situation 2), he shows some understanding of compensation —"No, there aren't more (in N) because there are some which are leaning against each other"—but this is not sufficient to lead to a permanent grasp of conservation. When he comes to the problem of quasi-continuous quantities (situation 3), CHR maintains that the two quantities are not the same, even as early as the initial situation, when experimenter and child are simultaneously adding seeds from the small glasses to the containers, and despite the fact that the experimenter explicitly recapitulates these repeated additions.

At the first post-test, in the conservation of liquids task CHR gives contradictory responses: "There's more in N because it's higher"; "They are both the same." However, he also gives a clear explanation of the co-variations: "There's as much to drink because it's in a bigger glass, it's more spread out."

Similarly, in the modeling clay task when the ball is flattened out into a "pancake," he says: "We've both got the same, but you have more because you've squashed it." Thus CHR relates the different factors, but does not manage to coordinate them, despite the help that might be derived from the use of the iterative method. In the second post-test, he answers all the questions correctly.

CHR, therefore, becomes acutely aware of the various difficulties inherent in the different situations of the training sessions and, in contrast to DEF or even DEL, does not regard iteration as a means for producing the correct answers to questions on numerical equality. DEF finds these obstacles insuperable, although he had apparently "succeeded" much better than CHR and, at first sight, i.e., solely on the basis of his "answers" and without taking into account his various arguments and obvious conflicts, DEF seemed more likely to make progress than CHR.

CONCLUDING REMARKS

For all its limitations, this experiment revealed types of responses, the importance of which will become clearer in some of the later experiments.

1. First, the training procedure produced two types of reactions, which resulted in two distinct kinds of change in the responses to the post-tests. The first type of reaction is found in children who have no difficulty with the situations of the training sessions, but whose explanations are based solely on the repeated one-to-one correspondence. The second type of reaction is found in children who hesitate when faced with the situations of the training sessions. From what they say, it seems that they cannot reconcile an understanding of the additive actions with the ensuing differences in the appearance of the collections. In certain cases, the conflict is resolved by a grasp of the meaning of the repetitive actions as well as of covariation and a possible return to the initial state. In others, the children fail to resolve the conflict and manage to give only a few correct answers.

What is the nature of the first type of reaction? Is it simply that the child stops focusing on the difference in appearance between the two collections and turns his attention to the correspondence between the adding actions of the experimenter and himself, which enables him to answer correctly? Is this change in focus sufficient to lead to an operatory understanding? Does it constitute a necessary and useful stage in the development of this concept, or is it simply the result of an experimental artifact which turns out to be a handicap for the child's future development because it directs the child's attention away from factors which he must understand before he can solve the problem in a truly operatory fashion? Such questions are also pertinent to the cognitive learning experiments carried out by Bruner and his team (Bruner et al., 1966).

By contrast, the second type of reaction is clearly due to a conflictual situation, i.e., what the children feel to be a contradiction between various aspects of the problem. Unlike the children showing the first type of reaction, those with the second type always make progress at the post-tests: at times, this is only partial, although stable, and at others it results in complete success.

2. This experiment also highlighted another interesting point about the changes in responses. The second post-test was intended to provide a means of checking whether the progress noted at the first test was in fact maintained; it was a surprise when some children (CEC, ROS, and DEF) gave *better* results at the second than at the first post-test. This delayed progress seems important and suggests the existence of internal processes of coordination which take place between the two tests, and which might be comparable to the coordination achieved by other children during the actual training sessions.

3. Some subjects had great difficulty in applying a reasoning which had proved adequate for problems dealing with discrete elements to other situations where quasi-continuous materials were used. This would suggest that the developmental link between the conservation of discrete and continuous quantities is neither simple nor direct. Further reference will be made to this question in the following chapters.

4. This experiment revealed a methodological difficulty. To assess the initial level of subjects, pre-tests consisting of two conservation tasks (liquids and modeling clay) are not sufficient.

Although a great deal of care was taken to effect a precise analysis of the intermediate level of responses (of children who essentially gave both correct and incorrect answers), it is difficult to evaluate the potential of a child whose answers are clearly nonoperatory.

Indeed, the responses of certain children during the training sessions are surprising when compared to the evaluation of their level on the basis of the pre-test. This unpredictable development raises a problem. Can these unforeseen responses be accounted for by shortcomings of our pre-test? Or are they due to differences in the children's individual potentials? In order to clarify this problem an attempt was made in several of the subsequent experiments to carry out a more detailed analysis of the child's initial level of reasoning during the pre-test, by using tasks directly related to the concept we wanted the children to learn as well as tasks dealing with other concepts that are generally acquired at the same ages.

5. This experiment also showed that it was advisable to select subjects for training who had at least reached a given level of development at the pre-test, e.g., the notion of quotity. Adequate exercises are easier to devise from such a baseline.

Similarly, the post-tests in this experiment are not totally satisfactory, since they remain too close to the situations presented in the training sessions. This makes it difficult to decide whether a child's success is due to the actualization of already existing possibilities, to his gradual familiarization with the experimental situation, or whether it is the result of genuine progress in reasoning. In the later experiments, some of these shortcomings have been remedied.

3 / From Numerical Equality to the Conservation of Matter

In this third experiment we also studied the acquisition of the concept of conservation of quantity. A series of exercises was presented which aimed at inciting the child to make direct use of his understanding of elementary numerical conservation in order to deal with problems of continuous quantity. A child who is beginning to understand that alteration of the configuration of a collection of objects does not change their number, but who has not yet grasped the idea that a change in the shape of, say, a ball of modeling clay does not alter the amount of modeling clay, might be helped to understand this latter conservation principle if bits of modeling clay were first simply juxtaposed, and then joined before finally being modified in shape. It was hoped that this would make the child realize that the total object is made up of smaller pieces which, even though they may be put together to make different shapes, can be formed again by breaking these up. If number is already conserved, it should not be difficult for the child to go on from this to the idea that the quantity of substance in the total object remains the same.

TRAINING PROCEDURE, TESTS, AND SELECTION OF SUBJECTS

In this experiment, the selection criteria for the subjects were more rigorous than those of previous studies, in that only subjects who had already acquired the concept of quotity or of number conservation (see Appendix, counter tests) but not yet that of conservation of quantity were selected. The post-tests, on the other hand, had the same shortcoming as in the previous experiment, namely, that they were the same as the pre-test. Furthermore, the same material (modeling clay) was used for the training sessions and for one of the tests. In the other one, however, liquid was used and so that test provided a more accurate indication of progress.

Materials. Small cylindrical pieces of modeling clay of different colors and two sizes, *a* and *b*, are used; *a* is approximately twice the size of *b* (both in length and in diameter). These objects, which in the experiment are referred to as "sweets," are made mechanically, so that there are no differences in size between the sweets of any one category.

Method. As in the experiment on elementary number (see Appendix), 8 sweets of the same size are put in a line. The experimenter asks the child to compare their number with the number in a pile of sweets of a different color and a different size (series I) or the same size (series II). If the child does not spontaneously put the two collections in a one-to-one correspondence, this is suggested to him.

By using two different sets, one with sweets of equal size and the other with sweets of unequal size, the experimenter presents two different types of situations to the children. The first series of situations consists of two sets of sweets differing in size and the second series of two sets of sweets of identical size but different colors. The problems of the first series are more difficult, although the experimental method is the same in both types of situation.

Once the child has put the two collections in one-to-one correspondence, he is asked questions concerning the numerical equality of the two sets and the inequality or equality of the quantity of modeling clay. The child is invited to compare one sweet from the first collection with the corresponding one from the second and so on for each pair of corresponding sweets, and then asked to generalize to the total quantity in both collections. In the first series, this quantity is different, since the sweets in one row are bigger than those in the other; in the second series, the quantity is the same, since the sweets are of identical size in the two collections. When the child has grasped this "initial situation," the experimenter presents the nine situations described below. In each situation, one of the collections—the reference collection, or collection A—remains unmodified; the other is called B. In some cases, the extremities of this collection coincide with those of the modified collection (unequal size and situation 7); in others, the extremities do not coincide (equal size and situations 3, 6, and 8).

1. The sweets of set B are joined in pairs, but remain clearly visible as individual elements.

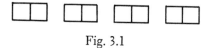

Fig. 3.1

2. The sweets are joined in groups of four.

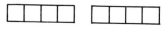

Fig. 3.2

3. All the sweets are joined together.

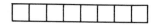

Fig. 3.3

4. Out of each pair of sweets, a new sweet is made (by reshaping the clay). Thus four elongated balls are obtained in which the two original elements are no longer distinguishable.

Fig. 3.4

5. Each set of four sweets is made into a new sweet. Thus two elongated balls are obtained.

Fig. 3.5

6. All the sweets are stuck together and made into a sausage of shorter length than row A.

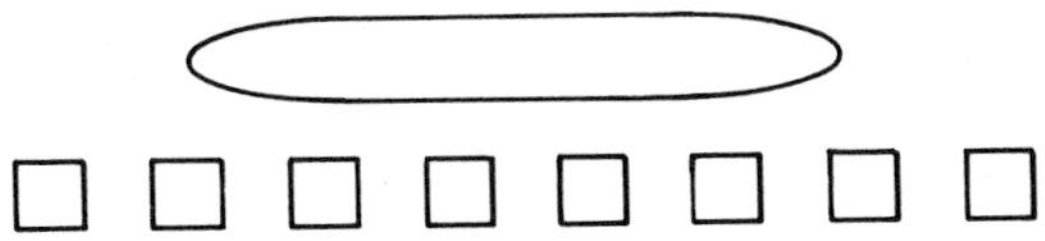

Fig. 3.6

7. The sausage is elongated so that its extremities coincide with those of A.

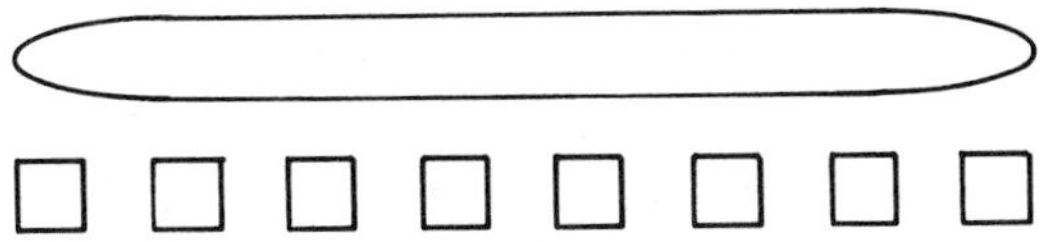

Fig. 3.7

8. The sausage is elongated even more so that its extremities now go beyond those of A.

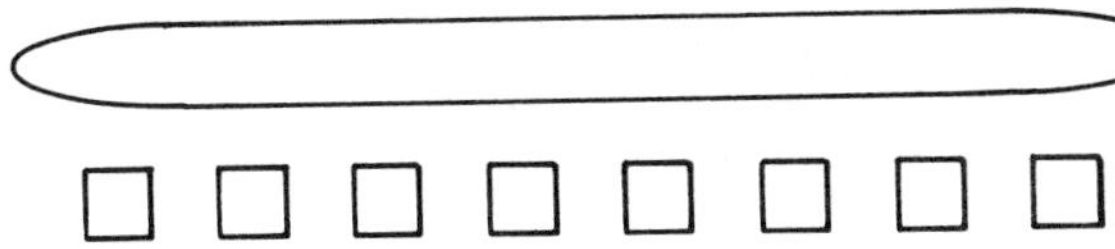

Fig. 3.8

9. The sausage is made into a ball.

After each change in shape of B, the experimenter asks the child whether there are the same number of sweets and the same amount of clay in the two collections. If the child gives incorrect answers to the questions in the first three situations, the experimenter returns to the initial situation. Some situations (4 and 5) may be omitted with more advanced subjects.

The experimenter asks the following questions, and, as usual, puts them in several different ways.

1. "Are there just as many . . . the same number of . . . or more or less sweets in the balls (or sausage) as here (reference set A)?"

2. "Is there the same amount of clay . . . would there be just as much to eat . . . in the sweets as in the sausage?"

Subjects and selection criteria. The 14 subjects selected, aged from 5;4 to 7;0 years, had at least grasped the concept of quotity, a necessary condition for the training sessions, but had not yet acquired conservation of quantity (modeling clay test).

Pre-test. The pre-test consisted of the following tasks: (1) elementary numerical conservation; material: counters (see Appendix); (2) conservation of continuous matter; material: modeling clay (see Appendix); (3) conservation of continuous matter; material: liquids (see Appendix).

Post-tests. The post-tests were the same as the pre-test.

Duration. Immediately after the pre-test the children were given three training sessions at weekly intervals, each lasting approximately 20 to 30 minutes. After these sessions, the first post-test was given, followed, six to eight weeks later, by the second.

RESULTS

COMPARISON OF PRE-TEST AND POST-TESTS

The children were divided into four groups according to their responses at the pre-test (see Table 3.1).

Level I (the lowest). The five children of this group had only reached the level of quotity in the conservation of number task and were clearly at the nonconservation level in those of liquids and modeling clay.

Level II (slightly more advanced). Four children differed from those of the above group in that they sometimes gave correct answers in the liquids task and were thus at an intermediate level for this concept, whereas in the number and modeling clay tasks their results were equivalent to those of level I. (This confirms that conservation of liquids is generally acquired slightly earlier than that of modeling clay, since these children had already reached the intermediate stage for the liquids when they were still clearly at a nonconservation level for the modeling clay.)

Level III. Two children were classed at this level; one had completely acquired conservation of liquids but had not yet fully grasped that of number. Their responses to the modeling clay task indicated nonconservation. It is important to note that in the pre-test the liquids task was always given at the end of the session, so that the actual pre-test may have been a learning experience, at least in the sense that the children became aware of, and to a certain extent familiar with, the problems of quantity.

Level IV. Three children unhesitatingly gave correct answers in the conservation of liquids task and were at an intermediate stage for that of modeling clay. These were the only children who at the beginning of the experiment had already acquired a true conservation of elementary number and were not just at the level of quotity for this concept.

The following responses were noted during post-test 1.

The five children of levels III and IV were all completely successful in the post-test problems of conservation of number, modeling clay, and liquids. This acquisition was perfectly stable, remaining unchanged at the second post-test. Only one child from level II did as well. Two of the children of the lowest level made no progress; the other subjects from levels I and II improved slightly. It is interesting that three of the children of levels I and II first showed progress in the liquids problems, which were not touched upon during the training sessions, where only modeling clay was used. Indeed, at no point during the training sessions did the experimenter bring up the question of relationships between containers and their contents, which is one of the features of the liquids task.

The children who made slight progress can be divided into two categories: the first, more advanced one includes all the subjects who increased their understanding of numerical conservation and gave more advanced arguments than those based on quotity or simple counting. These children also achieved either true conservation or an intermediate level in the liquids task, but made little or no progress in the modeling clay task. The second category includes the two

TABLE 3.1

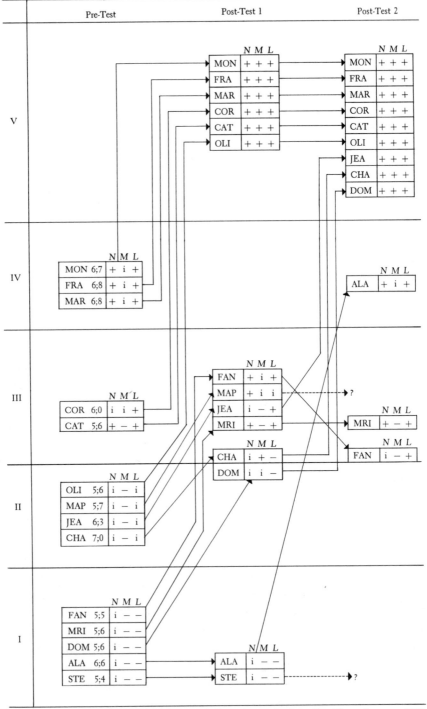

	Pre-Test	Post-Test 1	Post-Test 2

Note: N = numbers task; M = modeling clay task; L = liquids task; $-$ = NC response; i = Int response; $+$ = C response.

children who made no progress in number (remaining at the level of quotity) and liquids (remaining at a nonconservation level) but who made some progress in modeling clay (reaching an intermediate level).

At post-test 2 the following responses were noted.

All the children who were completely successful in the conservation of modeling clay task at the first post-test remained at the same level at the second: their acquisition was thus completely stable.

Only one of the two children who made no progress at the first post-test was given the second. This child then made spectacular progress, attaining true conservation of both elementary number and liquids and reaching an intermediate level for modeling clay.

Of the children who improved slightly, one remained at the same level at the second post-test, one regressed to a lower level (from C Int C to Int NC NC for number, modeling clay, and liquids respectively), and the others acquired conservation of modeling clay. This is another example of what has been termed "delayed progress."

The following points may be made.

1. Progress was clearly dependent upon the child's initial level. All five children of groups III and IV were completely successful at the first post-test, whereas only one of nine children in groups I and II reached this level.

2. The intermediate levels obtained through training sessions were unstable: only one child remained at the same level from post-test 1 to post-test 2. In fact, even though this child must be considered to have made partial progress, he did not remain at the intermediate stage for any one particular task, since he achieved conservation of elementary number and liquids but failed completely in the modeling clay task. Thus, at the second post-test no children were at the intermediate stage for any of the concepts.

3. The number of children who were completely successful was fairly high (six out of fourteen at the first post-test and nine at the second) and the acquisitions were stable. Furthermore, acquisition of conservation of modeling clay was always accompanied by that of liquids, which was generally mastered a little earlier than the former.

4. The percentage of success may have been due to the small differ-

ence between the ages at which conservation is acquired for liquids and for modeling clay. At the pre-test, nine of our subjects had already acquired, or were at an intermediate stage for, conservation of liquids, and only five were true nonconservers. None of these five completely acquired the concept at the first post-test and only one managed to do so at the second. The children who achieved conservation of modeling clay appeared to have made genuine progress, although on a small scale, since they already possessed, or were on the point of acquiring, conservation of liquids.

5. All but two of our subjects progressed in the problem of elementary numerical conservation to the point of giving correct answers supported by valid arguments.

Finally, the following responses of a control group of eight children who were given the same pre-test and two post-tests, but no training sessions, may be noted. These children showed some slight improvement in the liquids and modeling clay tasks, particularly in post-test 2, but none attained true conservation. The most important result, however, particularly when we consider the results of the training experiment, is that no child of the control group improved his understanding of number. All the children remained at the level of quotity at both the first and the second post-tests and did not modify their original responses in any way.

ANALYSIS OF THE RESPONSES DURING THE TRAINING SESSIONS

During the training sessions, the children encountered a number of difficulties which have been noted in other studies but which we had hardly expected in this type of training procedure.

As already mentioned, we had hoped that the training procedure used in this experiment (i.e., progressing from simple juxtaposition to modifications of shape) would make the children realize that an object can be thought of as consisting of several small ones whose number is conserved despite the fact that these small objects are grouped together in different ways. This realization could then be followed by the understanding that, regardless of how they are grouped, these small objects can be recovered by breaking up the whole, whose overall quantity must be conserved if the number of components is also conserved.

Since a number of children did indeed acquire conservation of modeling clay, it could be thought that this is indeed what occurs and that, consequently, there is a clear and direct link between the starting point (conservation of number, or at least the concept of quotity), the effects of the exercises of the training sessions, and the end result. If this were the case, the children's reaction to the training sessions could provide direct information on the processes of acquiring this conservation. In actual fact, for the advanced group of three subjects starting at level IV, progress was so rapid (just a little hesitation at the beginning followed immediately by correct and well-justified answers to all the questions) that virtually nothing could be inferred about the acquisition process. By contrast, we did observe some interesting reactions in the other groups, but these only suggested what might be the general difficulties facing a child at a particular level. These reactions, like the results of the post-test, were closely related to the child's initial level.

None of the children who initially were at levels I or II appeared to be aware of the progressive character of the actions performed (juxtaposition and modification). Some of them even found it difficult to admit that there were still the same number of "sweets" when these were joined in pairs, although the separate pieces remained clearly visible. Others had problems as soon as the experimenter made a "sausage" in which the individual elements could no longer be distinguished. All the children finally agreed that "you can get the sweets again if you cut it up," but this idea of a possible return to the former state did not affect their judgment of quantity of modeling clay. They evaluated the latter as if it were possible to compare directly a row of discrete elements with a continuous quantity. The different arguments of these children indicate the presence of a number of instructive substages.

The total quantity of modeling clay contained in a collection of pieces is generally evaluated by the number of the pieces and by their size. In the case of a row of elements, the number of elements is related to the length of the row and the space in between each of them. In the case of a single object, quantity is judged by its size, which in turn is evaluated from its dimensions. As the less advanced children make progress, they base their judgments on an increasing number of the above factors, i.e., number and size of elements, and begin to make partial compensations (often wrong) between them. They continue, however, to make direct comparisons between the total reference collection and one object of the modified collection without referring to the possibility of reestablishing the original row of elements. At a more advanced level, partial compensations become increasingly frequent, and the children are able to envisage partitioning actions by which the original elements can be reproduced. It is only at a higher level, when the children achieve conservation, that they realize that both number and quantity remain unchanged; at this point, the modifications of shape have been interiorized and are considered reversible.

The responses at the various sublevels have the following characteristics.

1. At sublevel 1, the children base their comparisons solely on size, in the following curious ways. They compare a single element in the reference row with a single element in the modified row, even if the latter has been made into one large object (sausage or ball). For example (unequal quantities, small blue pieces stuck together in pairs to be compared with a row of large red pieces): "There's more blue clay, because the blue balls are bigger"; and to prove his point the child puts one piece containing two blue pieces and one red sweet side by side. Or again (equal quantities, sausage shorter than the unchanged row): "There isn't the same amount, because the sausage is longer" (compared with a single piece in the unchanged row). It seems that these children attribute the "bigness" or "longness" of one single element to the whole collection. On the other hand, these children often base their judgments only on number (or rather numerosity) without paying attention to the size of the pieces. In this case, they give answers such as, for equal quantities, ball, "There isn't the same amount anymore because there're more blue sweets and only one red ball." Both types of reasoning are found in the same child at this first sublevel, but not for the same problem, since this would involve contradictory judgments of quantity such as: "There's more in the ball because it's bigger than one sweet" and "There's more in the sweets because there are several and there's only one ball."

2. At sublevel 2, the children base their answers on another comparison which to them remains valid a very long time, i.e., the comparison between the space occupied by the sausage to the length of the row, regardless of the spacing of the pieces. We had not expected to find such extensive use of this criterion. Indeed, if one makes a direct comparison between the unchanged row and the modified elements, without referring to the initial state and the type of action which modified it, then "length" is the most obvious characteristic common to the two collections, and the preponderance of evaluations based on "going beyond" or "stopping at the same point" is well known. Some children judge quantity solely on the basis of this criterion, as can be seen from the answer of CHA (7;0) (equal sizes, long red sausage and row of blue sweets): "If you eat the sausage you get more than if you eat the sweets, because the sausage is a lot longer than those blue sweets." She is therefore comparing the length of the total row to that of the sausage. In one sense, this constitutes progress, because the characteristics of any one element are no longer attributed to the whole and the only common characteristic of the sausage and sweets that can be directly compared is the length or the distance between extremities. However, this factor may be overshadowed by that of numerosity, e.g. (for unequal quantities, long sausage, row of sweets), ALA (6;6) says: "There, it's bigger (sausage) and there, it's smaller (pointing to the row of sweets), but there is still more there (sweets) because there are eight."

3. At sublevel 3, children occasionally combine length with numerosity, which leads them to make inadequate and rather curious compensations. CAT (5;6) (unequal quantities, row of blue sweets joined together in pairs and a row of red sweets) first judges by numerosity: "There isn't the same to eat because there are less blue ones." Then (unequal quantities, red sausage longer than a row of blue sweets) she says: "There's the same because there are a lot of blue ones and that's long" (compensation of length of sausage by the numerosity of the separate elements).

4. Finally, at sublevel 4, we noted references to the possibility of reconstituting the original collection. But despite the fact that when asked whether they can get as many sweets as before almost all the children agree that it is possible to return to the original number of

sweets, it is only at a more advanced level that this idea is used to support a judgment of quantity.

The above-mentioned sublevels are not always clearly distinct, and in fact some of the children (e.g., CAT, mentioned above) pass from one level to another during the course of a single session. Particularly in the case of the ball (situation 9), children very often combine reasoning based on a possible reconstitution action with partial compensations. This may be because here "length" is much less striking than in the situation where the modeling clay is made into a sausage. However, the reasoning that we have called an effective reconstitution possibility is at first applied only to the number of elements and not yet to their size (unequal quantities, ball, situation 9): DOM (5;6) explains, "It's the same because when you make little ones like that again you get the same, because you haven't taken anything away." It is, of course, only in situations where the objects of both collections were initially the same size that this reconstitution results in the correct answer. This is why the responses to series I are more instructive than those to series II, since they show that the children seem to have great difficulty in progressing from reasoning based on reconstitution to that indicating true reversibility, which was in fact the aim of the training sessions. The ability to imagine certain actions which will reconstitute the initial elements does not immediately and automatically lead to reversible operations. Evaluation methods based on the *hic et nunc* situation continue to be prevalent, dominated by factors such as length and numerosity, whose combination does not result in a correct notion of measurement.

EXCERPTS FROM PROTOCOLS

CHA (7;0)

At the pre-test, CHA has the concept of quotity, gives nonconservation responses for the modeling clay task and some conservation ones for the liquids problem, although these are not justified.

First Series, Unequal Quantities

After a few difficulties at the outset, CHA eventually admits that when the blue sweets are stuck together in pairs (with the separation still visible) their number remains the same. She also agrees that there is always less blue than red clay "because the red sweets are bigger and the blue ones smaller."

When the sausage is shorter than the row of sweets she agrees that you can always get back to the same number of sweets, "because you can cut it and squash the bits, that makes one blue one for each red one."

For the quantity of modeling clay she correctly judges that there is more red than blue clay (sausage), but her justification is strange: "more red, because they are only squashed a bit and the sausage is all squashed, that makes less and there are more red sweets." When the experimenter persists, she gives another reason: "Because the sausage, it's got less in it, the red sweets are more spread out." From her gestures, it is clear that by "spread out" she does not mean the spaces between the discrete elements, but is referring to the total place occupied by the row or its length.

When the sausage is the same length as the row, she judges that there is as much red as blue clay (wrong). "They're both the same, except that the red is made up of bits and the sausage is squashed, it's the same size."

When the sausage is longer than the row, she once again bases her judgment on length: this time "there's more blue to eat" (wrong—exact opposite since there is in fact more red clay).

When faced with the ball, she maintains that there is "more red to eat" (correct) and immediately afterward justifies this answer by referring to the reconstitution of the initial row: "Before, the ball was squashed (i.e., in a sausage) and before that it was little blue sweets."

Second Series, Equal Quantities

She again starts off by maintaining that you can get back the same number of sweets by breaking up the modeling clay. However, when the sausage is shorter than the row, she says: "More blue (sausage) because it's been squashed out." Immediately afterward, she refers to a possible reconstitution: "But when you cut it up (i.e., cut the sausage into bits) it's the same."

When the sausage is the same length as the row, she says: "There's the same to eat, and if you cut it up, that makes just as many sweets, they will be the same as those" (unchanged row).

When the sausage is longer than the row, length predominates, she says: "More to eat in the sausage, it's longer."

The difference in the types of responses is very clear when CHA's answers are compared with those of a subject of the control group who was a conserver in the pre-test and was not given the training exercises.

Pie (7;1)

When the sausage is longer than the row, and quantities are unequal, Pie says: "There's less in the sausage (correct) than in the sweets; from that (sausage) you can make the same as before, there was one blue for each red and the blue ones were smaller than the red ones."

For this child, the change in shape can be canceled out by the mental action of reverting to the initial state. Since this action is interiorized, he is no longer concerned with the concrete procedures required to carry it out. By contrast, for a subject of Cha's level the return to the original state is still envisaged as a physical rather than a mental action.

When Cha's difficulties are analyzed, it is clear that she no longer belongs to the category of subjects for whom the row and the single piece are always directly comparable. Her answers are generally based on the argument of a possible reconstruction of the initial elements. But how does she imagine this reconstitution? Certainly not as an interiorized action, i.e., a mental operation by which certain transformations are annulled. She thinks of the actual actions which must be accomplished in order to get back to the situation of separate elements. If the sausage is no longer than the row (unequal quantities), she suggests: "You've got to cut it and then squash each bit out to make one blue sweet for each red one." If the sausage is the same length as the row (equal quantities), she maintains: "You've got to cut it up and then you'll have sweets which will be the same as those there." In the situations with the sausage, her judgment of quantity of modeling clay is always based on the space occupied and the reconstitution is imagined to fit in with the length of the two rows, regardless of the fact that there are empty spaces between the different elements of the rows.

It seems that Cha also bases her judgment on the factor of length when she maintains that she can recover the discrete elements. When she says that one has to "cut it and then squash it out," she seems to mean: "You've got to cut it so that you have the same number of bits and these bits, you've then got to squash them out so that they take up the same length (as the other ones) and then there'll be the same quantity." If, however, the sausage is the same length as the row,

96

she maintains that the sweets of the right size will be recovered immediately, without having to "squash them" out. Quantity is therefore judged according to length (if the sausage and the row are laid out one above the other), and length is estimated by dividing the object into units whose size does not need to remain constant. CHA does, however, give correct answers in the situations with the ball, where length is not a predominant factor. The same type of reasoning was also noted in other children.

CONCLUDING REMARKS

The main conclusions to be drawn from this experiment follow.

1. There is a close connection between the children's initial level and their post-test results. All the children from the more advanced levels (III and IV) completely acquire the concept at post-test 1, as opposed to only one from level II and none from level I.

2. Genuine operatory schemes, i.e., interiorized and reversible mental actions, appear to be preceded, first, by an awareness of the possibility of executing a particular action which reconstitutes the initial situation and, second, by the ability to envisage the same action mentally, still applied only to the same particular concrete situation as previously; finally, this action becomes interiorized and reversible and so no longer linked to a specific situation, with the result that it can be generalized to other situations and can thus become an operatory scheme.

In situations 6–9 of the present experiment, it is difficult to carry out the specific concrete action which reconstitutes the original situation (the sausage or ball would have to be divided into eight identical pieces of a certain shape). The difference between an awareness of possible reconstitution actions and a reversible operation is therefore particularly clear in the children's behavior.

3. Topological aspects of the situations presented, such as contiguity and ordinal relations, dominate the child's reasoning. This was a finding that we had not anticipated from what we already

knew about the difficulties of conservation of quantity problems. Moreover, for the questions on the number of elements the children also remained attached to the spatial aspect longer than would have been expected from the results of the regular numerical conservation tasks. The children found it very difficult to dissociate the total length of the row from the number of elements; this is particularly clear with the least advanced subjects, who all thought it is possible to compare the sausage directly (i.e., without returning mentally to the separate elements from which it was formed) with the row of separate elements. It is this dissociation between length and number which seems to have been furthered by the training sessions, since progress at the post-tests always implied both an improvement in the number concept and in conservation of modeling clay.

4. The intermediate levels lack the stability of either conservation or nonconservation, and the second post-test shows regression or further progress, a phenomenon whose importance was stressed in the previous experiment. As has already been pointed out, it seems that the delayed progress may be accounted for by internal regulatory mechanisms.

5. Several sublevels or types of responses were found in the responses given during the training sessions. The children who make little or no progress judge quantity on the basis of a single criterion (not always the same in the various situations) and in most cases this results in incorrect answers. By contrast, those children who make more progress hesitate and show signs of an internal conflict, because they are basing their judgments on several contradictory criteria (e.g., length and numerosity). This conflict then leads to curious inadequate compensations, which attempt to combine criteria which, from the adult's point of view, cannot be combined. Such compromise responses were also observed in other experiments.

These results clarify to a certain extent the problem of the relationship between the conservation of a small collection of discrete elements and that of a quantity of matter (e.g., modeling clay). It is fairly clear from the reactions to the training sessions that conservation of matter does not derive directly from numerical conservation. Rather, there appears to exist a primitive nondifferentiation of numerosity, space occupied (or length of a linear display), and quantity. The phase of nondifferentiation is followed by a slow process of dissociation whose duration depends on the types of situation presented. For a long time, the child's understanding of number remains influenced by spatial and particularly topological aspects of the concrete display, until finally the concept of arithmetical number, as a synthesis of the construction of classes and of relations, is acquired. The child's idea of the space occupied by an object or a collection of objects continues to be influenced by such topological aspects until he becomes able to grasp the concept of measuring, which implies a division into units of constant size. (This problem will be discussed in Chapter 6.) Similarly, the concept of continuous quantity remains influenced by topological notions until the child becomes capable of regarding a quantity of matter as an agglomerate of interchangeable units whose particular position can result in an increase along one dimension accompanied necessarily by a decrease along another dimension.

It seems therefore that conservation of continuous quantity is developed by means of a process of gradual differentiation rather than being derived directly from numerical evaluation. The main finding of this study is the existence of several processes of differentiation, all necessary for a correct evaluation of quantity, that are activated at different moments of development.

This development, instead of being described as linear, is more appropriately described as a branching system in which various dissociations appear at different times. An adequate system of quantifications can be formed only as a result of the various dissociations.

4 / Verbal Training Procedure for Conservation of Continuous Quantities

This research* differs from other Genevan studies in that its aim was to discover whether language training could influence the reasoning process. A different experimental method was therefore necessary. Since all cognitive training had to be avoided, no conservation problems were presented, no transformations were effected, and there was no true dialogue with the experimenter, nor any attempt to arouse conflicts in the child's mind. The children were simply encouraged to use certain expressions for the description of continuous or discontinuous quantities.

In conservation experiments, certain expressions are used both by the experimenter and by the child, and it has often been supposed that nonconservation is simply a result of the child's inability to understand and use the correct expressions. However, because the various conservation concepts are acquired at different ages and because the same expressions are used in all conservation tasks, this argument is not very convincing. How does it happen that a particular child uses and understands terms such as "more" and "less," "just as much," and "the same amount" in the adult sense when he is talking, e.g., about weight, while when talking about volume he appears to interpret them differently? There can certainly be no question of the difficulty being purely verbal. However, the acquisition of the correct semantic value of these expressions is in itself an interesting problem, and it cannot be concluded a priori that verbal training will have no influence on cognitive structuring (cf. Bruner et al., 1966).

Our first task was to draw up a list of words which are used in conservation experiments. These consist essentially of expressions that

* This chapter is based on a longer report of the experiment (Sinclair, 1967).

describe and compare quantities and dimensions (such as width, height, etc.) and may be divided into two groups.

Expressions for describing continuous and discontinuous quantities and dimensions include:

objective terms: numbers and measures

subjective terms: e.g., *beaucoup* (a lot), *peu* (little), and adjectives such as *long* (long), *court* (short), *gros* (large), *grand* (big), *petit* (small), etc.

Expressions for comparing quantities and dimensions include: *plus* (more), *moins* (less, fewer), *autant* (as much, as many), *trop* (too much, too many), etc.

These expressions of comparison are used in French with or without an adjective, depending upon the nonlinguistic context: without an adjective to make a comparison between two collections of objects, two continuous quantities, or two weights; and with an adjective for the comparison of dimensions or any other property common to two objects.*

Descriptive terms are used both to evaluate only one quantity (he has a lot of marbles) and to compare two (he has a lot of marbles, she's only got a few).

Comparative terms, by contrast, are used only to compare two quantities or objects. Without an adjective, the comparison bears on the number of objects—*il a plus de billes qu'elle* (he's got more beads than she has); or on the quantity—*il a plus de sirop qu'elle* (he's got more juice than she has). With an adjective the comparison describes a feature common to two objects: *A est plus grand que B* (A is bigger than B).

With comparative terms the difference between two objects or collections is indicated objectively and explicitly, but not necessarily quantified. With descriptive terms, both objective and subjective evaluations of dimensions or quantities are possible, but only an implicit comparison is made, e.g.: *A a quatre billes, B a six billes* (A has four beads, B has six beads).

In the first experiment, the comprehension and use of these expres-

* In French, the comparative of all adjectives is formed by preposing the word *plus*.

101

sions by children at both the conservation and nonconservation levels were studied.

USE AND UNDERSTANDING OF THE EXPRESSIONS OF QUANTITATIVE COMPARISONS: PRELIMINARY INVESTIGATION

The children were presented with a series of situations in which they had to compare quantities or dimensions. The visual aspects of the situations were clear and any difference in quantity or size very obvious. No change was made in the position or shape of the objects; thus the verbal investigation did not involve the problem of conservation. The main difficulty for the children was that in some situations there was only one difference between the objects, while in others there were two.

METHOD

Materials. The materials were two dolls, a girl and a boy; modeling clay; marbles of two sizes, and pencils of different lengths and widths.

For the study of the children's use of quantitative terms the method was as follows. The experimenter explained that he would give things to two dolls, such as bits of modeling clay, marbles, and pencils, and that he wanted the child to tell him what the dolls had received. Ten situations were presented:

Modeling clay
    a. Equal quantities (oo).
    b. Unequal quantities (oO).

Marbles
    a. Unequal numbers of marbles of the same size (oo oooo).
    b. Equal numbers of marbles of different sizes (oo OO).
    c. Unequal numbers of marbles of different sizes with more large and fewer small (OOOO oo).
    d. Unequal numbers of marbles of different sizes with more small and fewer large (oooo OO).

Pencils
    a. One long, thin pencil and one long, thin pencil.
    b. One short, thin pencil and one short, thick pencil.

c. One short, thin pencil and one long, thick pencil.

d. One short, thick pencil and one long, thin pencil.

The experimenter never used the terms "more," "less," "as much," "the same," but asked the questions in this form: "You see, mommy gave modeling clay to the girl and the boy, is it fair? Are they both happy? Why? Why not? Who isn't happy? Why?" In general, the instructions were grasped fairly rapidly and it was not necessary to repeat them for each situation. For the pencils, the child was asked: "How are they different?"

In the situations where there were two differences (c and d for marbles and pencils), the child sometimes mentioned only one, whereupon the experimenter asked, "Don't you see anything else different?" But he did not insist and if the child answered, "No," he simply went on to the following situation. The order of the three types of situations (modeling clay, marbles, pencils) was varied, but that of the different questions on each type remained constant. These descriptive items were followed by the liquids conservation task (see Appendix), so that the child's operatory level could be determined.

Having discovered the children's spontaneous use of language in the above situations, we then tried to determine how much the children understood of the expressions used by the experimenter. The children were asked to carry out simple instructions using the materials described above. The experimenter used the expressions most often encountered with children possessing conservation.

Modeling clay

1. *Donne plus de pâte à la fille et moins au garçon.*
   ("Give more modeling clay to the girl and less to the boy.")
2. *Donne la même chose (autant) aux deux poupées.*
   ("Give the same to the two dolls"; or "Give as much to the girl as to the boy.")

Marbles

1. *Donne plus de billes à la fille qu'au garçon;* or *Donne plus de billes à la fille et moins au garçon.*
   ("Give the girl more marbles than the boy"; or "Give more marbles to the girl and fewer to the boy.")
2. *Donne de plus petites billes à la fille et de plus grosses au garçon.*

103

("Give the smaller marbles to the girl and the bigger ones to the boy.")

3. *Donne plus* (*et*) *de plus grosses billes à la fille et moins* (*et*) *de plus petites au garçon.*

   ("Give more of the bigger marbles to the girl and fewer of the smaller ones to the boy.")

4. *Donne moins mais de plus grosses billes à la fille et plus mais de plus petites au garçon.*

   ("Give fewer but larger marbles to the girl and more but smaller ones to the boy.")

Pencils

The experimenter chooses:

1. a short, thin pencil and says: *Cherche un crayon plus long* ("Find a longer pencil");

2. a long, thin pencil and says: *Cherche un crayon plus gros* ("Find a thicker pencil");

3. a long, thick pencil and says: *Cherche un crayon plus court et plus mince* ("Find a shorter and thinner pencil");

4. a short, thick pencil and says: *Cherche un crayon plus long mais plus mince* ("Find a longer but thinner pencil").

Subjects. Eighty-eight children (aged 4;6 to 8;0) took part in this experiment. They attended first and second year kindergarten and first and second year primary schools in Geneva and were considered to be of normal intelligence by their teachers. French was their mother tongue.

RESULTS

Description of Responses

This preliminary investigation produced the following results. All the children except one managed to carry out the instructions correctly. The youngest were 4;6 years old and it seems therefore that, at least from this age, the terms are understood in the above situations. By contrast, there were systematic differences between the expressions conserving and nonconserving children chose to describe the situations, and these fall into three categories.

1. *The use of descriptive or comparative terms.* In the modeling clay situation, most of the children who had already acquired conservation answered, *Il a plus de pâte, elle a moins* ("He's got more modeling clay, she's got less"), using a comparative; while most of the nonconserving children answered, *Il a beaucoup, elle a peu (pas beaucoup)* ("He's got a lot, she has a little [not a lot]"), using descriptive terms. In the marbles situation the same preferences were noted, with the difference that a few more nonconserving children used the words *plus* ("more") and *moins* ("less").

2. *The use of differentiated or undifferentiated terms.* In the pencils problems, the conserving children used two pairs of opposites to describe the differences in length and width, e.g., long/short, thick/thin. Those at a nonconservation level often used undifferentiated terms, with the same word indicating length in one situation and thickness in another, e.g., big/little, thick/little. In this case, "little" was used a first time in the sense of "short" and immediately afterward in the sense of "thin." However, the difference between the conserving and nonconserving groups was not as marked here as in their use of comparatives.

3. *The use of two- or four-part structures.* In the situations where the child was asked to describe two differences at the same time (marbles c and d, number and size; pencils c and d, length and thickness), the conserving children chose the following form for the pencils: "This pencil is long but thin, the other is short but fat"; whereas the nonconservers said: "This pencil is long, that one is short, this one is thin, that one is fat," if they were capable of describing both differences and of using differentiated terms.

Quantitative Results

Table 4.1 shows the percentage of subjects giving the more advanced type of answer in the different situations, i.e., comparative terms for the modeling clay, two-part structures for situations c and d of marbles and pencils, and differentiated terms for situations c and d of pencils. The eighty-eight subjects are grouped into three

TABLE 4.1

Conservation Level	Comparatives for Modeling Clay	Two-Part Structures				Differentiated Terms		Number of Subjects
		Marbles		Pencils		Pencils		
		c	d	c	d	c	d	
C	71	100	100	82	82	94	100	17
Int	12.5	19	44	19	31	25	37	16
NC	9.0	11	13	7	16	18	27	55

categories: conservation, C; nonconservation, NC; and intermediate, Int.

The fact that during this preliminary investigation the language of the conserving children clearly differed from that of the nonconserving ones gave rise to the following questions: (1) Is it possible to teach nonconserving children the verbal expressions for quantitative comparisons that are spontaneously used by conservers? (2) If this is the case, will a change in their verbal patterns lead to a change in their conservation answers? As our aim was to try and study the verbal factor, there had to be as little similarity as possible between the situations presented in the training sessions and those of the pre-test and post-tests. Since the training sessions involved descriptions of the situations that had been presented during the preliminary investigations (quantities of modeling clay, numbers of marbles, and sizes of pencils) the liquids conservation task was used in the pre-test and post-tests, followed, in certain cases, by the modeling clay task. The essential difference between the training sessions and the pre-test and post-tests was that during the former the children were required to describe static situations where all the differences were clearly visible, whereas in the latter one of two initially identical quantities was "transformed" (modified in shape).

LEARNING STUDY

TRAINING PROCEDURE AND TESTS

There were three teaching sessions separated by four to seven days. The method used was in no way comparable to those of the cognitive learning experiments, but consisted simply in encouraging the child to use the expressions proposed by the experimenter.

First Session: Pre-Test

The child was first asked to describe the above ten situations and then his conservation level was determined by means of the liquids pouring problem (pre-test).

Second Session

The child was required to carry out instructions in a series of ten situations and, after each, was asked to say what he had done. As he very often transposed the instructions into his own language (e.g., for the instruction, "Give more to one and less to the other," the child said, "I gave a lot to one and only a little bit to the other"), the experimenter frequently had to ask such questions as "But how did I ask, how did I say it?"

Having noted in previous experiments that it is in the situation where there is only one ball of modeling clay which the experimenter gradually makes larger that the nonconserving children first begin to use the terms "more" and "less" in their descriptions, we added the following situations to this second session.

Modeling clay. The experimenter gave one of the two dolls a little ball of modeling clay and then gradually made it larger. Each time he added some clay to the ball, he asked the child to tell him what the doll had received, whether or not she was happy and why. In another situation, the experimenter started with a large ball which he then gradually made smaller.

Marbles. The experimenter gave one of the dolls some marbles and then added or took away, one by one, a number of marbles, again asking the child to give a description each time the situation changed. To encourage him to express in one sentence the two differences in any given situation, items c and d of marbles and pencils were repeated several times. If the child mentioned only one of the two dimensions, the experimenter would try to get him to refer to the second. For example, in the situation where one of the dolls has more and larger marbles than the other, a child might say: "The boy isn't happy because he's got three marbles"; whereupon the experimenter

107

would ask, "What are those of the girl like?" If the child started with a four-part description and said, e.g., in the situation with two pencils differing both in length and width, "That one's longer and the other is . . . ," the experimenter would try to make him use a two-part syntactic structure by saying: "Yes, it's longer and what else is it?"

Third Session

In this session, several parts of the preceding one were repeated, namely, the instruction to give more clay to one doll and less to the other, the child's repetition of this instruction, the items dealing with a progressive increase and decrease of the quantity of clay in one ball, and the description of items c and d of marbles and pencils.

At the end of the session, the experimenter gave the child the first post-test, i.e., the liquids conservation task. After an interval of two weeks, this post-test was repeated.

RESULTS

Comparison of Pre-Test and Post-Tests

Table 4.2 shows the progress made from pre-test to post-test 2 for 31 subjects. In the two post-tests, one subject who was NC at the

TABLE 4.2

Pre-Test		Post-Test 1			Post-Test 2		
	M	NC	Int	C	NC	Int	C
NC	28	18	7	3	18	7	3 (+1, −1)
Int	1	0	0	1	0	0	1
C	2	—	—	2	—	—	2

pre-test attained conservation in the first post-test, but then reverted to nonconservation responses in the second; one subject remained at the nonconservation level at the first post-test but achieved conservation at the second. The performance of all the other children was the same in both post-tests. The two children who in the pre-test answered correctly but did not provide any justifications (in reply to the question "How do you know that there's the same to drink?", they simply said, "I know" or "I can see") maintained their correct answers in the two post-tests and also justified them by arguments of identity and compensation.

Analysis of the Responses during the Training Sessions

The following summaries of protocols illustrate the behavior of (1) a child who progresses from NC to C; (2) a child who progresses from NC to Int; and (3) a child who remains at the nonconservation stage but alters his arguments. This last example is given in detail and provides a clear illustration of what happens during the training session.

EXCERPTS FROM PROTOCOLS

Example 1: Progress from NC to C

ERI (6;0)

Pre-Test

Although ERI gives incorrect answers he already takes account of the two dimensions of width and height ("More in this [narrow] glass, it's a bit closer, so that makes more to drink").

Post-Test

ERI unhesitatingly gives conservation answers based on the two arguments of compensation and reversibility ("The glass is bigger, that's further apart, but it's the same to drink. When you put it back in the other glass it'll be the same").

Example 2: Progress from NC to Int

JEP (6;2)

Pre-Test

First JEP concentrates on the height ("more in the thin glass") then on the width ("No, less"); he then wavers between the two dimensions before finally basing his incorrect answer on the height of the liquid.

Post-Test 1

Again, he starts off considering the height and the width separately, but eventually relates them—"That's thinner, so that makes it bigger (pointing to the height), we've got the same to drink because we've both got the same juice." However, as soon as the experimenter suggests a nonconservation argument, JEP regresses to a lower level and affirms, "It isn't the same, that's bigger, but it's not as tall as that, that makes it smaller, he's got less."

Example 3: Remaining at NC but Altering Arguments

CRI (5;4)

Pre-Test

In CRI's descriptions, her use of terms is typical of the preconservation pattern. For the modeling clay balls of two different sizes, she says: "That one's bigger, that one's smaller"; for those of the same size, she says: "That one's bigger and that one's also bigger," and so does not use the expression "the same"; when the experimenter asks her if she is sure, she says: "It's right." For the four marbles (situation d: OO oooo) she says: "The boy's happy, the girl isn't because she's only got two marbles." Only after questioning does she add: "They're big." Thus the answer remains incomplete and cannot be classified as either a two-part or a four-part structure. She describes the two pencils of the same width but different length as "a large one and a small one"; when faced with those which differ in width only, she says: "It's the same length." When the experimenter asks for more details, she refers to the width: "This one's bigger, the other one's smaller"; there is thus an undifferentiated opposition, since she uses the term "small" both for the description of length and for that of width. Where the pencils differ in both length and thickness (long and thick, short and thin), she says: "That one's thicker and that one (the other pencil) is smaller, and that one (first pencil) is bigger and that one (the other) is smaller"; here again there is an undifferentiated opposition, and this time we note a four-part structure.

Conservation Pre-Test

CRI is clearly at the nonconservation stage, basing her arguments solely on the level of the liquid (narrow glass): "They haven't got the same"— "Who has more?"—"The girl, it's bigger" (indicating the level of the water).

Learning

CRI makes slow but sure progress with language.

For the modeling clay, she correctly carries out the instruction "Give the boy more than the girl"; but when she is asked how she did this, she answers, "I gave a big one and a middle-sized one." However, during the exercise with just one ball of clay which the experimenter progressively makes larger or smaller, she uses the comparatives "more" and "less" spontaneously, if rather sporadically. When the quantity becomes very small, she says "a tiny little bit."

For the marbles, she carries out the instructions correctly, but when asked what she did or even what she was asked to do, she uses numbers. With only one doll and one collection of marbles, she begins to use the comparative terms systematically and with ease: *Il est plus plus plus content, il a plus* ("He gets more more more happy, he's got more"). From then on, but only at the experimenter's suggestion, she uses the comparative terms in the appropriate situations, and once again correctly complies with all the instructions. She then manages to describe the differences in number and size fairly easily, using a two-part structure: "The girl has big marbles, but less."

For the pencils, she correctly carries out the instructions. Seeking a term to describe the difference in size, she tries "fat," "wide," where wide seems to mean thin. At the experimenter's suggestion, she adopts "thin" and immediately uses a two-part structure: "This one's smaller and thinner and the other's longer and it's fatter."

By the third session, therefore, CRI has learned the use of simple comparatives for the description of the marbles, but not yet for the modeling clay. She uses two-part structures and differentiated oppositions for both marbles and pencils.

Conservation Post-Test

CRI is still at her original level for conservation, but the justifications for her answers have changed. For a narrow glass: "They haven't got the same"—"Who has more?"—"The girl"—"Why?"—"Because it (the narrow glass) is longer and thinner." For a wide glass: "The girl's got more, the boy (wide glass) hasn't got more, he's got a little bit"—"Why?"—"The glass is fatter, when you put water in it, that makes it not more" (*pas plus*). The opposition "more/not more" appears constructed along the lines of "a lot/not a lot."

CRI's protocol is typical of almost all the subjects who made no operatory progress at the post-test. Some children made neither operatory nor verbal progress and used the higher-level expressions only sporadically at the experimenter's insistence. For each new question they returned to typical nonconservation expressions. All the other subjects, however, definitely benefited from the verbal exercises, regardless of whether they made operatory progress. Since the descriptive terms are linguistically perfectly correct, except for the undifferentiated use of adjectives, one cannot count the nonuse of comparatives as an error. Nor can it be assumed that the use of comparatives is necessarily more than a simple imitation of the model given by the experimenter. As can be shown from the figures in Table 4.1, 29 percent of conserving children used "a lot" and "a little" instead of "more" and "less"; the use of noncomparative descriptions is by itself no obstacle to the acquisition of conservation. Moreover, most children used the proposed terms either sporadically or frequently at the end of the training sessions, and only very few used them either always or never. Consequently it is impossible to give a table comparing the level of language after training and the level of conservation. It also is difficult to measure the rapidity and ease with which the children learned because of the flexible ways in which the training methods were adapted to each child. However, if we judge by the number of repetitions required for the various situations, we can make three observations.

1. The children found it most difficult to use the simple comparatives *plus* and *moins* when dealing with the modeling clay. The experimenter's instructions, expressed in these terms, were always correctly carried out, but if he asked immediately afterward, "What did I ask you to do?" the child looked at the portions of clay and said, "I've given a lot to one and only a little to the other." Even when the experimenter added, "You gave more to one and . . . ," the child often finished the sentence ". . . and not a lot, only a little to the other."

It seems in keeping with preconservation reasoning that children use a comparative term very early and completely spontaneously in the situations where modeling clay is added to one of the balls. In evaluating quantities, the reasoning at this level is directed by the ordinal aspect of the situation, i.e., by what "goes beyond." It is easier to realize that something has got bigger if one has witnessed the concrete act of adding than to grasp that despite the fact that one quantity was acted upon, no quantitative difference has resulted.

Furthermore, the quantitative implications of an identical repetition of any action, known as iteration, also appear to be grasped very early. In situations where the experimenter successively adds many little bits of modeling clay to the ball, there is both the concrete act of adding and that of iteration. It is therefore not surprising that the spontaneous language of the young child contains many examples of the word "more" in the sense of "again." The "more" can convey a concrete addition ("I want more") or the request for the repetition or iteration of a pleasant action ("Sing one more"). By contrast, the child finds it more difficult to deal with an iterated subtraction where more actions result in less quantity. The use of the word "less" comes later, with children using the expression *plus moins* ("more less") in the sense of "even less" (Donaldson and Wales, 1970).

2. It proved much easier to teach the children to use differentiated terms such as "fat"/"thin" or "long"/"short." A minimal number of repetitions and often only a little prompting by the experimenter was sufficient. For instance, the simple suggestion "Wouldn't it be better to say thin, instead of small?" often resulted in the child's permanently adopting the term. If the children started off using unconventional differentiated terms, as, for example, "high" and "low" for "wide" and "thin" (pencils), the experimenter did not insist that they replace them by the accepted terms. He simply made sure that there was no verbal confusion between length and width.

3. Finally, our subjects found it less difficult to learn the differentiated terms than to use a two-part structure for items c and d of marbles and pencils. We had the impression that, at the end of the training sessions, this type of structure was in some cases still only a passive imitation of the model; the child would pronounce the first part of the sentence, stop and ponder, often looking at or touching the other object and then looking at the experimenter, before finally finishing the sentence in the way we wanted.

DISCUSSION OF THE CHILDREN'S CONSERVATION LEVELS AND
CONCLUDING REMARKS

The results show that three subjects progressed from nonconservation to conservation; however, one of them regressed to the intermediate level at the second post-test. By contrast, one child, still nonconserving at the first post-test, reached conservation at the second.

Seven children progressed from nonconservation to the intermediate level. This result should, however, be treated with caution for the reasons already mentioned: the pre-test was fairly rapid and perhaps a child's competence may not have been fully realized or his progress might simply have been due to a progressive familiarization with the experimental situation, etc.

Nine children remained nonconserving but, like CRI, whose protocol is quoted above, modified their arguments in the post-tests. In the first post-test, all of them referred to the covariation of the dimensions (higher level, narrower glass). They noticed and described the dimensions of the glasses and the level of the liquid and sometimes even explained why the liquid went higher in the narrow glass. This did not lead them to the idea of compensation, which requires an operatory construction based on a coordination rather than a covariation. We think that this effect of our training procedure is instructive, particularly for the following reasons.

1. The subjects who progressed to the intermediate stage of conservation were clearly aware of the covariation of the dimensions. This led to a temporary coordination expressed in the form of the compensation argument resulting in a conservation answer. Only one of them justified his correct answer by "If you put it back it will be the same," an argument often given alone or initially in other experiments. All the others supported their conservation answers only by compensation arguments.

2. The children who achieved conservation started off by giving the compensation argument, but then, without any prompting from the experimenter, added those of identity or reversibility.

3. It was quite easy to teach nonconserving children the differentiated terms, but, as we saw during our preliminary investigation, the use of such terms is the least reliable indication of conservation.

The following conclusions may be drawn from these observations.

1. The hypothesis that a child needs only to understand and use correctly certain expressions to attain conservation should be discarded. However, there seems to be a clear parallel between the structuring of the cognitive operations and the acquisition of the terms necessary for their expression. As long as we remain at the level of the lexicon (differentiated terms), verbal learning is easy; however, as soon as we come to a more structural level, then verbal training is faced with the same obstacles as the acquisition of the concept itself, namely lack of coordination and of decentration.

2. Acquisition at the level of the lexicon enables a child to direct his attention toward the relevant aspects of the situation (argument of covariation).

3. Verbal training helps some children who have already acquired conservation but are unable to justify their answers to give clear explanations during the post-test. This effect of verbal training is well known. The very nature of language permits rapid coding and an efficient storing and retrieval of data, as has been realized by many researchers and educators.

The effect of directing a child's attention toward the relevant aspects of the situation has also been demonstrated in discrimination and classification experiments. It is quite possible, but in our opinion not yet conclusively proved, that such training may really help the child acquire the concept. In some cases, however, he simply concentrates on a new aspect of the problem which may seem more adequate because of its greater complexity, but which still requires the same coordination with the other elements of the situation as the original one. Indeed, some children seemed to be more certain of their incorrect answers during the post-tests than the pre-test, producing what they thought to be a completely coherent argument: "That makes more to drink because the liquid goes higher; it goes higher because the glass is thin." The real danger here, we think, lies in the fact that it is possible to combine verbal training, which directs the child's attention to the relevant factors, with certain other procedures, such as masking the disturbing factors or using the same material and type of questions in both the training and the post-tests. This combination may result in pseudo-conservation answers in the post-tests.

Several of the experiments conducted by Bruner (1964) and his team seem to be based on this method and do not, in our opinion, result in the true acquisition of operatory structures, but simply in correct answers in a specific situation. The child's attention is directed to the relevant information and then, by conditioning, he is led to use this information to produce a correct answer. We do not deny that verbal training can sometimes result in a truly operatory acquisition. But in evaluating the responses, great care must be taken to observe all the necessary precautions outlined in the methodology section of the Introduction; otherwise, the results of verbal training may easily be misinterpreted.

5 / Cross-Cultural Study of Conservation Concepts: Continuous Quantities and Length

The aim of the research (Bovet, 1967, 1971) discussed in this chapter was to study the development of certain basic concepts in a different cultural environment from that where the original cross-sectional and learning experiments had been carried out. The opportunity to conduct research in Africa provided such an environment: the main distinction concerned schooling and literacy, since the Algerian subjects who participated in the experiments came from a completely illiterate population.

Several such studies have already been published. In Iran, Mosheni (1966) compared a group of Teheran schoolchildren with a group of rural unschooled children as regards their responses to certain IQ tests and some of the Piagetian conservation tasks. In Hong Kong, Goodnow (1962) used Piagetian tasks of the concrete and formal operational levels to compare several groups of children whose level of schooling, when judged by Western standards, ranged from very low to average. In Italy, Peluffo (1962) carried out several comparative studies on children with different degrees of schooling. In Australia, De Lemos (1966) and Dasen (1972) gave several conservation tasks to aborigine children, again with various degrees of schooling. In Senegal, Greenfield and Bruner (Bruner et al., 1966) tried to find out how unschooled children understood conservation. We shall discuss this last study in greater detail because it dealt with the same concepts whose development we investigated in Algiers.

In general, it has been found that unschooled children succeed at the Piagetian tasks at somewhat later ages than the children studied in Geneva. Also, IQ results do not seem to correspond to the levels of reasoning obtained by means of the Piagetian tasks. However, very little is known about the reasons for differences in speed of cognitive development, and as yet, few attempts have been made to find out whether differences in stimulation by the environment in general and schooling in particular affect only the speed or also the course of development. Does the development of the fundamental mental operations follow one particular pattern, regardless of the type and amount of schooling a child may receive, or, on the contrary, are there different ways of acquiring a particular type of reasoning?

The importance given to the question of possible differences in the acquisition process guided the method of investigation: not only were a number of Piagetian tasks presented to 51 unschooled children between the ages of six and twelve, providing cross-sectional results ranging from frank nonoperatory answers to solutions belonging to the higher level of concrete operations, but the subjects also took part in a training procedure. Two different types of conservation tasks were studied in this way: conservation of physical quantities (liquids and modeling clay; see Appendix) and conservation of length (see Appendix). These particular problems were chosen because it is possible that, according to the activities with which a specific population is familiar, certain concepts may follow the same developmental course in that population as that found in our schoolchildren, whereas others may be subject to a different one. The handling of continuous quantities is a familiar activity in the population studied, in contrast with the measurement of length, which in general appears to be more typical of a "school-taught" notion.

CONSERVATION OF CONTINUOUS QUANTITIES

EXPERIMENTAL PHASES

Three different experimental phases were devoted to the study of concepts of conservation of continuous quantities.

Part 1

a. The traditional procedure for the conservation of liquids was used: starting from equal quantities in identical glasses the experimenter (or the subject) poured the liquid from one of the glasses into a glass with a different diameter, and/or starting from different quantities he poured the contents of the glass with the bigger quantity into a wider glass (see Appendix). For this task, both the household glasses with which the subjects were familiar and glasses identical to those used in the Genevan experiments were used. As it turned out, the subjects had no trouble in dealing with the latter.

b. For the conservation of solids, the traditional procedure was also followed (see Appendix) except that instead of modeling clay, bars of chocolate were used; the only modification presented was to break these into small pieces.

Part 2

a. One full and several empty glasses of different dimensions were shown and the children were asked to indicate, on each of the empty glasses, how high the liquid would come if it were poured into the glass. Six predictions were asked for, and after each prediction the liquid was actually poured and the children could see how right or wrong they had been.

b. The child was asked to pour approximately equal quantities of the liquid into pairs of glasses which differed either in diameter, in height, or in both dimensions.

Part 3

After the exercises of part 2, the conservation tasks of part 1 were repeated.

The interviews were conducted in Arabic, by psychology students of Algiers University who had been trained in the method of questioning and were perfectly competent. The difficulties encountered by the youngest subjects when asked to explain and justify their answers to the conservation questions cannot be ascribed to lack of skill on the experimenters' part. The situations presented in part 2 were therefore doubly informative: not only did they serve as a training procedure, but since they do not demand any verbal responses, they provided a different way of grasping the subjects' modes of reasoning.

RESULTS

Results of Part 1 for Children of Six to Eight Years

The youngest subjects (six to seven years) consistently judged the quantities unequal after modification, referring to the general change in appearance or mentioning one of the dimensions. This type of response is also characteristic of Genevan children at a frank preconservation level.

Children of seven to eight years unhesitatingly gave correct answers to the conservation problem. Despite helpful questioning, it was impossible to obtain verbal comments and explanations. Since it is difficult to evaluate the reasoning behind conservation answers unaccompanied by justifications, these subjects (and some of the younger ones) were presented with part 2 problems, which ask for manipulation rather than verbal explanation.

Results of Part 2 for Children of Six to Eight Years

Like their Genevan counterparts, the youngest subjects did not pay any attention to the diameter of the glasses when they were asked to make predictions regarding the height of the liquid level, and when they had to pour approximately equal quantities themselves, they made only a global estimate.

Children of seven to eight years were quite inconsistent in their answers to the prediction problems, and they did not seem to learn from their errors. In the pouring problems these subjects either paid attention to only one dimension (usually the height of the liquid) or filled both glasses completely, disregarding the difference in dimensions.

These reactions to the prediction and pouring problems threw doubt on the value of the conservation answers in part 1, since, according to Genevan data, pouring and prediction problems are generally correctly solved at the same time as conservation problems.

Results of Part 1 for Children of Eight to Eleven Years

Subjects eight to nine years old gave the same type of answers as the intermediate-level subjects in Geneva. These children either took one of the dimensions into account, or focused on the action of

120

pouring. When the child was giving all his attention to the fact that all the liquid was poured into another glass, he answered the conservation questions correctly, but as soon as he observed the difference in the levels of liquids he denied equality. Apparently, this group gave responses of a lower level than the younger subjects. Children of ten to eleven years were capable of higher-level coordinations, and although they still had hesitations, tended toward explicit conservation answers.

These different responses to part 1 problems can be classified as follows:

6–7 years	7–8 years	8–9 years	10–11 years
NC	C	Int	Int+, C

Compared to Genevan results, this is highly unusual, because of the reappearance of nonconservation answers after the conserving responses of the seven-to-eight-year-old subjects.

Results of Part 2 for Children of Eight to Eleven Years

Children of eight to nine years were hesitant in the prediction problems, but gradually, after the first opportunities of checking their answers, they progressed. In the pouring problems, their responses were characteristic of the intermediate stage: they had some idea of compensating for the smaller diameter of the glass by pouring the liquid to a slightly higher level.

The subjects ten to eleven years old gave responses of the same level to both prediction and pouring problems, i.e., although they still hesitated and sometimes made mistakes, they explicitly mentioned both the dimensions and the necessity for compensation.

Results of Part 3

Repetition of the conservation tasks of part 1, after the training and the familiarization with the situation provided by part 2, produced the following results.

The six-to-seven-year-old subjects gave the same type of nonconservation answers as they had given in part 1. No progress or change was observed.

The seven-to-eight-year-old subjects now gave either nonconserving or intermediate responses, mentioning such aspects as the height of the liquids and the dimensions of the glasses, to which they had made no reference in part 1. Although superficially they had regressed from conservation to intermediate responses, this change in their approach to the problem should be seen as progress. Instead of simply disregarding the figural aspect of the situation, they now tried to take it into account and understood the problem better than they had at first. From this point of view, it is not surprising that they now behaved like the eight-to-nine-year-old subjects in part 1.

The eight-to-nine-year-old subjects progressed toward conservation, and gave the same type of Int+ answers as are often obtained with Genevan subjects who, starting from an Int− level, progress toward Int+ and C.

Most of the ten-to-eleven-year-old subjects gave frank conservation answers in part 3, despite a few hesitations. They were capable of giving explicit justifications for their correct conservation judgments.

The part 3 results were thus as follows:

6–7 years	7–8 years	8–9 years	10–11 years
NC	NC, Int	Int+	C

Compared to the results of part 1, those of part 3 reproduce the regular developmental trend. The precocious conserving judgments have disappeared after the exercises of part 2 and have changed into NC or Int responses, followed by Int+ and finally by C responses.

COMPARISON OF GENEVAN AND ALGERIAN RESULTS

The difference between the Genevan results and those of the Algerian subjects in part 1 can be interpreted in the light of their reactions to the part 2 problems. The youngest subjects focus on the final result and establish no connection between the final state, the modifying action, and the initial situation; at this level, the Algerian subjects' reactions are typical of children elsewhere. The next group of Algerian subjects, however, show a response pattern not encountered in schoolchildren: they appear to focus on the initial equality (or inequality), and link this initial state of affairs to the final outcome through the action of "pouring all the liquid." These precocious conservation judgments lack a main feature of operatory conservation—the integration of the dimensional aspects into the reasoning process. Although these subjects are further advanced than the youngest group, their reactions to the prediction and pouring problems show that in their conservation task responses they simply disregarded what to Genevan children of that age are incompatible features of the total situation. The Genevan data never show a massive regression in conservation judgments from a younger group to an older group, nor do we notice such regressions in training experiments.

From eight to nine years onward, subjects display the usual developmental pattern, starting with responses still close to nonconservation, and proceeding to an intermediate stage before reaching, around the age of ten, a conserving level. The same pattern is found in the results of part 3—i.e., after the exercises of part 2, when the precocious conserving answers disappear to give way to NC or Int— responses, under the influence of the newly installed awareness of the dimensional aspects. Despite this difference in the developmental trend, it does not seem that the Algerian subjects showed a way of acquiring conservation totally different from that which has been found elsewhere in schoolchildren. Apart from the phenomenon of precocious conservation judgments, in which the action link between the initial and final states overrides the puzzle of the differing heights and diameters, the developmental sequence and its end product are the same. The difference appears to be mainly in a temporary reversal of the succession of various foci of attention.

CONSERVATION OF LENGTH

EXPERIMENTAL PHASES

The deviation from the general developmental sequence found with the unschooled children in Algiers can be further elucidated by their responses to problems of length. Once again, the concept was studied in three phases.

In part 1 traditional conservation questions were asked after two sticks, A and B (of equal or of different lengths), had been placed directly underneath one another, and A then broken into pieces which were arranged in a zig-zag line beneath B.

In part 2, using pieces of sticks, the subjects had to construct straight roads of the same length as the experimenter's zig-zag road, starting from a predetermined point underneath the latter (see Fig. 5.1).

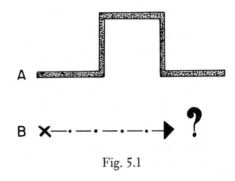

Fig. 5.1

In part 3 the conservation task of part 1 was repeated.

RESULTS

The five-to-six-year-old and seven-to-eight-year-old subjects were presented only with part 1; all their responses displayed the frank non-conservational pattern, based on the "going beyond" principle.

The eight-to-ten-year-old and the ten-to-twelve-year-old subjects were further advanced and gave answers that approached an intermediate level. In part 2 they had difficulty in going beyond the end point of the model, but after a period of hesitations, the necessity for compensation began to be understood. In part 3 the eight-to-ten-year-old subjects generally reached an Int level, and the ten-to-twelve year-old children generally either gave frank conservation answers or showed an Int+ response pattern. Nothing resembling the precocious conserving responses in the conservation of quantities problems was found in this experiment; the succession of stages was regular, and part 2 resulted in some gradual progress in the subjects' response patterns.

The ages of acquisition differed from Genevan findings (Inhelder, 1963), where the children generally acquired conservation of length between eight and nine years of age (68 percent success at eight years and 96 percent at nine years). The unschooled Algerian children did not reach category C before they were ten to twelve years old. The Algerian experiments in conservation of physical quantities (liquids and solids) and of length thus seem to point to different developmental patterns, one differing from and the other parallel to those observed in Geneva. Such differences in the development of two distinct concepts are of far more interest for cross-cultural research than variations in the ages at which children in different populations acquire certain concepts.

From an epistemological point of view, two aspects of the above results have to be stressed. The first is that the deviation of the Algerian sample from the developmental pattern for the conservation of liquids, as established on the basis of research in Geneva, is only temporary; the findings indicate a subsequent return to the regular pattern with an intermediate period of both correct and incorrect answers followed by the acquisition of conservation. The second is that after the training sessions, the children who had originally given the unusual precocious conservation answers gave responses similar to those of the younger Genevan children (intermediate level); all children therefore seem to go through this intermediate stage before they finally achieve conservation.

EXCERPTS FROM PROTOCOLS

Examples of Precocious Conservation Answers

Rac (7;7)

In part 1, Rac gives conservation answers, but offers no other explanation than "because" (which is apparently just as frequently used by Arabic-speaking children as by those who speak French or English). He sometimes hesitates, when the experimenter attracts his attention to the different heights of the liquid levels, but, on the whole, maintains his judgment of equality. In the situations where bars of chocolate are used, Rac is less sure of himself, but here too most of his responses are conserving. In part 2, for the pouring problems Rac at first pours the liquid in such a way that he appears to be trying to compensate by the height of the level for the differences in diameter; however, progressively RAC focuses more and more on the height of the level, and finally carefully pours the liquid in his glass so that it reaches the same level as that in the model glass. In the prediction problems RAC is quite inconsistent; sometimes he appears to have a good idea of the level to which the liquid will rise, but usually without being able to give an explanation (when he does try to explain, he refers to nonpertinent features, such as the height of the glasses); on other occasions his predictions are flagrantly wrong. Despite numerous opportunities of seeing the error of his predictions, RAC does not make any progress. In part 3 RAC gives nonconserving responses, even though the experimenter reminds him of the initial equality of the original quantities.

This is one example of the breakdown of initially correct answers and of general ambiguity and lack of consistency in the reasoning processes. There are glimpses of what appears to be operatory understanding, but when these are considered in the context of the child's reactions to the nonverbal problems they appear to be due to a disregard of what should be an integral part of the solution.

ZAH (8;0)

To the first conservation of liquids questions ZAH gives conservation answers, despite several objections and suggestions from the experimenter as to the apparent inequality of the quantities. Although she is astonished when she sees what happens when the experimenter pours the liquid into another glass, she continues to give correct answers (without any justification).

In the pouring problems of part 2 she starts off by filling two glasses of different diameters but the same height right to the top in order to have the same quantity in each. She first maintains their equality, and only after the experimenter has drawn her attention to the different diameters does she judge the quantities unequal. However, when the same situation is repeated, she carefully fills both glasses, this time not to the top but to the same level. Later on, she quickly pours part of the liquid from a bottle into one of the glasses (narrow and tall) and the rest into the other (wide and short). The result suggests that she has compensated for the difference in the shape of the glasses, since the levels turn out to be more or less correct. However, she judges the resulting levels unequal, compares the levels alone, and "corrects" the situation by making them the same.

She does this several times in subsequent problems. Sometimes she completely fills both glasses and firmly maintains the equality of the two quantities of liquid. Sometimes she quickly pours out two quantities without paying attention to the levels, but when the experimenter asks her to compare the quantities she judges them unequal.

Her responses to the prediction problems are sometimes more or less right, sometimes wrong. ZAH does not provide any explanations and makes no progress.

When the conservation problems are repeated in part 3 ZAH gives clear nonconservation responses.

This is a typical example of a child who in part 1 gives conservation answers, but whose lack of operatory reasoning becomes clear in the problems of pouring and prediction and who finally regresses to solutions based on either the height of the liquid or the diameter of the glasses without any coordination between the two dimensions.

Examples of Initial NC Responses Becoming Int or Operatory C+

LEI (9;6)

In part 1 LEI gives a nonconservation response to the liquids situation in the first problem. In a subsequent situation dealing with number conservation (this problem was presented to several children), she wavers between an answer based on the general appearance of the lay-out of the objects and one based on operatory reasoning. The same type of response occurs in the problems dealing with the breaking up of the bar of chocolate.

In part 3 LEI still frequently gives incorrect answers because she focuses her attention on the figural aspects of the liquid in the glasses. The exercises of part 2 were not sufficient to ensure progress beyond the intermediate stage.

ARA ZOR (10;3)

ARA ZOR starts off with nonconservation responses in part 1; but little by little she becomes aware of the differentiation to be made between the figural aspects of the situation and the quantification. Her final answers in part 3 are all correct and accompanied by explicit justifications.

The part 2 problems served to bring to the surface a capacity for operatory reasoning of which ARA ZOR had already given signs in part 1 and which was unambiguously established in part 3.

CONCLUDING REMARKS

Differences in the ages of acquisition of various concepts have been frequently noted in cross-cultural research and seem to be governed by the amount of general cognitive stimulation the child receives in his everyday life. It is sometimes sufficient to ask the right question at the right moment in order to activate mental processes lying dormant through lack of stimulation. In the experimental situation, therefore, it is necessary to repeat questions several times, in a variety of different ways, so as to elicit the use of unfamiliar types of reasoning. Similarly, the use of exercises such as those of the prediction and pouring problems might, in many cases, correct the impression, derived from the results of a single test, of the existence of an important time lag. Use of the various training procedures that have resulted in an acceleration of the developmental rate with subjects in Geneva might well help children who appear to be rather far behind to catch up with their more favored contemporaries. Finally, it must not be forgotten that unschooled subjects are completely unfamiliar with the testing situations, for which schools offer at least certain parallels.

Far more interesting is the phenomenon of precocious conservation found in the six-to-seven-year-old Algerian subjects. As we have seen, after a number of exercises these children apparently "progress" to nonconservation answers based precisely on the perceptual features which they had at first disregarded and which they cannot yet coordinate with the modifying actions. Furthermore, an older group of Algerian children also gave nonconservation responses for the same reasons. From then on, development of the conservation notion is the same as in Geneva, that is, it is characterized by a gradual comparison of the dimensions which later results in their coordination by compensation—an indication of conservation based on a system of operations. This interpretation is, however, different from that given by Bruner, who underlines the fact that increased attention paid to the perceptual features "is followed by a drastic and systematic reduction of the importance of such features." In our opinion, it is because the child becomes able to regard the results of the pouring as the final state of a continuous process of change that he can integrate all the aspects of the situation. As a result he makes fewer references to the dimensions as such, not because he attaches less importance to them than previously, but because he has understood the nature of their coordination.

We also think that, both with the screening and with the pouring procedure used by Bruner and Greenfield with their unschooled subjects, a shift of attention occurs; with the former method the shift is from one perceptual feature to others, and with the latter from one aspect of the action to another. In the pouring method, which led many subjects from NC to C+ (Bruner et al., 1966, p. 247), the children are asked to pour the liquid in equal quantities into two glasses and then from one glass into another of a different shape. When the experimenter pours out the initial equal quantities and then pours the liquid from one glass to another, the children base their answers on the most obvious aspects of the situation, i.e., the ensuing changes in the overall appearance, and this leads to non-conservation answers. When the child himself carries out all the actions, he spontaneously pays greater attention to the initial action of making the quantities equal, since this is a difficult task. Consequently, less attention is paid to the easier action of pouring the liquid into another glass. The change observed by Bruner and Greenfield from NC to C+ in the pouring procedure does not mean that the child has made progress in coordinating all the aspects of the situation, but rather that his attention has simply been shifted from the modifying activity to the equalizing action.

Briefly, both the screening and the pouring procedures used by Bruner and Greenfield, which they feel are responsible for an acquisition of conservation, seem to us simply to be directing the child's attention to the particular aspect of the situation which elicits correct *answers* to the conservation question; it is doubtful, however, whether these responses indicate a better *understanding* of the problem.

According to this interpretation, Greenfield's results (Bruner et al., 1966, p. 233) may well be similar to those obtained with the Algerian subjects for the liquids conservation problem. For the eight-to-nine year-old unschooled children, Greenfield notes 45 percent C responses (a figure which seems high in comparison with our Int— results at that age, and 50 percent for the eleven-to-thirteen-year-olds, which, by contrast, seems an astonishingly low figure, showing virtually no progress when compared with the figure for the eight-year-olds. These results could be explained if the eight-year-olds' successes, as our own findings lead us to believe, were in fact conservations which were not based on a system of operations. On the other hand, we think it quite plausible that, had a group of nine-to-ten-year-olds been questioned, these children would have provided responses of an intermediate level corresponding to the Int and Int+ answers of our eight-to-ten-year-olds. Finally, the results of the eleven-to-thirteen-year-olds, i.e., those of the subsequent developmental stage, probably indicate truly operatory solutions quite different from those obtained at eight years of age. Thus Greenfield's results of 45–50 percent success between eight and eleven to thirteen years, which at first sight seem to be static, would be masking a progressive change in the reasoning processes underlying the apparently similar answers.

The foregoing comments throw some light on the justifications given by Bruner's subjects. His table (Bruner et al., 1966, p. 237) shows that what he terms "perceptual reasons" disappear with age in the schooled groups while they increase in the unschooled group. We disagree with Bruner when he considers that the reduction of the number of such arguments constitutes progress and that training should aim at their elimination. On the contrary, we think that such arguments are essential. It seems fairly revealing of Bruner's approach that the children's justifications are categorized solely on the basis of the form in which they are expressed. In our opinion, the justifications take on importance only when considered in the context of all the child's reactions to the various conservation problems. If the child uses them to back up a nonconservation answer, this shows that he has reached the stage of reasoning based on the possibility of an empirical return to the initial state and that he is paying attention to, but not compensating for, the reciprocal variations of the dimensions. If, on the other hand, the child uses these same arguments to back up a conservation answer, this shows that he has understood the concepts of compensation and true reversibility. The discussion shows once again that, in order to determine the child's cognitive level, total response patterns should be taken into account.

6 / From Elementary Number Conservation to the Conservation of Length

The conservation experiments of the previous chapters yielded results which make us wary of too simplistic an interpretation of a chronological order of acquisition. Clearly, the fact that elementary number is conserved well before continuous quantity does not mean that the latter concept is derived directly from the former. A complex system of interdependent relationships links the two notions. Conservation of length—a unidimensional continuous quantity—is usually acquired at a slightly later age than that of matter. Once again, the question of a link with the earlier conservation has to be explored. When elementary number conservation has been acquired, can the system of operations bearing on a (still restricted) number of elements be extended directly to the conservation of a number of elements which, when put together, form a certain "length"? Or does conservation of length also show complex relationships with earlier conservations?

The concept of number is not equivalent to, nor contemporaneous with, that of the conservation of limited numerical quantities. Similarly, conservation of length is not equivalent to the concept of measurement. The concept of number, in the sense of an understanding of natural numbers and the operations which can be performed upon them, is slowly built up from the first elementary number conservations (see Piaget and Szeminska, 1941, and Piaget, Inhelder, and Szeminska, 1948). The concept of measurement implies several steps: first, a unit has to be partitioned off from the object to be quantified, and then this unit has to be displaced without overlaps or empty intervals; second, these continuous units form inclusions—

131

the first bit measured is included in the bit that comprises two units, and so on. The learning experiments on conservation of length* were designed to explore the psychological reality underlying the theoretical parallel between number and measurement, and between numerical conservation and conservation of length.

PRELIMINARY EXPERIMENTS

In many, if not all, conservation problems one of the factors that account for nonconservation is the tendency to make ordinal judgments based on ideas of *going beyond, overtaking,* and so on. The level of the liquid poured into the narrow glass "goes beyond" that of the liquid poured into the wider glass; the row of counters that have been spread out "goes further than" the other row. In the conservation of length problems (see Appendix) this type of judgment is particularly tenacious. When one length of wire is twisted into a zigzag and put directly underneath a straight, much shorter bit of wire, the two lengths are judged to be equal, "because they go just as far." Similarly, when one of two sticks, which are placed directly parallel to and underneath one another, is pushed slightly forward, that one is judged to be longer, "because it goes further." In a first approach to the learning experiments on length, situations were designed to assess the particular strength of the ordinal judgments as regards conservation of length. The numerical conservation problem was made more difficult by using 20 to 30 elements and by displacing the elements in one of the straight lines so as to make a zigzag. The length conservation situation was made easier by using, instead of wire or sticks, a collection of six matches put end to end (eliminating the difficulty of the partitioning operation). Apart from the fact that the matches touched each other and thus formed, in a certain sense, a continuous line, the situation used for numerical judgments appeared more complex (20–30 objects) than that used for judgments of length (six matches only).

* Other authors have carried out learning experiments on conservation of length (e.g., Braine [1959, 1964], Smedslund [1963a and b, 1965] but with different aims and methods).

SITUATIONS PRESENTED

a. *Number.* Starting with two equal collections, A and B (see Fig. 6.1), the experimenter rearranged B as shown in parts 1 and 2 of Fig. 6.1 and then asked questions about the number of elements: "Are there the same in A and B?" etc.

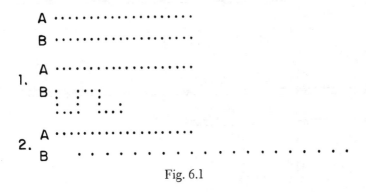

Fig. 6.1

b. *Length.* Starting with two identical arrangements of matches (see Fig. 6.2), the experimenter altered B as shown in parts 1 and 2 of Fig. 6.2 and asked the child questions about the length of the "roads": "Are they the same length, or is one longer than the other?" etc.

The twelve children selected for this preliminary experiment had previously succeeded in a simple elementary number conservation problem and failed when faced with a conservation of continuous length problem involving two changes in shape of the wire. (See Appendix.)

The main results were as follows.

a. Despite the large number of objects, almost all the subjects gave conservation judgments; a few initial errors were spontaneously corrected. They gave the same arguments as in the simple counters test, despite the particularly misleading spatial arrangements: "Here you've pushed them into a zigzag and there it's stayed straight" (compensation); "You haven't added anything or taken anything away" (identity); and "You can make the straight line zigzag as well, then that'll be the same" (reversibility).

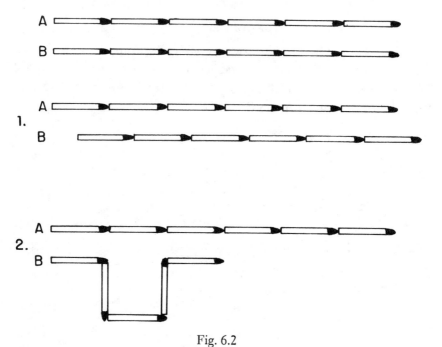

Fig. 6.2

b. For some children, questions on conservation of length in this simplified situation proved easy. Focusing on the six identical matches, they quickly realized that counting the matches provided them with the correct answers, which they maintained, even when the experimenter tried to make them change their minds ("But look! That one goes much further").

For other children, however, there seemed to be no connection between the problems of number and those of length. When asked about number, the "going beyond" aspect did not lead them into error, but when asked about length, they proved incapable of applying the same type of reasoning and continued to judge the length of the "roads" according to whether or not they "went just as far." Whereas they spontaneously suggested that one could count the matches to check their judgments in the number tasks, it did not occur to them to do so in the length situations. Often they even declined to do so when the experimenter suggested it. Those who finally did adopt this suggestion remained unconvinced by their own findings and gave contradictory answers—changing from inequality judgments (based on the ordinal principle) to equality judgments (based on counting) and vice versa. Frequent returns to the number situations, where their logical convictions remained unshaken, had no effect on their answers to the length problems; the striking figural similarity of the two situations did not help them connect the two types of questions.

This preliminary experiment suggested several possibilities for further investigation. In the first place, it confirmed the persistence of ordinal judgments of the "going beyond" type whenever questions are asked about length, even when the lengths to be compared are broken up into countable units. This tendency to draw conclusions about respective lengths from the correspondence (or the absence thereof) between extremities appears possible only if the two lengths are arranged as in the original experiment and the experiment just described, i.e., directly underneath one another. How would the children react if roads of equal length but of different contours were presented on different corners of the table? In the second place, it seemed possible that those subjects who used the counting method simply shifted their attention from the extremities of the seemingly continuous lines to the individual matches and their countability. Their correct answers could be interpreted as pseudo-successes in conservation of length, since they might have translated the problem into a question of conservation of number. What would happen if instead of using matches of identical size, we presented them with lengths made up out of unequal elements? Finally, we wondered whether the tendency to approach questions on length in a different manner from questions on number would still be observed if questions on number and length were asked in the same situation. These considerations led to a first learning experiment where three different types of situations were used.

INITIAL TRAINING PROCEDURE

The experiment just described led to a trial training procedure, which was presented to a group of children who had succeeded in elementary number conservation and failed in conservation of length. A certain number of variations were introduced, and no effort was made to keep the procedure uniform for all the subjects: consequently, no quantitative results will be given, but the different re-actions to the various situations will be described. The most inter-esting situations were subsequently chosen to construct a regular training procedure. Three displays were presented to the subjects.

Situation a. Two sheets of paper (40 x 30 cm) are placed in front of the subject. Either the experimenter, or the child following his instructions, lays out two roads, A and B, on the first sheet, one straight, one in a zigzag, placed directly above each other, each made up of four matches of equal size (5 cm). On the second sheet, road

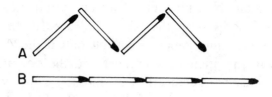

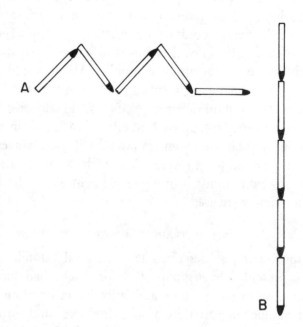

Fig. 6.3

A is placed in the same way, but road B is laid out vertically at the extreme edge of the paper. The latter situation will be referred to as "separate lay-out" and the former as "close lay-out" (see Fig. 6.3). The subject is asked to compare the lengths of the roads, first in the close lay-out, then in the separate lay-out. The close lay-out often leads to a judgment of inequality ("Road B is longer, it goes further"), whereas in the separate lay-out the roads are judged to be of equal length, since no comparison of points of arrival is possible and the display suggests counting of the matches. The experimenter then tries to make the subject compare these two different ways of judging. The same situation can be used as a construction task: the experimenter lays out the zigzag road, and the child is asked to construct a road of the same length either directly underneath or at the edge of the paper.

Situation b. The same close lay-out and separate lay-out are used, but the roads are made up of matches of different length (5 and 7 cm). The same questions are asked as in situation a and the same instructions are given.

Situation c. Two straight lines of sticks with tiny houses glued onto them are laid out, consisting of the same number of sticks, one di-

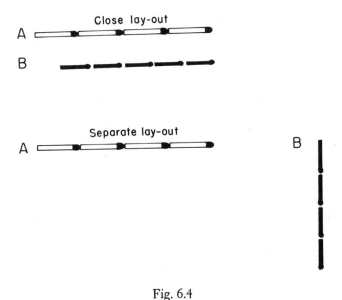

Fig. 6.4

rectly underneath the other. The experimenter rearranges the sticks of road A, changing its contours, and asks conservation questions regarding both the number of houses and the length of the roads:

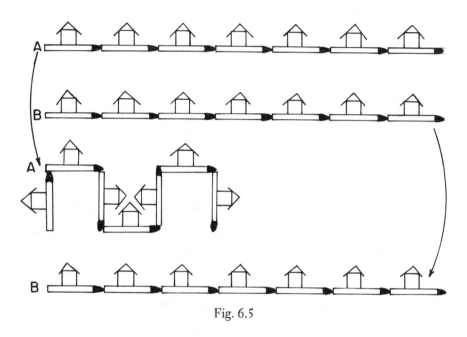

Fig. 6.5

"Are there the same number of houses here as there? Just as many? Show me, how did you find out?"; and "Is this road just as long as the other, is there just as far to walk here as there, or is it different?" The experimenter goes back and forth between questions on length and number, according to the answers the subjects give.

ANALYSIS OF THE RESPONSES DURING THE TRAINING SESSIONS

Various reactions were noted during this training procedure, many of which indicated an awareness on the part of the children of the inconsistency of their answers. Reasoning based on counting entered into conflict with that based on the ordinal principle; answers given to questions on number were felt to be in contradiction with answers given to questions on length. In several cases, these conflicts led to new insights. In others, the conflicts remained unsolved, and some children did not seem to be aware of the contradiction in their answers. Examples of these different reactions to the various training situations are the following.

As expected, in the separate lay-out all the subjects gave correct answers based on the number of matches. When the close lay-out was presented immediately afterward, conflicts often arose. One subject, Duv (6;6), expressed this conflict particularly clearly. Presented with a situation where four matches in the top road are in a straight line and six matches in the bottom road are in a zigzag pattern, with the beginning and end points coinciding and all matches of equal length (Fig. 6.6), Duv said: "The roads are exactly the same . . .

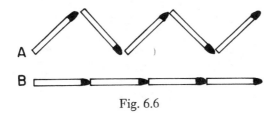

Fig. 6.6

except that you've put a bit more in the bottom one so that they're the same length." An involved bit of reasoning, based on the coincidence of the end points, but showing awareness of the difference in the number of matches. It left the child rather perplexed; after a moment's hesitation, he said: "But then, why are they the same? That's what I'm wondering about . . ."

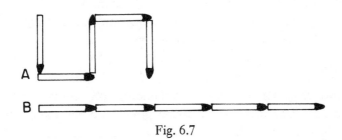

Fig. 6.7

In the next situation (Fig. 6.7), the same child seemed to have decided in favor of a judgment based on counting: "The roads are the same, five matches and five matches." When the experimenter told him that another child had said that road B was longer "because it goes further," he was amused: "That's really funny, there's the same number of matches and he thinks that the roads aren't the same!" But when the experimenter returned to the situation of Fig. 6.6, the child once again returned to an ordinal estimate and maintained that the two roads were the same length. Only when he was asked to construct roads rather than give judgments did he get real insight into his own difficulties.

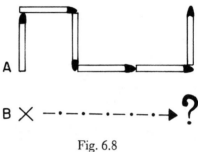

Fig. 6.8

When in the following situation (Fig. 6.8) he had to make a straight road of the same length as the zigzag road A, starting at B, he ran his finger along the matches of A and put down the same number for his straight road, B. When he was again invited to give a judgment about length in the first situation, he proceeded in the same way, pointing to the successive pairings of the matches in both roads. Finally he took one match away from A and said: "Now it's the same," though B still "goes further" than A. When the experimenter reminded him of his earlier conviction that A (five matches) and B (four matches) were the same length, he gave an explanation of the crux of his problem: "Because I didn't count properly, because they came to the same place." In fact, he had counted perfectly correctly, but had been incapable of reconciling the fact that the number of matches was not the same with the idea that if the ends of the roads coincided they must be of equal length.

From then on, this child appeared to have mastered the problem and gave correct answers to all questions. His post-test confirmed this acquisition.

Often children who started to count the matches when faced with the separate lay-out did not feel any conflict in the more difficult situations. For CHA (6;11), e.g., counting immediately gave way to judgments based on the order of the end points. In the construction problem in Fig. 6.8 she correctly laid out her road, saying: "Because I counted six (in A) and then six (for B)." As soon as she had finished, however, she seemed to discover the lack of coincidence between the end points and, judging the roads of different lengths, removed enough matches from B to make the ends coincide.

Other children went on to apply the counting procedure to every problem. However, they did so regardless of whether or not it was appropriate. For instance, when CAT (6;6) was asked about the lengths in situation b (Fig. 6.9), she replied: "B's got further to walk

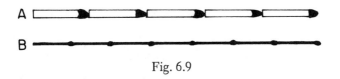

Fig. 6.9

because there are seven and A's got less because there're five." She continued to give answers based on counting to several further questions, even when these were formulated in terms of "being just as tired or not when one walks on A and B."

Finally, some children became increasingly confused as the experimenter passed from one situation to another. The number of possible criteria from which to choose, suggested in turn by the different situations (number of matches, coincidence of the end points of the roads, length of the individual matches, link between the original lay-out and its subsequent modification for the conservation problems), disturbed them to such an extent that they ended up by giving answers about which they themselves were clearly not happy. For example, ANN (7;3), in situation b (see Fig. 6.10), when asked, "Who's got further to walk?" after much hesitation replied, "B's got further to go," pointing to the five small matches, in a tone of voice which betrayed her resigned perplexity.

Situation c brought further confirmation of the fact that, for certain children, questions bearing on number have nothing in common

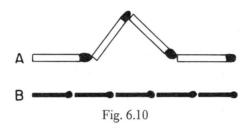

Fig. 6.10

with questions bearing on length. All those who had made no real progress in situations a and b gave the same response pattern in c: that is, they answered correctly all the questions about the number of houses and incorrectly all those concerning length, which they judged by the order of the ends of the roads.

ANALYSIS OF THE RESPONSES TO THE POST-TESTS

The post-tests consisted of problems of continuous length (wire; see Appendix). The responses were often surprising, since, in many cases, it was precisely those children who had become increasingly confused during the training sessions who made clear progress, while those who had used counting from the beginning of these sessions and shown no signs of conflict reverted to the same responses as they had given in the pre-test. There were, of course, other children who gradually grasped the various aspects of the problems; their mistakes led to an awareness of what was involved and they often gave completely correct answers in the post-tests.

The final training procedure took the findings of the preliminary experiments into account, particularly regarding the following points.

1. The responses of the children who were given the opportunity of comparing the *close* and *separate* lay-outs led us to include exercises in which all the lay-outs remain in front of the child throughout the entire training session so that at any time he can make comparisons between his solutions to the various problems.

2. Of the three types of problems used in the first experiment (i.e., the "building" of a road of the same length as the experimenter's model; evaluation of the respective lengths of two roads both laid out by the experimenter, and problems of conservation of length), the first one ("building" a road) seemed to lead to the most interesting

responses. Therefore only this type of problem was used in the training procedure for the final experiment.

3. It seemed essential to use matches of different lengths in order to obtain an accurate assessment of the children's responses. Generally, the children were given matches five-sevenths the length of those of the experimenter. The spontaneous reactions of some of the subjects, who tried to see how many times a small match could fit into a larger one, led us to include an easier situation where the children's matches were half the length of those of the experimenter.

4. In order to get a better idea of how the important principles of equal units of measurement and of compensation were handled, a situation in which the model was made up of matches of various lengths was also presented.

FINAL EXPERIMENT

TRAINING PROCEDURE, TESTS, AND SELECTION OF SUBJECTS

Problems

In the problems of the second training procedure the child is always asked to build a road "of the same length as" or "just as long as" the model, or to build his road "so that there's no further to walk on it than on the other."

Problem 1

For all the situations matches are used, those given to the child being shorter than those used in the model (exact proportion: 5:7 or 4.3 cm:6 cm).

a. *Complex close lay-out.* The child has to build a straight road of the same length as the zigzag model road, starting directly underneath one of the end points of the model road (see Fig. 6.11). The general lay-out of this model is such that the most obvious solution is to make the end points coincide. Furthermore, as the child's matches are shorter than those in the model (four short matches placed in his straight road "go just as far" as the five long ones of the zigzag model), counting alone cannot result in the correct answer,

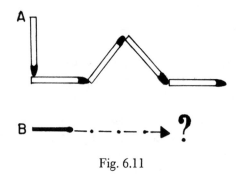

Fig. 6.11

although it can help the child overcome the tendency to concentrate on the end points. The correct answer can be derived from situation c.

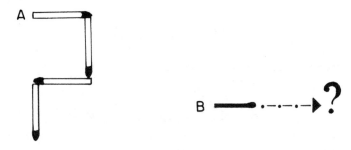

Fig. 6.12

b. *Separate lay-out.* In this situation (see Fig. 6.12) the road to be constructed is not directly underneath the model. This lay-out does not suggest the ordinal ("going just as far") criterion, but the numerical comparison; however, since the child's matches are not of the same length as those of the model road, they cannot serve as units as such. A rough visual estimate can be made, and the correct solution can be derived from situation c.

c. *Simple close lay-out.* In this situation, where both roads are

Fig. 6.13

144

straight with their initial end points coinciding, the ordinal criterion gives the correct solution immediately. Since the model road in a was made up of the same number of matches as that in c, the latter situation provides the answer for a if the child has grasped the principle of transitivity.

Problems a, b, and c were sometimes made easier by using matches of 3 cm and 6 cm.

Problem 2

The model is always made up of matches of various lengths and the child is given a collection which includes five matches identical to those used by the experimenter.

a. *Complex close lay-out.*

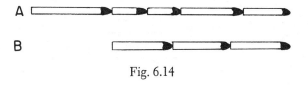

Fig. 6.14

b. *Separate lay-out.*

Fig. 6.15

c. *Simple close lay-out.*

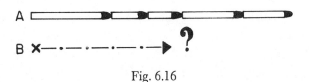

Fig. 6.16

145

In a the child can build the correct road by three methods: (1) He can use a staggered one-to-one correspondence, starting with an identical match and following the same order (see Fig. 6.17). (2) He

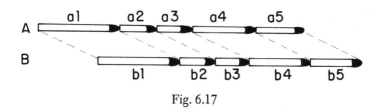

Fig. 6.17

can start with a match identical to the second one in the model (a^2) and then at the end select a match identical to a^1 (see Fig. 6.18); (of-

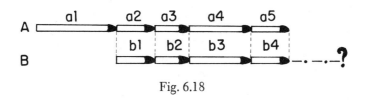

Fig. 6.18

ten the children chose the last match haphazardly). (3) He can use his matches in a different order (see Fig. 6.19); (here, too, the choice

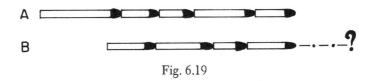

Fig. 6.19

of the last match is the most difficult).

In lay-out b the problem can be solved by a one-to-one copy.

Problem 3

The model consists of a straight length of wire, while the child has matches of various lengths and has to start his road further to the right than the model. To find the correct solution, some idea of measurement is necessary: one either starts at the indicated point, makes the end of one's road coincide with the model and then adds a match of the same length as the difference between the starting points of the two lines, or one first constructs a road directly underneath the wire and then displaces the whole construction so as to comply with the imposed starting point. For this last problem only one lay-out is used (see Fig. 6.20).

Fig. 6.20

For problems 1 and 2 the three lay-outs a, b, and c remain in front of the child throughout the training. After the child has proposed his initial solutions, the experimenter returns to all three lay-outs and asks for comparisons. If necessary, he points out that the child has used different and sometimes incompatible methods of solving the problems.

Selection of Subjects

Sixteen subjects were chosen, aged between 5;4 and 7;4 years. Thirteen were in the first grade and one in the second grade of a Genevan primary school and the two youngest were in the second year of a Genevan kindergarten.

The subjects were selected on the basis of two criteria.

1. A correct solution of two or three conservation of number problems. Two identical glasses, A and B, were filled with exactly the same number of beads, by the one-to-one or two-to-two iterative method. The contents of A were then poured into another glass, W (wider diameter) or N (narrower diameter), and the child was asked questions about the number of beads in the two glasses. After a return to the initial situation of A = B, the contents of A and B were poured simultaneously into W and N and the same conservation questions were asked. The children's answers had to be consistently correct and accompanied by clear explanations.

2. An incorrect solution of the problem of conservation of continu-

ous lengths using two strips of modeling clay (see Appendix). The length problems were again presented in a first post-test immediately after training and then once more, under the same experimental conditions, in a second post-test after an interval of four to six weeks. A different version of the conservation of length test from that described by Piaget, Inhelder, and Szeminska (1948, chap. 7) was used so as to avoid presenting situations which bore too close a resemblance to those of the training situations and also so as to be able to distinguish between "conservation" answers based on the identity of the object (on the fact that the object that had been moved was still the same) and those indicating the presence of a system of mental operations underlying a true understanding of conservation of length.

All the subjects took part in three to four training sessions given twice a week, each lasting 15–20 minutes.

RESULTS

Comparison of Pre-Test and Post-Tests

As described in the Appendix, we distinguished between nonconservation (NC), intermediate (Int), and conservation (C) responses. In the Int category, a distinction was made between Int− responses (i.e., those in which the child is either hesitant or gives right answers regarding the first change of shape but wrong ones regarding the second) and Int+ responses (i.e., those in which the answer is completely correct for the first change in shape, but hesitant or wrong for the second) (see Table 6.1). All the subjects found it more difficult to solve the second problem than the first. A comparison of the results of the two post-tests (see Table 6.1) reveals the phenomenon of delayed progress (also observed in the other experiments). Five children (EMM, HEN, PER, CHR, ROD) improved their performance at the second post-test. At the second post-test six subjects reached complete acquisition, seven partial acquisition (four Int− and three Int+), and only two subjects remained at the NC level (one subject, BEE, was not given post-test 2).

The results of a control group who took no part in the training but were given the same pre-test and post-tests were very different from

TABLE 6.1

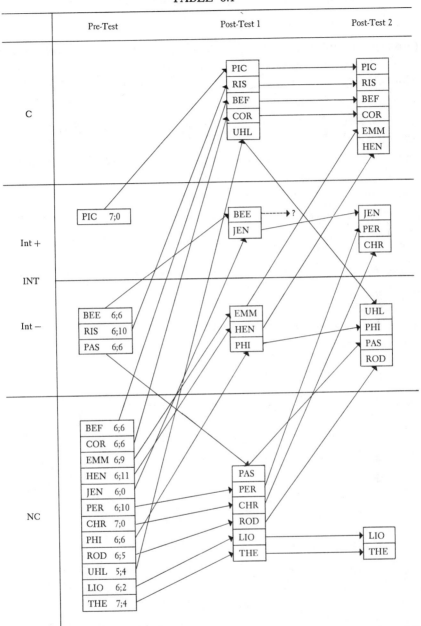

those of the experimental group. Two subjects of the control group gave conservation answers at the second post-test; they had, however, already been very close to conservation at the pre-test, where they had given arguments based on reversibility and compensation. Some of the subjects hesitated between correct and wrong answers in the pre-test, without any explanations; in the second post-test, these children gave no correct answers at all, but they were sure of themselves and explained their answers. One child, for example, judged two roads to be of equal length "because they go to there and there (pointing to the two final ends which coincide) . . . because they come to the same length . . . before (i.e., before the change) that didn't come up to here, but now it does . . . because I can see where the roads arrive; you don't have to look at the bends, I just look at the end."

Apart from this change in explanations, and from the slight progress made by the two subjects mentioned above, the subjects of the control group did not modify their responses from pre-test to post-tests.

Analysis of the Responses during the Training Sessions

First of all, problems 2 and 3 will be discussed, as they turned out to be easier than problem 1. Problem 1 will be discussed more extensively since the mental processes involved in a transition from a lower to a higher level of conservation of length were most clearly revealed in the reactions to these problems.

The following responses were noted in problems 2 and 3.

The most primitive type of response was to make road B start at the imposed point, but stop in coincidence with the end point of A.

At a slightly more advanced level, the children first produced the primitive solution, but then judged B too short and added another match. Having done this, they incorrectly judged that B was now longer than A. They continued to waver between the two solutions.

At the next level, the children immediately made their road go beyond road A. But since they had to work with matches of various lengths, they could not simply pick any match and place it at the end of their road B to make the correct compensation; they had to find one of exactly the right length. Several children chose their final match at random, arriving at an approximate solution.

At the most advanced levels, various methods were used to produce a correct solution, as for example in Fig. 6.17.

In problem 3, where there was only the close lay-out, the accurate solution was obtained either by measuring the length between the left ends of the sticks, or by making B protrude beyond A by an estimated amount which the children then checked by moving one of the roads so that the left ends of the sticks coincided. If necessary, B was modified and then returned to its original position. This type of solution shows that the child is capable of reasoning based on conservation.

The experimenter switched back and forth from one problem to another. Throughout the session, the child's solutions remained in front of him on the table. Several children made some progress in problem 2, but only rarely does there seem to be a close relationship between the post-test results and the responses during this exercise. A correspondence does exist in the case of the children who showed no progress at all at the post-tests, and then gave low-level responses to problems 2 and 3. It also exists in the case of the children who gave the most advanced solutions to problems 2 and 3 and then made excellent progress at the post-tests.

Problem 1 elicited a variety of responses which indicated clearly the nature of the difficulties of those situations and showed the conflicts arising in the children's minds when they had to compare their different solutions. The different types of solutions can be described as follows, in developmental order.

In situation a (complex close lay-out), 14 (out of 16) subjects began by making a road which stopped exactly underneath the end of the model road, made up of five long matches (this requires four of their short matches). They declared that their roads were just as long as the model (see Fig. 6.21). The experimenter then went on to the separate lay-out (b), where most of the children spontaneously counted the matches in the model and used the same number for their straight road. When the experimenter asked them how they

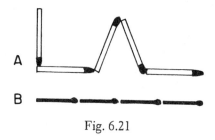

Fig. 6.21

had gone about making the two roads as equal as possible, they said they had counted: "There were five matches in your road, so I counted five for the other one."

The experimenter then returned to the complex close lay-out of situation a (which was still on the table) and if the child did not spontaneously start to count the matches, counting was suggested and usually carried out correctly: four short matches and five long ones. This led to two types of reactions. Some children saw nothing wrong in using the same number of matches in A and B in lay-out b but a different number in lay-out a. At a more advanced level, others attempted to correct their construction in a by using the same number of matches as in the model. But the idea that "going beyond" means "being longer" is so overpowering that instead of simply adding a match to their road they invented various compromise solutions: (1) breaking the last match of their road in two pieces, so that both roads had the same number of matches, but neither went beyond the other (Fig. 6.22); (2) adding a fifth match, but placing it so that it

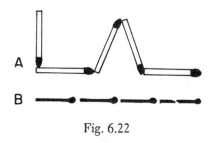

Fig. 6.22

did not protrude beyond the model (Fig. 6.23); (3) adding a bit of a fifth match so that the protrusion was hardly noticeable (Fig. 6.24).

Sometimes the children found these compromise solutions rather

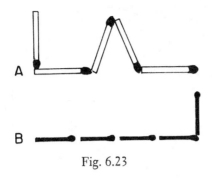

Fig. 6.23

unsatisfactory, as for example Dɪᴅ (5;4), one of the subjects given the initial training procedure who, although he could not find a better solution, declared: "It's not very much the same."

At a more advanced level, the children added the fifth match even though this made their road go beyond the model, explaining: "Even if it goes a bit further, there are the same number of matches here (pointing to roads A and B in lay-out b) and here (lay-out a); there are five and five."

This last solution constitutes a step forward since the difficulty of the overpowering "going beyond" principle is overcome; however, it is far from perfect, since the total length is simply judged by the number of matches (their quite noticeable difference in length is ignored).

In the simple close lay-out (c) (Fig. 6.13), two types of construction were made.

1. Some children immediately constructed a road of the correct length, its end points coinciding with those of the model; when asked to explain how they knew that this was the right solution, they answered, quite legitimately: "I can see that the two lines are the same: two straight roads." However, when the experimenter asked them to

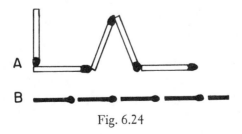

Fig. 6.24

count the matches in both the roads, they were reluctant to count beyond five in road B, and quite perplexed to find that there were five matches in A, but seven in B.

2. Other children started by counting the matches in A and then used the same number of matches to make B. When they discovered that using five of their matches made B shorter than A, they were puzzled and very hesitant about adding two more to B: "I don't think it can be done . . ." (BEN, 6;5, one of the subjects given the initial training procedure).

Nevertheless, in this simple lay-out all subjects finally found the correct solution: "There are more red matches (B), but the roads both come to the same place." Most subjects were also able to explain why there should be more matches in road B than in road A, using a compensation argument: "With big matches, you don't have to put so many; you have to use more of the little ones." At this point, the experimenter returned to the separate lay-out. Now the children often "discovered" the difference in size of the matches and added one or two matches to their road "because my matches are smaller than yours, so I've got to put a few more, if I don't . . . if I put the same number . . . that makes a smaller road."

If in lay-out a the child had used the same number of smaller matches for his road B as there were in A (five), so that his road already went beyond B, although it was still too short, the experimenter returned to this situation. When the children realized that in the separate lay-out (b) it was not sufficient to use five of the short matches they had taken a major step forward in understanding the problem. Consequently, it was interesting to see how this understanding would affect their responses to situation a. The following reactions were noted.

1. Having realized the need to compensate for the shorter length by a greater number, some children now added matches to their road, B. Sometimes they even exaggerated, making their own road go way beyond the model.

2. Other children became confused when situation a was repeated after situation c and continued to hesitate between the various solutions, including the most elementary one of making the ends of the roads coincide.

3. Others hesitated between two solutions. They first used the same number of matches as in the model, then added some more, then took them away again, etc. The experimenter then tried to help these subjects by giving them matches which were half the size of his. This often had the desired effect: the child realized that two of his matches were equivalent to one of the experimenter's and produced the correct solution. After this, a final return to the five-sevenths matches resulted in many completely correct solutions.

4. The most advanced children immediately realized the error of using the same number of matches and added one or two matches to their roads in situation a. The experimenter then asked them, once again, to compare c and a. At this point, some of these children still could not deduce the correct solution for a from situation c; but since they understood the need to compensate for the shorter length of their matches by using a greater number, they explained how they solved the problem by referring to a qualitative compensation. Others used the information about the necessary number of matches obtained in situation c to solve situation a; their arguments referred explicitly to the transitivity relationship obtaining between situations a and c. Consequently, it was not necessary to use the simpler material (matches half the size of those of the experimenter) with these subjects.

EXCERPTS FROM PROTOCOLS

The first protocol is an example of the behavior of those subjects who encounter great difficulties at an elementary level.

Lɪo (6;2)

In problem 1.a Lɪo constructs his road so that its end points coincide with those of the experimenter's road. In problem 1.b he uses the same number of matches for his road, B, as there are in A, but when he has finished he announces (correctly) that his road is shorter. However, this does not help him find a better solution, and he keeps his construction as it is, saying, "I copied it the way it is, there are four." In situation c he starts counting the matches he uses for his straight road, begins to hesitate when he has put down five (the number in A), but nevertheless continues until his road reaches the end point of A, then takes two matches away, explaining, "Because there are five green ones there, and like that five red ones here," although he adds, "The green ones are longer than the red ones." Lɪo is aware of the importance of the difference in length of the matches, but he does not know what to do about it. He proposes changing A, and agrees to look at the total length of both roads only after much hesitation, finally adding two matches. When the experimenter goes back to situation b he once again starts counting, continues to judge his road as being shorter, but does not accept the experimenter's suggestion of adding at least one match to his road. For situation a he once again constructs a road whose end points coincide with those of A. With the matches half the size of those of the experimenter, a slight progress is obtained for lay-out c, where Lɪo does agree without so much hesitation to use a different number for his road from that in the model. But in situation b he again uses the same number as in the model, and in situation a he makes the end points of his road coincide with those of the model. He is not happy with his solutions, but he can neither correct them spontaneously nor accept the experimenter's suggestions.

Lɪo reacts to problems 2 and 3 in the same way as to problem 1, and his results at the post-tests are exactly the same as at the pre-test.

Lɪo's protocol illustrates the elementary types of reactions to the problems, i.e., the alternative use of the "going just as far" criterion and the counting method. Apart from some hesitations, Lɪo does not seem aware of the contradictions in his different solutions, and no progress is noted.

The next protocol illustrates the way a subject who in the second post-test reaches the Int+ level reacts to the training problems.

Per (6;10)

In situation 1.a Per spontaneously uses six of her small matches; but then she judges her road to be too long, because it goes further than the model. Her next idea is to arrange her matches in the same shape as those in A. When the experimenter reminds her that her road must be straight, she starts her construction to the left of the model road. Once again she is reminded of the instruction, and she finally opts for the solution where the end points of her road coincide with those of the model. She points out, however, that if road B were to be laid out in the same zigzag as A, A would go further. In lay-out 1.b (A made up of four matches) she uses five matches for road B, and explains that her matches are smaller than the experimenter's. However, when she counts again to check her solution, she starts to waver between the simple numerical solution and her own idea of compensating for the shorter length of her matches: "You need more red matches and less green ones, because the red ones are smaller."

Returning to situation 1.a she gives up the compensation idea and constructs her road according to the numerical principle: five matches, as in the model. In lay-out 1.c she immediately makes a road whose end points coincide with the model, without counting, and when the experimenter attracts her attention to the difference in number, she explains without hesitation: "The green matches are bigger, so you can put more red ones." Throughout various comparisons between 1.a and 1.c she maintains her (correct) solution for c, but tries various compromise solutions for a. For example, she breaks some of her matches into bits, and constructs a road with the same number of matches and bits of matches as the model, without having to make it go beyond the latter. She also proposes making road B with the same zigzags as road A, or, inversely, to change the model road to a straight one. Finally she opts for a solution with the correct number in which her road starts to the left of the model and stops beyond it, and she explains: "They are the same length, because one starts first (pointing to the first sequential match in A) and the other goes further at the end" (see Fig. 6.25).

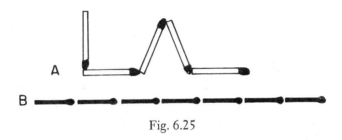

Fig. 6.25

With matches half the size of the experimenter's, PER gives the same type of compromise solution. She realizes that two of her matches fill the same space as one of the experimenter's, but when she has to solve the problem of Fig. 6.26 she uses three matches for her road instead of four, since with four her road "goes too far," and then she tries to obviate the difficulty by using four matches but putting them down two by two, as is

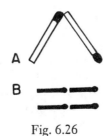

Fig. 6.26

157

shown in Fig. 6.26. These simplified situations do not help PER, and when the situations of problem 1 are taken up once more, she continues to use compensation arguments, but never arrives at the correct solution. In situation 1.a she uses six matches (instead of seven, for the five matches in the experimenter's road) and explains: "This one starts first, so the other one has to go a bit further and . . . and also this one has a point (a)."

Similarly, in problem 2 she makes her road go further than the model, but she cannot establish a precise relation between "starting first" and "going further" at the end. In problem 3 it is only after a suggestion from the experimenter that she adopts the solution of a preliminary parallel construction and then a displacement of her road. Once she has solved the problem in this way, she judges correctly that the roads are indeed of the same length.

In the first post-test she still gives wrong answers, judging by the "going beyond" principle; but in the second post-test she reaches level Int+. Even though she does not yet give conservation judgments in all the situations, she has made notable progress in the interval between the two tests.

PER's reactions to the training procedure are intermediate between those of LIO and those of EMM (given below): she does not simply judge either by "going beyond" or by number, but still finds only approximate solutions to problems 2 and 3, and in problem 1 tries various compromises to reconcile the numbers of matches, their difference in length, and her desire to have the two roads start and stop at the same point.

The last example illustrates the reactions of a subject who reaches the conservation level in post-test 2, but who appears to have great difficulties during the training procedure.

EMM (6;9)

In situation 1.a EMM's first reaction is to construct her road so that its end points coincide with those of the model; in 1.b, on the other hand, she explains spontaneously that she has to use more matches for her road because her matches are smaller than the experimenter's. Coming back to 1.a, she adds a match to her road, but takes it away again because "the road goes too far." In lay-out 1.c she first uses the same number of matches as in the model, but quickly adds two more, explaining: "The red ones are smaller and the green ones are bigger." When once again asked to think about situation 1.a, she takes only number into account, and is now so obsessed by this criterion that when presented with situation c she takes away two matches and maintains, despite the obvious difference in length, that "the roads are the same, it's right, because there are five matches and five matches." After a comparison between one green and one red match she adds only one match to her construction (six as against five in the model)—a compromise solution, since the difference in length is now less, and the difference in number not too great. With the matches that are half the size of the experimenter's EMM first constructs her road in 1.a once again on the coincidence principle; in 1.b, however, she shows insight: "When you have two small matches it's as if you had one big one," and she gives the correct solution. She manages to do the same for lay-out 1.a after much hesitation.

When the experimenter goes back to problem 1 using the five-sevenths matches, she finally admits the necessity of compensating for their shorter length by a greater number, but the "going beyond" principle remains too strong, and she chooses the compromise of breaking her matches into little bits.

In problem 2 she continues to be confused by the apparent contradiction between counting, compensation for the shorter length of her matches, and the fact that the roads "do not go just as far." She spontaneously finds the solution of making her road start from the same point as the model and then shifting the whole construction to the right. Even so, when she has to defend her solution against the experimenter's argument, she is not very convinced.

Problem 3, by contrast, is immediately solved. First she chooses a last match of approximately the right length, but when asked to explain, she demonstrates that the last match of her road protrudes as far beyond the end point of the model road as it lags behind the model at the start.

In post-test 1 she is still very hesitant and reaches level Int—. In post-test 2 she answers all the questions correctly and gives excellent explanations.

It seems strange that a child who succeeds so well in the second post-test should have had so much difficulty during the training sessions: at first, EMM is convinced that the roads must have the same number of matches, then she begins to coordinate the number with the length of the individual matches, but she can apply this only to the simple problems. In the complex situations, her solutions are either based on a single criterion or are the result of a compromise between several criteria. The results of EMM's first post-test tally with her reactions to the training sessions, but during the interval between the first and second post-test an internal process of reorganization seems to have occurred which results in excellent progress at post-test 2, where all her solutions are correct.*

Complementary Experiments

Reversal of the Order of Presentation of the Different Lay-outs

To check whether the predominance of the counting behavior was due to the order of presentation, the order of the situations in problem 1 was reversed and lay-out c was presented first. The responses of six subjects given this order of presentation were comparable to those given above. One example will suffice to illustrate this.

SER (6;3)

In the simple lay-out 1.c, SER spontaneously makes a correct road B. In explanation he simply says, "I saw (it)," and thinks there is no point in counting the matches, as suggested by the experimenter. In the separate lay-out 1.b he refers spontaneously to the number of matches—"I counted, there are five (A) and five (B), it's the same length"—which shows that he takes no account of the size of the matches; but in 1.c he does: "The red ones are smaller and you've got to put more." When the experimenter goes on to the complex lay-out 1.a he stops his road to coincide with the model and comments: "I saw by the ends, without counting." Comparison with his solution in 1.b leads him to add another match to his road, which now has the same number of matches as the model; but since his road goes beyond the experimenter's he cannot make up his mind, taking the extra match away and then adding it again.

After a comparison between one of his matches and one of the experimenter's, SER explains his correct solution to problem 1.c: "The red ones are smaller, you need more." He then manages to transpose this reasoning to b: "I counted but I put one more (in B) because the red ones (A) are longer." In the complex lay-out 1.a he again ends his road at the same place as the model without counting the matches. When he is reminded that for 1.b he counted, he considers that this is of no use in 1.a and answers: "Yes (I counted in 1.b) because it was harder, here it's easier."

Although this order of presentation might be expected to make the solution of problem 1.a (complex lay-out) easier, this did not turn out to be so. Presenting the simple lay-out first, which suggests the correct solution almost automatically and provides the right answer

---

* These examples were selected to illustrate particular difficulties. Other subjects gave correct answers straightaway during the training procedure and reached C at the first post-test.

to problem 1.c (if the subject thinks of counting the matches), and then presenting 1.b (the separate lay-out), where almost all subjects start counting spontaneously, did not suggest an application of the counting procedure to problem 1.a. On the contrary, the same difficulties appeared, and the tendency to adopt different ways of solving the different problems seemed even stronger. The child has to realize the necessity of a compensation between the length of the individual matches and their number, and he has to become aware of the insufficiency of the "going just as far" principle. The comparison between the lengths of the different matches suggests the idea of measurement. Lay-out 1.b suggests the counting of units that make up a length. The complex lay-out demands the coordination of these aspects of comparisons of length. However, in the correct solution to this problem the straight road "goes so far beyond" the zigzag model that even if the necessity of a compensation between the length of the units and their number is already understood many children cannot apply this principle. When they are led to make several comparisons between the different situations these children can overcome this difficulty, but the order in which the comparisons are made is immaterial.

Experiment on the Relationship between the Different Stages Observed with the Traditional Conservation of Length Task and with the Construction Tasks of the Training Procedure

An exploratory experiment was designed to determine whether, for subjects who had not followed a training procedure, the questions asked in the conservation of length task (as described in the Appendix) and in the construction problems (as described in the training procedure) were of equal difficulty. For example, would one find that certain children gave conservation answers but still constructed roads on the primitive "going just as far" principle? Or would correct answers in the conservation questions always go together with correct constructions?

The conservation of length task (see Appendix) and the construction problem 1.a (see p. 143) were presented, in a single session, to 12 subjects between the ages of 7;4 and 8;5 (see Piaget and Inhelder, 1966, chap. 8, sec. 6).

161

Five subjects gave correct answers to both questions of the conservation of length task. Four of these subjects immediately constructed straight roads that went well beyond the end point of the zigzag model. One subject did not make his road long enough, but still made it continue beyond the end point of the model and refused the solution based on the "going just as far" principle proposed by the experimenter.

Two subjects gave the right answer to one of the problems in the conservation task only after some hesitation. When faced with the construction problem they at first made the end points of the roads coincide, but then spontaneously judged their straight road to be shorter than the model, and added the necessary matches.

Five subjects were classified Int for the standard conservation problems: they either answered one question correctly but hesitated or gave the wrong answer to the second, or else they hesitated for both problems. These children had similar difficulties in the construction problem, i.e., they started off by making the end point of their straight road coincide with that of the model, then changed their minds as a result of the experimenter's questions, and finally made their road go beyond the model. Their hesitations, however, showed that they were not yet fully convinced of the correctness of this solution, and that the tendency to judge by the "going beyond" principle was still strong.

This experiment showed the existence of a close correspondence between the behavior of the subjects in the two different types of problems.

CONCLUDING REMARKS

The experiments on the learning of conservation of length throw light on two connected questions. The first one concerns the nature of the connection between operatory structures dealing with discontinuous units and those that deal with a continuous quantity, i.e., length. The second concerns the ways in which children construct the concept of length and that of measurement in the case of a unidimensional quantification.

Since children seem to have the same types of difficulties in both the tasks of elementary conservation of number and those of conservation of length (i.e., there is a tendency to judge both number and length according to ordinal criteria such as "going beyond" or "going just as far"), one might be tempted to believe that the only additional difficulty in the length problems is that length involves a continuous quantity. According to this hypothesis, children who already possess an elementary conservation of number should have little trouble in reaching understanding of conservation of length problems if the lengths are broken down into clearly distinct units (the matches) and lined up so that they touch each other (the roads).

The preliminary experiment showed that this was not the case. The subjects were able to give correct answers to conservation questions concerning large collections of elements, even when these elements (paper balls or beads) had been placed in glasses and then poured into other glasses of different shapes and sizes. Despite these correct answers for large collections, however, some of the children could not solve the problems dealing with the length of a road, even when it was made up of a number of separate elements which were contiguous but nevertheless perceptually clearly distinct.

What is more, some of the children who managed to solve the problems in which the roads were made up of small contiguous elements of equal length did not seem to have really overcome the difficulties caused by the coincidence or noncoincidence of the end points. They appeared to have decided to pay no attention to the fact that one of the roads went beyond the other and simply counted the matches, which in the experiment happened to lead to a correct solution. When matches of different lengths were used the real character of these solutions became clear.

The results of the learning experiment therefore run counter to the hypothesis that, in children's judgments of length, the strength of the ordinal criterion is solely due to the fact that length is a continuous quantity. Moreover, the findings also show that in the case of conservation of length there is no direct developmental link between the concept of continuous quantity and that of number.

Length differs from global numerical quantity both by its continuous nature and by the fact that it has to be quantified through the use of units. A child's understanding of this second specific property is constructed by means of a differentiation between the global "size" of the object and that of its measurable length. Length may be conserved only when its quantifiable nature is understood, and this conservation implies an understanding of the use of units of length. The results of the learning experiment provide us with some information about this problem.

Whereas at the lowest level the subjects simply used the division into units introduced by the experimenter, the more advanced subjects understood the dimensional value of the units; they knew that they could not immediately conclude that two roads were the same length if they were made of the same number of matches, but that they had to decide whether these matches were all of the same length. Moreover, the children who succeeded in the post-tests generally understood that the correct number of matches to be used in problem 1.a could be deduced from lay-out 1.c (see Fig. 6.27) by using the transitivity principle. For these subjects, understanding of conservation of length appears to go together with an understanding of measurement. Their explanations, which refer, on the one hand, to

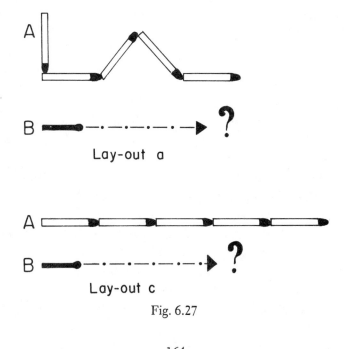

Fig. 6.27

the length of the individual units and the total length of the road ("You need more small matches than long ones to make a road of the same length") and, on the other, refer to transitivity in order to find the correct number of matches necessary in lay-out 1.a, indicate a coordination of partition and displacement from which, in Piaget's opinion, derives the principle of measurement.

The training study also provides information on the processes by which a higher level of reasoning is reached.

At the lowest level, the subjects reacted to questions on number ("Are there the same number of matches, or are there more here or there?") and questions on length ("Are the two roads just as long or is one longer than the other?") as if they concerned two entirely different problems. In the construction problems, these subjects either made up their roads according to the "going just as far" principle (in lay-out 1.a) or by the counting method (in the separate lay-out 1.b). They did not appear to feel any contradiction between their different solutions, despite the multiple comparisons between situations and despite the experimenter's suggestions.

At the second level, the comparisons between the various situations and the experimenter's questions appeared to have some effect, because the subjects became aware of the contradictions in their answers. At this level, however, they were not yet able to solve the internal conflict.

At the third level, the children started to produce what have been called "compromise" solutions in order to solve the conflict. These solutions provide more information on the nature of the conflicts. It seems that different conceptual schemes were activated, depending on the particular question asked or the lay-out presented. In some situations, it is sufficient to use either counting or the coincidence of start and finish to obtain the correct solution (e.g., counting in the situation with matches of uniform length, or ordinal relationships in the simple close lay-out 1.c). In other situations, however, the two schemes have to be coordinated (e.g., in the complex close lay-out 1.a with matches of uniform length), while in yet other cases, the principle of measurement has to be understood (e.g., in the complex close lay-out 1.a). The compromise solutions indicate that the conflict between the two schemes was only partially resolved at this level, since the ordinal principle is sufficient to solve the problem only when both lengths are straight, and the counting, although adequate when the units are identical, is not sufficient in the situations where they are different.

At the highest level, the children began to make the necessary coordinations and to give the correct solutions both during the training sessions and at the post-tests. The most difficult problem of the training procedure (complex close lay-out 1.a) can be resolved only through a grasp of the principle of measurement.

The responses observed in the conservation of length training study clarify the general processes underlying the transition to a higher level of reasoning. Both in especially contrived situations and in normal everyday life conflicts can arise between different conceptual schemes, some of which are more developed than others. A first effort to combine and reconcile the conflicting schemes results in inadequate compromises, which indicate the beginning of a coordination between certain previously unconnected schemes. Subsequently, the various schemes are integrated into a new and more advanced cognitive structure.

The training procedure of the conservation of length study proved to be one of the most instructive, highlighting developmental processes in action. The preliminary studies showed us which schemes were used for each particular problem and, as a result, we devised exercises that we believed would activate these schemes. We also hoped that the method of switching back and forth between the problems and of giving the child the opportunity of comparing his different solutions would elicit conflicts in his mind. Once particular conceptual schemes are known to be applied in certain situations, it is possible to devise problems that activate these schemes and to induce conflicts by comparing solutions based on different principles. Questions and discussions at certain crucial points in the learning process can induce an awareness of contradictions, and provide the impetus for higher-level coordinations leading to new cognitive structures.

7 / Class Inclusion Training and Its Influence on Conservation

Traditionally, the various branches of science have been regarded as separate disciplines (evolving at different rates, as is evidenced by the more rapid advances in mathematics compared with those in physics); today there is a growing tendency to try and find links between them. The ever closer connection between logic and mathematics is an example of this trend.

Piaget is a well-known advocate of such an interdisciplinary approach, and so it is hardly surprising that Genevan psychologists should decide to include in this research into learning a study of the psychological, and particularly developmental, links between concepts with different structural characteristics. The general cognitive structures, such as the system of concrete operations, account for the fundamental competence that allows the establishment of concepts, but these concepts can take various forms, depending upon the particular type of problem to be solved.

We decided to compare conservation concepts with concepts of the logic of classes. A preliminary experimental study (briefly summarized below) indicated the psychological interest of such an approach, and a theoretical analysis of the problems that were finally selected showed their structural adequacy for comparison purposes.

In the first studies, the exercises presented to the children concerned only the specific concepts that we wanted them to acquire, and the post-tests evaluated only the amount of progress they had made in acquiring these concepts. The children's reactions to the training procedures revealed, to a certain extent, how a particular

167

notion develops, starting from one acquired earlier, when both belong to the same area of cognitive structuration. It therefore appeared probable that a similar technique could be used to study the links between concepts which are acquired more or less at the same time but are not of the same type. In particular, learning studies might provide information on the degree of structural similarity between such concepts and on their psychological interrelationships.

Consequently, a second set of experiments was designed in order to investigate whether the exercises used to accelerate the acquisition of a specific concept would also have an effect on a concept that is based on the same system of operations but belongs to a different structural type.

In the first, exploratory, experiment three groups of four subjects (ages 4;11 to 5;11) were selected. These children were all at approximately the same level, and at the pre-test had at a minimum reached the quotity level for elementary number conservation and at a maximum reached an intermediate level for other conservation problems. Pre-test and post-tests included problems on elementary number conservation, conservation of the quantity of matter (modeling clay), seriation, dichotomy, quantification of inclusion, and conservation of length (see Appendix). One group of subjects was given exercises in seriation and classification, a second group was given exercises in conservation, and a third group served as a control and was given only the pre-test and post-tests.

The training procedure for the seriation-classification group consisted of a series of logical exercises dealing with these two specific concepts. The first exercises included problems of simple seriation and single criterion sorting tasks. These were followed by more complicated exercises culminating in problems of seriation with two criteria and multiple classifications presented in the form of matrices. In certain situations there was a small collection of objects whose figurative differences were so slight that a careful comparison was required to detect them, and in others, a larger collection, where it was easier to distinguish between the objects. The children were asked to do three things: (1) to sort and seriate a collection of objects; (2) to complete an unfinished seriation or matrix by selecting the missing objects; and (3) to correct completed matrices or seriations in which mistakes had deliberately been introduced by the experimenter.

In the seriation exercises, for example, the children were asked to order correctly a series of toy boats with hulls and masts of different sizes (in one series the boats with larger hulls had longer masts, and in another those with larger hulls had shorter masts).

In the conservation exercises, the experimenter placed in front of the child two collections of objects in an irregular pattern, using the method of repeated one-to-one correspondence (putting one object of one collection down at the same time as one object of the other collection). In the first situations, the numerical one-to-one correspondence remained visible, while in later situations, the equivalence could only be deduced from the iterative method. Subsequently, liquids were used (once again the iterative method was employed, with small measuring glasses); in the final situations the physical appearance of the quantities of liquid to be judged suggested wrong answers, so that only an understanding of the implications of the iterative method could lead to correct judgments. The children were asked not only to give judgments on quantity, but also to set up collections of objects and to find a method of obtaining either equal (or unequal) quantities of liquid in glasses of different shapes. It was hoped that these exercises would provide the children with challenging opportunities to apply the multiplicative and additive operations necessary for the understanding of the transformation system underlying conservation concepts.

The results may be summarized as follows.

1. The conservation group made considerable progress from the pre-test to the first post-test in the conservation problems (number and quantity of matter), which had been covered by the exercises, but virtually no progress in solving problems with which they had had no help. In post-test 2, however, they gave more advanced answers to the latter, whereas little or no change was noted in the conservation tasks.

2. Similarly, at the first post-test the seriation-classification group had made considerable progress in seriation and dichotomy, but scarcely any progress in conservation. Once again, at the second post-test no change occurred in the solutions given to the seriation and

dichotomy problems, although a great deal of progress was noted in conservation tasks.

3. In the case of the control group, progress was slight but regular throughout the three testing sessions.

Generally speaking, therefore, in the case of the two groups given training, at post-test 1 the children made clear progress only in the problems covered in their training sessions, while at post-test 2 some progress was noted in the other problems.

These results were encouraging. The experimental procedure, however, was complicated and lengthy, as it had been found necessary to increase the number of training sessions to 12, each lasting approximately 20 minutes. Moreover, each group consisted of only four subjects. It was therefore decided to restrict the scope of the comparison by concentrating on fewer concepts, to increase the number of subjects, and to give to one group exercises in conservation of matter, and to another exercises in class inclusion.

For the conservation concepts, a modified and improved version was used of a procedure that had already provided interesting results, particularly in the research described in Chapter 2. Since a suitable training procedure had not yet been devised for the concept of quantification of inclusion, preliminary experiments had to be carried out before one was found which produced results comparable to those of the conservation training. Appropriate tests were also prepared.

The original quantification of inclusion task used in cross-sectional research (Piaget and Inhelder, 1959) had two versions. In one the material consisted of flowers, e.g., ten daisies and two roses (question: "In this bunch, are there more daisies or more flowers?"—cf. Appendix). In the other, the material consisted of wooden beads of two different colors (question: "Are there more wooden beads, or more red beads?"). The problem in both cases is, however, the same: given a class B, made up of the two subclasses A and A' (A has more elements than A'), the child is asked to compare the number of objects in subclass A with the number in class B. Children frequently say that there are more A elements, e.g., "more daisies." A psychological explanation of this error is that the child who starts to evaluate A mentally subtracts it from the entire collection B; the latter then ceases to exist as a class and consequently the child can only compare

A to A', instead of comparing A to B. (Of course, children give this particular incorrect answer only when A has more objects than A'. If $A = A'$, then the children often answer incorrectly that there are as many A's as B's.) Until the age of eight or nine, many children are incapable of conserving a logical whole when they are concentrating on one of its parts. In their logical analysis of the problem Piaget and Inhelder (1959) point out that in the case of a class B, of which A and A are subclasses, two operations can be carried out: the direct operation $A + A' = B$, and its inverse, $B - A' = A$. These operations lead to the deduction that B is bigger than A and that B is also bigger than A'. The existence of an inclusion relation between class A and class B guarantees the accuracy of the following statements: "All A' elements are B's" and "there are fewer A's than B's. Understanding of these statements is an indication of the acquisition of the additive grouping of the concrete operations of classes, a very general logical structure which is also a prerequisite for the grasp of conservation concepts. (In the case of conservation, however, the child must also understand the concept of reciprocal relationships.)

There are, however, some fundamental differences between the concept of conservation of matter and that of class inclusion. The former concept is applied to situations which have a temporal and causal aspect: children who have acquired conservation understand that a change in the shape of a physical object leaves its quantity unchanged, and this understanding implies that they are capable of linking two states by a reversible mental transformation. The concept of class inclusion, on the other hand, is applied to situations in which all the information is present from the outset: a correct understanding of class inclusion implies that each element is regarded as belonging to both a subclass and a more general class; moreover, a comparison of the number of objects in B with the number in A (comparison of their cardinality) implies a change of criteria, since the criteria of the subclass include all those of class B plus a number of others. When the acquisition of class inclusion is compared with that of elementary number conservation (the first notion of invariance acquired well before the concept of quantification of inclusion), it seems that one of the difficulties of inclusion lies in the need to apprehend the logical simultaneity of two different level classes. In the same way, one of the difficulties in the seriation task stems from the necessity of regarding an element *b* as being at the same time bigger than *a* and smaller than *c*.

A comparative study of the development of the concepts of quantification of inclusion and conservation of continuous matter can thus be justified from both the psychological and the logical point of view. The two concepts are acquired at approximately the same ages and they have certain structural features in common (the concrete operatory grouping), but they are not of the same type and children encounter different difficulties in the course of their acquisition.

PRELIMINARY LEARNING EXPERIMENT ON THE QUANTIFICATION OF INCLUSION

There are a number of difficulties in using as the basis for a learning experiment the original task of quantification of class inclusion (see Appendix) with flowers or beads as the experimental material. First, the child is somewhat taken aback by the formulation of inclusion problems, even after a series of introductory questions. Second, the original questions lead to right or wrong answers, or to hesitations between the two ("More daisies . . . no more flowers . . . no more daisies, there are ten of them . . ."); they do not allow for any intermediary or compromise solutions.

To devise a training procedure comparable to those of the other experiments, situations had to be imagined where the children would be active, and where they would perform actions that could be progressively corrected. The following basic situation was chosen for this purpose.

The experimenter gives one doll a collection of fruit* made up of two subclasses, e.g., two apples and four peaches; he then asks the child to give another doll "more apples but just as many *fruits*, the same amount to eat." To solve this problem, the number of *fruits* in the total collection must be the same as the total number of *fruits* of

---

* This experiment cannot be carried out using *fruit* in English because the plural of *fruit* is *fruit*, unless the reference is different kinds of fruit, when *fruits* is correct. The authors suggest that sweets may be used (chocolates, toffees, etc.). However, for the purpose of this description and in order not to complicate the text, the plural of *fruit* will be *fruits*, that is two apples = two *fruits*.

the other doll, but the number of *fruits* in the two subclasses of B must be varied by a reciprocal adjustment. When A's are added B is increased (if apples are added, the number of *fruits* is increased because apples are *fruits*); consequently, if the number of B is to be kept constant, some A's have to be taken away (when peaches are taken away, the number of *fruits* is reduced because peaches are also *fruits*).

This situation allows several variations. Instead of asking the child to give more A's, the experimenter can ask him to give fewer A's. Instead of having two clearly defined subclasses, one can be defined positively and the other negatively; on the one hand, two apples and, for instance, on the other, an orange, a pear, an apricot, and a peach (that is to say, four "nonapples"). Furthermore, the instructions can be formulated naturally, and in several different ways: "You have to give her more apples, because she likes apples best, but they must both get just as much to eat, neither must be jealous of the other, they must both be happy," etc. Moreover, these situations are particularly suitable for training, since they are easier to understand than the problems of the well-known flower test (see Appendix).

The second part of the training procedure aimed at facilitating the comparison between the cardinal of a general class and that of one of its subclasses. As was observed in the original experiment, once children have mentally isolated one of the subclasses of a total collection, they can no longer compare the number of elements in subclass A with the number in the total class, B, but only with the number in its complementary subclass, A'. A first step toward this difficult operation would be to compare the subclass A of one specific collection, B_1, to another collection, B_2, identical to the first. In other words, the child would be helped if we were to present, for example, two collections, each consisting of four apples and two peaches, and then ask if the apples in B_1 were more or less numerous than the *fruits* in B_2. This question may be put very naturally when there are two collections, by simply asking the child whether the person (or doll) who eats all the apples in the first collection, B_1, eats more, or less, or as much as, whoever eats all the *fruits* in the second collection, B_2.

To favor rapid decentration from subclass to total class, a number of other questions were asked concerning the situation where two identical collections were present. Finally, one of the collections was removed, and the original inclusion question was asked in two slightly different formulations.

Materials. The following items were used:

ten apples (L);

eight peaches (P);

two plums, two lemons, two tangerines, and one apricot (O, i.e., other fruit, nonapples and nonpeaches);

two dolls, a girl and a boy;

two baskets.

Parts of the Training Procedure

The training procedure consisted of three parts. In the first part, the child himself made up collections of fruit following the experimenter's instructions; in the second, the experimenter asked questions about two numerically equal collections of fruit; and in the third, the experimenter asked questions about a single collection.

First Part

In all the situations, the experimenter starts off by putting into the basket of one of the dolls a collection of fruit consisting of two subclasses, A and A', one of which has more fruit than the other. He then asks the child to give the other doll a collection of fruit made up of the same number as the model, but whose subclasses have a different distribution. The following situations were presented.

Experimenter's
collection   Instructions

1. LLPPPP   "Give more apples, but the same number of *fruits.*"
2. LLOOOO As above.
3. LLLLPP   "Give fewer apples, but just as many *fruits.*"
4. LLLLOO As above.

The following variations were presented, depending upon the child's specific difficulties.

   a. Less fruit in the model collection, e.g., LLP.

b. Arrangement of the fruit in two straight rows, one directly beneath the other, so as to facilitate a numerical comparison between the two collections.

c. A simple instruction for each collection in the above arrangement: "Show me the apples" and "Show me the *fruits*."

d. Substitution of the instruction "Give *only* apples, but just as many *fruits*" for "Give *more* apples, but just as many *fruits*."

e. Substitution of the instruction "Give as many *fruits*, but *no* apples at all" for "Give *fewer* apples, but just as many *fruits*."

Second Part

Questions were asked about two different collections.

1. The following questions were asked about collections LLPPPP and LLLLPP:

"Does someone have more apples?"

"Does someone have more *fruits*?"

"Does someone have more peaches?"

"Does someone have more *fruits*?"

If the child made a mistake, the experimenter said:

"Show me the apples, show me the *fruits*."

2. The same questions as for item 1 above were asked for collections LLLOOOO and LLLLOOO.

3. For collections LLLLPP and LLLLPP the experimenter asked:

"The boy eats all his apples and the girl eats all her *fruits*, who eats more?"

4. The same questions as for item 3 above were asked for collections LLLOOOO and LLLOOOO.

Third Part

The following questions were asked when only one collection of fruit was presented.

1. LLLLPP.

"If the doll wants to eat the most, what must she say: I'm going to eat all my apples, or I'm going to eat all my *fruits*?"

"In the doll's basket are there more apples or more *fruits*?"

If the child made a mistake, the experimenter said:

"Show me the apples; show me the peaches; show me the *fruits*."

2. LLLLOOO. The same questions as those in situation 1 above were asked.

All the children were asked questions 1 to 4, whereas the variations a to e were presented only if a child had difficulties. After each incorrect answer the experimenter would immediately say something like, "Are you sure?" "Look carefully at what you've done"; and it was only after the child really thought he had given the right answer and had spontaneously repeated the instructions correctly, or, alternatively, after the experimenter had repeated them, that the latter drew the child's attention to his mistake. At this point, the experimenter would say, for instance: "But look, I don't think the two dolls are very happy, they both want to have the same amount to eat, that's not right." From then on, the variations were presented. The questions dealing with two collections were phrased in such a way that the child himself generally realized that his answers were contradictory. If not, the experimenter reminded him: "Do you remember what you said before? You said . . . and now you say . . . Which is right?" or "Can you say it in another way?" When the child gave wrong answers, the questions dealing with a single collection were again followed first by "Are you sure?" etc., and then by "You say more apples, you mean more apples than what?" The experimenter continued by repeating the instructions once again and saying things such as "Show me all the apples, show me all the peaches, show me all the *fruits*"; and finally he presented variations such as "Show me what the boy eats when he eats all his apples, and show me what he eats when he eats all his *fruits*." If the child still made a mistake, the number of *fruits* was again reduced, to a minimum of three; if, on the other hand, the child was successful, the number was increased.

Duration. The training procedure was presented immediately after the pre-test and was divided between two sessions, each lasting approximately half an hour. They were separated by a one-week interval.

Pre-Test and Selection of Subjects

As mentioned in the introduction, it is necessary for a pre-test to be sufficiently discriminating to allow the responses to be categorized on a finer scale than simply that of "success" or "failure." On the other hand, it should not be so elaborate that it becomes an exercise in itself. Consequently, the pre-test started with the three regular questions of the quantification of inclusion task (see Appendix), which enabled us to eliminate children who had already acquired the concept. Twelve children aged from 5;9 to 7;9 years were retained for the learning experiment. It was possible to determine their initial substage from their responses to the four situations where they themselves have to make up collections of fruit. These situations are the first items of the training procedure and thus serve a dual purpose.

Post-Tests

At first, the post-test was an exact replica of the pre-test, where flowers were the material and the original questions were asked. Later, however, additional questions were included, based on a different material, for which the child was required to use a similar, although more extensive, mental structure. These additional questions referred to the following toy animals: three dachshunds, two Alsatians, a cow, a pig, and a goat. The experimenter asked the following questions: "Are there more dogs or more dachshunds?" when all the dogs were presented; and "Are there more animals or more dogs?" when all the animals were shown.

As in the case of the fruit, we first made sure that the children knew the names of all the different animals presented as well as the generic term for the whole collection (*animals*).

This material, which is suitable for questions dealing with a three-level system of inclusion, seemed more appropriate than the flower task for evaluating the post-test responses, since the latter task differs only in content from that of the fruit. We still felt, however, that the children could be successful by using a limited strategy and could give responses based on the following reasoning: "I find the name that goes for the whole collection; that's what you've got to say when you're asked what there's more of."

Consequently, we added the following questions, which had proved to be the most difficult during the preliminary investigations. Using one collection of objects (either fruit, flowers, or animals, made up of two subclasses, each containing the same number of objects), the experimenter asked the child whether there were more A's or more B's. Using a collection of identical objects so that A is the same as B (e.g., eight apples), the experimenter asked: "Now in this basket, are there more apples or more *fruits*?"; in this situation, what had been a correct answer in all the previous situations, i.e., "more *fruits* because they are all *fruits*," is wrong because here there are, of course, "as many apples as *fruits*."

One final problem was added to the post-test: if the children correctly answered the question "Are there more fruits or more apples?" when referring to a collection of six, or eight or sometimes ten, apples and two peaches, the experimenter would ask: "How many more *fruits* are there?" This problem was suggested to us by one of the children, who after having correctly solved all the other problems, said, when presented with a collection of six apples and two peaches: "There are more *fruits* than apples, and I know how many more, two, the two peaches."

The children were given a second post-test, which was identical to the first, after an interval of three to five weeks.

RESULTS

Analysis of the Responses to the First Part of the Training Procedure

In the situation where one of the dolls is given the collection LLPPP, and the experimenter asks the child "to give the other doll more apples but just as many *fruits*," the types of responses can be categorized in the following order.

I.a. The most elementary type of response is given by children who make an identical collection to that of the experimenter, using exactly the same fruit. Here it seems that the children are concentrating all their attention on only one part of the instruction, "just as many fruits," and that for them "the same number," "just as many," or "as much to eat" all signify a qualitative as well as a quantitative equivalence. Some of the children start off by giving this type of solution and are unable to modify their collections, while others modify them to a certain extent when they realize that they have failed to carry out

178

the instructions correctly. More often than not, however, this type of solution is given by children after they have already given a different incorrect answer (category I.b or II). Some children then realize that this solution is still not correct and declare that it is impossible to "give more apples, but just as many *fruits*."

I.b. Here the children seem to take account only of the other part of the instruction, "give more apples." Their collections, in fact, contain only A's, the total number of which is less than that of the experimenter (e.g., LLLL for LLPPPP). Some of them change their collection to make it identical with the experimenter's (category I.a); others cannot make up a collection with the same number of fruit, not even an identical one. Yet another modification of this solution, this time correct, is provided by the children who add A's until their number is equal to that of the fruit in the experimenter's collection. In this way, the difficulty of adjusting the relative number of the two subclasses is avoided; by reducing subclass A' to zero, the child simply makes that of A contain the same number of elements as class B. This is a rather interesting solution, often given as a first answer, and will be discussed below (category IV).

II. Here the children increase the number of elements in A but keep the same number in A', so that their total collection has more fruit than that of the experimenter (e.g., for LLPPP the child gives LLLLPPP). This clearly corresponds to the mistake made by children who when answering the original question whether there are more flowers or more roses say, "More roses." Because they are concentrating on subclass A and comparing it with subclass A' they are unable to take account of the whole B. When asked to give more peaches but the same number of *fruits* (experimenter's collection: LLLLPP), one child gives LLLLPPPPP and explains: "I thought fruits are apples and since there are four I put four and then gave more peaches." This type of solution was frequent, and in fact occurred fifteen times during the pilot study, with nine of the twelve subjects. In two cases the child followed up this response by making an identical collection, which is the only way these children can reestablish the numerical equality. Some children realize their error and eventually manage to give a correct solution. In other cases, no progress is made; the children either decide that no correct solution can be found or, despite the experimenter's objections, they refuse to modify their answers ("Yes, I'm sure, they both have the same amount of fruit").

III. Here the children understand that if they increase subclass A they must necessarily reduce subclass A'. They often say this themselves: "More apples, then I have to give him fewer peaches; then nobody will be jealous." But this compensation remains qualitative, i.e., either the child does not manage to adjust the number of *fruits* in his collection to make it equal to the experimenter's (e.g., for LLPPPP, "Give more apples but the same amount of *fruits*," he gives LLLLPPP); or else, if the experimenter proposes such a collection the child accepts the solution as correct. Most of these children rapidly overcome this difficulty and arrive at a correct solution of the V.a or V.b type (see below).

The following responses constitute correct answers.

IV. The child makes up a collection equal to that of the experimenter, but containing only one type of fruit (e.g., for LLPPPP, he makes LLLLLL). In some rare cases, this is a I.b type of answer, where the child gives the right number of A's purely by chance, but if this is so, he is unable to justify or modify his answer. Generally speaking, however, it seems that this answer indicates a true understanding of the problem since the child apparently realizes that his collection must include the same number of *fruits* as the experimenter's, even though he avoids the difficulty of adjusting the relative number of fruit in A and A' by making a collection where A = B. In other words, this solution avoids the adjustment of the "whole" and "some," and the child now has a collection in which all the *fruits* are apples and all the apples are *fruits*. Usually, children adopting this solution have no great difficulty finding another correct solution (V.a or V.b) if the experimenter uses so many apples for his own collection that the child does not have enough of them to make up his collection without adding other kinds of fruit. While some children immediately complete their collection with other types of fruit, others look, or ask, for more apples, but nevertheless eventually find the correct solution ("I'll give him apricots, that comes to the same thing, I think that he'll have enough *fruits*"). These hesitations show that the child still has some difficulty in realizing that the most restrictive criterion of the subclass is irrelevant for the total class or, in other words, that in relation to class B (*fruits*) all the items are interchangeable.

V.a. Here the child produces a correct solution by reversing the cardinals of A and A', e.g., for LLPPPP, he gives PPLLLL; for LPPPP, he gives PLLLL, etc. Of course, several situations have to be presented before the experimenter can be sure of the child's intention to produce such symmetric solutions. When the experimenter's collection contains a mixed subclass, this type of solution is less satisfyingly symmetrical, and when in the experimenter's collection the two subclasses are numerically equal, it is wrong (applied to LLLPPP this formula results in an identical collection PPPLLL). These situations may be used in order to help the child overcome the desire for symmetry and agree that each subclass can consist of any number of elements, provided that the total, B, is equal to that of the experimenter.

V.b. The child immediately understands the necessary relationship between A and A'.

Comparison of Pre-Test and Post-Tests

Table 7.1 shows in terms of success $(+)$ and failure $(-)$ the children's responses to the seven problems of the first post-test and the types of justifications they gave. The results of the second post-test are generally identical to those of the first; in the rare cases where there was a change, this is indicated beneath the first answer.

Table 7.2 shows the results of the pre-test and post-tests grouped into the following categories.*

IV. Correct solutions to all the problems.

III. No mistakes for the questions about the quantification of inclusion for the fruit, flowers, and animal situations (two-level inclusion) and for the situation where $A = A'$, but incorrect responses to the question "How many more?" and/or to the problem where $A = B$.

II. Several mistakes in different problems, but corrections either

---

* These categories concern the post-test results and not the responses (I to V) to the training procedure.

TABLE 7.1

Symbols used

+	correct answer	−	wrong answer
0	no answer	−, +	child spontaneously corrects his answer

− × +   experimenter's intervention: he either says, "Show me the B's," or reduces the number of elements

Subjects		Fruits	Flowers	Dogs	Animals	How Many?	A = A'	A = B
Cor 7;5	(1)	+	+	+	+	+	+	+
	(2)	+	+	+	+	+	+	+
Mar 7;0	(1)	+	+	+	+	+	+	0
	(2)	+	+	+	+	+	+	0
Ser 7;9	(1)	+	+	−, +	+	+	+	+
	(2)	+	+	+	+	+	+	−, +
Wal 6;6	(1)	+	+	+	+	−	+	− × +
	(2)	+	+	+	+	−	+	−
Min 6;0	(1)	+	+	+	+	− × +	+	−
Gab 6;1	(1)	− × +	− × +	−, +	+	+	− × +	0
Jos 7;8	(1)	− × +	+	−, +	+	−, +	− × +	−
Dom 6;0	(1)	− × +	+	+	−, +	−	− × +	−
	(2)	+	+	+	−, +	−	−	−
Mic 6;1	(1)	+	−	+ ?	+ ?	−	−	0
	(2)	+	−	−, +	−	−	−	0
Ber 6;6	(1)	+, −	−	0	−	−	−	0
	(2)	−, +	−	0	−	−	−	0
Phi 6;2	(1)	− × +	−	0	0	0	0	0
	(2)	−	−	0	0	0	−	0
Ant 7;0	(1)	−	−	0	0	0	0	0
	(2)	−	−	0	0	0	−	0

Justifications

More fruits, because we put a lot of *fruits*; there are still peaches (A'), that makes more *fruits*.   Cor

There are other fruits than apples (A): that makes more *fruits*.   Mar

Because it's all together, there are more *fruits*.   Ser

Because those (the apples, A) are *fruits* as well, they are all *fruits*.   Wal

Because there are only *fruits*, that makes more.   Min

Because all of those are *fruits* (counting).   Gab

Because they are all *fruits* (counting).   Dom

There are more fruits, because there are fewer peaches than apples.   Mic

More fruits, because there aren't very many *fruits*.   Ber

No justification.   Phi

No justification.   Ant

TABLE 7.2

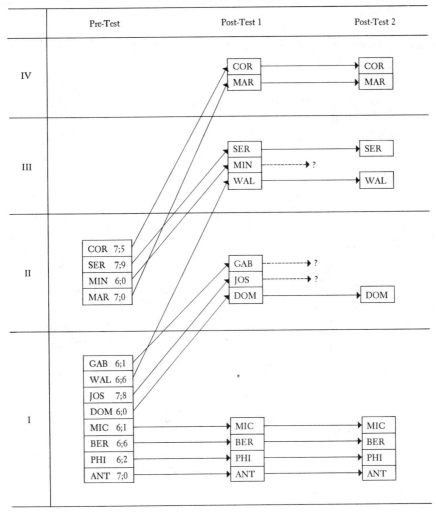

spontaneously or after an intervention of the experimenter; complete failure in the problem where $A = B$.

I. Mistakes in all the problems; some changes, but no real correction after the experimenter's interventions. The most difficult situations (two-level inclusion and the situation where $A = B$) were not always presented to the children of the lowest level since they did not seem to understand the questions, and the experimenter did not understand their answers. For example, to the question "Are there more flowers or more daisies?" (eight daisies, two roses), Mic replied: "More flowers because there are more daisies than roses." When the experimenter took away the roses and repeated the question, he said: "There are more flowers because there aren't very many of them."

Justifications. Certain types of justifications correspond to the above categories of answers.

When the class-inclusion problem is given in its original form, many children who give the correct solution justify their answer by saying (in the situation with eight daisies and two roses): "There are more flowers, because the daisies are also flowers." Although during the training sessions this argument also appeared frequently, it was conspicuously absent in the post-test (only one subject referred to it). In the situation where $A = B$ the incompleteness of this argument is revealed: it remains, of course, correct to say that apples are also fruit, but from this statement it is impossible to deduce whether there are more apples than fruit or only apples. Psychologically, it seems that in a situation such as LLLLPP, the argument "apples are also fruit" is used by children who somehow reason with themselves in the following way: they are first tempted to answer, "There are more apples," because, having once focused their attention on the subclass apples, they have mentally put it on one side, so that they then compare it with the remaining subclass, peaches; then they seem to remember that apples are also fruit and that therefore the number of apples should not simply be compared with the number of peaches. Logically, this argument seems to be no more than a repetition of the proposition "apples are fruit," without combining it with the proposition "some *fruits* are apples." Consequently, this type of reasoning does lead to the conservation of the total class, B, but through reiteration of the operation $A + A' = B$, which served to constitute B in the first place. A momentary focus of attention on A' (for example, some peaches)—which without a following decentration would lead to the wrong answer: "More apples, because there are only some fruits"—gives way to a new way of considering A: apples are also fruit, A' (peaches) $+ A$ (apples) $= B$ (fruit); therefore there are more fruits.

By contrast, the children who say there are "More *fruits* than apples, because there are also other *fruits*; there aren't only apples" do not feel the need to argue against the idea that once the apples have been mentally collected together, it is only the peaches which are *fruits*, since they maintain simultaneously both propositions ("Apples are *fruits*" and "Some *fruits* are apples," or, in other words, "There are some *fruits* which are not apples"). These children seem to have understood both the direct operation $A + A' = B$ and the inverse operations $B - A = A'$ and $B - A' = A$; they are capable of reasoning that "if you took away the apples, the other *fruits* would remain" and that "if you took away the other *fruits*, the apples would remain." Only the subject who in the post-test progressed to category IV put forward these completely logical arguments.

It goes without saying that without training the "incomplete" argument remains a valid justification of a correct answer. It is only after several training sessions that this type of reasoning, if it persists, has to be interpreted as an argument *ad hominem*. A justification that is frequently given for correct answers (during both the training and the post-tests) is: "They are all flowers (or *fruits*)." The children often accompanied this argument with a gesture of both hands embracing the whole collection, and when the experimenter said, "But look, aren't there a lot of apples?" they replied, "But only those are apples" with another gesture, holding their hands much closer together. This spatial argument is given by category III children, who incorrectly answer the question "How many more?" and/or that involving the situation where $A = B$, and by those in category II, who all give incorrect responses in the latter situation and also make mistakes in other post-test questions. At this level, counting is also used as an argument: "There are eight *fruits* and only six apples, I counted them all." These children continue to feel the need to count before answering and have not really mastered the problems, even though as long as they count correctly they give the right answer; the counting method even provided some correct answers to the difficult question "How many more?"

Finally, the children in category I give no justifications at all, and it is difficult to understand what they really mean by answers such as: "There are more dogs because there are fewer dachshunds." Despite this lack of coherent reasoning throughout the training sessions, they nevertheless gave a few correct answers in the post-tests for situations where the same material was used as during training. Once again, this shows how easy it is to overestimate the child's operatory level on the basis of his answers to problems which have already been presented during training procedures.

Analysis of the Responses to the Entire Training Procedure

Order of Difficulty

The order of presentation of the various items of the training sessions corresponded to an increasing order of difficulty. The easiest items were those where the child himself had to make up collections with the same number of elements as those of the experimenter. Next came the questions involving two identical collections which, as mentioned above, led to a comparison of the total class of one collection with a subclass of the other and to a comparison of the total class of one collection with a subclass of the same collection. The questions relating to a single collection proved more difficult and it was at this point that the problem of logical simultaneity arose, i.e., when the child had to realize that the same apples which counted as "apples" also had to count as "fruit." Several children from category I were unable to overcome this difficulty.

Different Types of Solutions

The children used several methods to solve the problems, some of which resulted in excellent progress, while others seemed to lead to an impasse. For the training situations to be effective, the experimenter had to find ways to help the children realize their mistakes. To make those subjects who had given type II solutions notice the numerical inequality of the two collections, they were asked to count both collections. (Some children did this without the experimenter suggesting it.) This method, however, produced surprising results: when the child, with the experimenter's help, had successfully adjusted the number of elements in the two subclasses and thus obtained two collections of B's, each with the same number of elements, one collection was hidden and the experimenter asked the child, who had just said, "The two dolls are happy; they've both got the same," to indicate how many *fruits* there were in the hidden collection. Surprisingly, several children answered: "There are eight, I gave him two extra apples." By contrast, this regression toward a non-conservation of the whole was not noted in children who established a sort of one-to-one visual correspondence between the fruit of the two collections by arranging the fruit in the baskets or on the table, so that the equality could be evaluated fairly easily. Consequently, this method, rather than the counting method, was adopted by the experimenter.

Another method which some subjects used of their own accord and which we had not previously thought of was a substitution method. Sometimes the child first copied the experimenter's collection exactly (category I.a) and then exchanged one or several *fruits* of this collection for one or several other *fruits*, so that his final collection would conform to the instructions; e.g., when shown the collection LLPPP, one child who was asked to "give more apples, but just as many *fruits*" started by making the collection LLPPPP, thought again and then took one peach away and put an apple in its place (correct solution). Other children did the same thing, but mentally: one child immediately gave the correct solution, LLLLPP (symmetrical type V) and said: "I took away two peaches (in fact he had done this mentally although he spoke as if he had actually carried the action out) and I put two apples instead." This process of substitution, applied to the total subclass and not to its component elements, seems to underlie the following explanation given by a child to justify his symmetrical solution: "I'll do the opposite, then it will be O.K." (experimenter's collection LPPPP; instruction: "Give more apples, but the same number of fruits"; solution PLLLL). This method does not result in a correct solution for the more difficult situation where the experimenter's collection has as many elements in A as in A'. This situation was therefore chosen as one of the items of the post-tests.

The most advanced solution to the problem of the first part of the training procedure consists in the immediate use of other types of fruit (apricots, etc.) when the elements in either A or A' of the experimenter's collection are not available or when it contains a mixture. Indeed, the only child who adopted this solution of his own accord during the first training session was also the only one to give immediately correct answers to the questions in the final part of the training procedure. We therefore tried to elicit this type of solution during the experiment, either by presenting a model collection which forced the child to choose different fruit (for example, by selecting for the model collection the only two apricots available) or by asking the child if he could choose his fruit in another way, or by replacing several of the child's *fruits* and asking him if the new collection still complied with the instructions.

Verbal Responses

The questions asked about the two collections allowed the children to switch their attention rapidly from a subclass to the general class, and these changes in the focus of attention sometimes led to a first adjustment of the reasoning processes. The fact that the child had himself made up two collections following the instruction that "nobody must be jealous, the two dolls should have just as much fruit to eat," and the fact that he had to focus alternately on the classes and subclasses combined to make him realize the contradiction in his responses. For example, in the case of the collections LLPPPP for the boy doll and LLLLPP for the girl doll, the following dialogue was noted: "Does someone have more apples?"—"*Yes, the girl.*"—"Does someone have more *fruits?*"—"*Yes, the boy.*"—"Does someone have more peaches?"—"*Yes, the boy.*"—"Does someone have more *fruits?*" —"*Yes, the girl . . . oh! no . . . they've both got more fruits . . . no, they've both got the same.*"

The questions asked about a single collection are by far the most difficult. Here again, some of the children wanted to count, although this somewhat lengthy process did not seem to lead to a true understanding of the problem. These children first of all counted the subclass (e.g., "There are four apples") and then the total class ("There are six *fruits*."). But some of them then went on to say that there were still "more apples than *fruits*"; others answered correctly only as long as there were only a few items (six or seven). When at the end of the training procedure the experimenter continued to add apples to his collection and asked after each addition, "Are there more fruits or more apples?" there came a point when the child said: "Now there must be more apples, you've put in such a lot." This type of response is quite different from that of the children who succeeded in all the situations of the post-test and who, when the collection reached, e.g., ten apples and one peach, started to laugh and said: "But of course, there are more *fruits* than apples, there's always that one peach."

Several excerpts from protocols are shown below to give an idea of the proceedings of the training sessions.

Dom (6;0)

First session. Experimenter's collection: LLPPPP; instruction: "Give the boy more apples, but just as many *fruits*."

The child starts off by giving the doll five apples, then stops, takes a peach and puts it in the basket, takes two other peaches, hesitates and puts only one of them in the basket (type III solution, qualitative compensation).

"How is it now, are both dolls happy?"—*"They've got the same thing."* —"Can you remember what I said? What did the boy want to have?"— *"You said they've both got to have the same thing."*—"Look carefully, do they both really have just as much fruit to eat?" (Dom seems to compare the fruit without counting.)—"No."—"What can we do so that they do have just as much fruit to eat?"—*"You should take away an apple from the girl"* (correct, symmetrical solution).—"Now, who's got what?"— *"One's got four peaches and the other four apples and one's got two peaches and the other two apples."*—"Right. Now we'll change and I'll give this to the boy (LLOOOO) and the girl wants more apples, but just as many *fruits*" (Dom starts off by giving the girl four apples and then selects exactly the same fruit as in the experimenter's collection, LLLL-OOOO; type II solution, since A' is regarded as *fruits*). "What have you done now?"—*"I've given more apples."* (Note that while she made a qualitative compensation in the first situation and repeated the part of the instruction which concerned "the same number of *fruits*," this time she

repeats the part "more apples.")—"Can you remember what I've just said?"
—"*More apples and . . . just as many fruits.*"—"Show me the girl's
apples." (She does this correctly.) "Show me the girl's *fruits.*" (The child
points only to the OOOO.) The experimenter then says, "Are those really
all her *fruits?*"—"*No . . . there are the apples as well.*"—"Yes, that's
right. That makes how many?"—"*Six for the girl*" (wrong).—"You're
sure? Look carefully."—"*No Eight.*"—"Yes. Then who has more *fruits?*"—
"*The girl.*"—"Then what must you do so that they both have just as
many *fruits,* but the girl has more apples?"—(No reply.)—"Do you think
we could take some of the girl's *fruits* away?"—(She hesitates and cannot
decide what to do.)—"Watch, I'm going to do it, you tell me if it's right."
(Experimenter takes away two O's, correct answer.) "Is that right? Have
they both got as many *fruits* now?"—". . . *Yes*" (not very convinced).—
"We'll do it once more. Watch. I'm giving this to the boy (LLOOOO)
and you give the girl more apples, but just as many *fruits;* you see, she
loves apples, but nobody must be jealous." (The child gives LLLLOO,
the two O's being identical to the two O's of the experimenter's collection.) "Good. Now, what's the girl got?"—"*Four apples, one peach, and
one tangerine.*"—"Yes. What did I tell you to give her?"—"*More apples,
but just as many fruits.*"—"Good. How many's she got now?"—"*Six*" (correct).—(Experimenter hides the boy's basket.) "And the boy, how many's
he got?"—". . . (Hesitates.) . . . *Five?*"—"You're sure? Think . . . (experimenter uncovers the boy's basket) . . . look!"—"*Six too.*"—"And
now, I'm giving the boy this (PPPPLL) and the girl wants fewer peaches;
she doesn't like them all that much, but she still wants just as much fruit."
—(Immediately.) "*Then I'll give her more apples.*"—"That's up to you,
as long as she has fewer peaches, but as many *fruits.*"—(The child gives
PPLLLL, symmetrical solution.)—"Is that right?"—"*Yes.*"—"How do
you know?"—"*There, there're four peaches (points) and there, there are
four apples (points) and the boy's got two apples, and the girl's got two
peaches.*"

Other types of solutions (I, II, IV) are illustrated by the following
excerpt.

Wal (6;6)

First session. Experimenter's collection, given to the girl: PPPPLL; instruction: "Give the boy more apples, but just as many *fruits.*"

(Wal gives the boy an identical collection, PPPPLL, type I solution.)
—"What have you given him?"—"*Two apples and four peaches.*"—"Can
you remember what I've just said?"—"*He's to have the same as the girl.*"—
"The same of what?"—"*The same of the other fruits.*"—"He wanted just

as many *fruits* to eat as the girl, but he wanted to have more apples than she."—"*We've got to add some then.*"—"Go on."—(WAL adds four apples, LLLLLLPP, type II solution.)—"Do you think that's right?"— ". . . *No.*"—(Experimenter repeats instruction.)—(WAL takes away all the fruit he had given the boy, ponders, and then seems to make a discovery.) "*We've got to give just apples, then?*" (Gives LLLLLL.)—"There you are. Now, how is it?"—"*Now, he's got more apples than the girl.*"— "Right. Do they have the same number of *fruits*?"—"*No, one's got more.*" (WAL's insight turns out to be short-lived.)—"Who?"—"*The boy, I gave him two extra apples.*"—"You're sure? How many *fruits* has he got then?"— (Without looking.) "*He's got eight.*"—"Have a good look and count them carefully."—(Surprised.) "*He's got six, too.*"—"Yes, you see, you did do the right thing."

This subject went on to give several type IV solutions without repeating the mistake of thinking that one of the dolls has more fruit. However, he again had difficulties when the experimenter presented new collections and there were no longer enough apples for him to give the other doll only one sort of fruit; he had great difficulty in completing the collection with other fruits.

PHI (6;2)

PHI is successful in the simple situations where he has to make up a collection and always invokes compensation: "*It's right, the girl has less peaches but more apples and the boy's got more peaches but fewer apples.*" He is then questioned on two collections (LLPPPP and PPLLLL) which he has himself made up: "Does someone have more *fruits*?"—"*No, they've got the same.*"—"Do you know how many?"—"*Yes, they've got six.*"— "Show me the boy's *fruits*."—(Points correctly.)—"Show me the girl's *fruits.*"—(Points correctly.)—Experimenter takes away one of the collections and asks with reference to LLPPPP: "And in this basket, are there more fruits or more peaches?"—"*There are more peaches.*"—"Show me the *fruits*; how many?"—(Indicates correctly.) "*There are six.*"—"And how many peaches?"—"*Four.*"—"Now then, when will he eat the most? When he eats all his fruit or when he eats all his peaches?"—"*When he eats all his peaches.*"—"One time, he ate all his fruit. Show me what he ate."—(Indicates correctly all the fruit.)—"Another time, he ate all his peaches. Show me what he ate."—(Indicates correctly the peaches.)— "Now then, when does he eat the most?"—"*When he eats his peaches.*"

PHI, like all children who made little or no progress at the first post-test, never managed to overcome this difficulty. Some children seem

191

to have flashes of insight when the question is phrased in the following way: "What should he say to eat the most: I'm going to eat my *fruits* or I'm going to eat my apples?" When the action is thus explicitly placed in the future, they no longer seem to regard the result of a mental action (putting the apples together, separating them from the total collection, eating them, etc.) as being equivalent to that of a real action ("She's eaten her apples, only the peaches are left"), although this understanding is only temporary.

CONCLUSIONS OF THE PRELIMINARY EXPERIMENT

Class inclusion problems are purely logical, as opposed to conservation problems, where objects (or reality in general) are of greater importance. It may well be that acquisition processes of logical concepts can never be rendered as evident as those of more physical notions. Certainly, this experiment gives less direct information on the transitions toward higher-level constructs than, for example, the experiment on the conservation of length. However, the specific difficulties children encounter in mastering the inclusion problems emerge rather clearly.

The most difficult situation was that where the child had to compare the subclasses and the total class within only one collection. A psychologically important feature of this problem is its "simultaneity," e.g., the fact that each element A belongs *at the same time* to the subclass A and to the more general class B. In seriation problems, it was noted (Piaget and Inhelder, 1968) that children can easily understand that of two identical elements P and P', one is smaller than an element Q and the other is larger than an element O, but they have more difficulty in grasping that one element P is "at the same time" bigger than O and smaller than Q. Similarly, in the case of class inclusion, some of the subjects were quite capable of making comparisons between two collections and compared correctly the number of elements of a subclass A, belonging to a collection of elements, B, with the number of elements in the total class B of another collection identical to the first; but they were incapable of making this same comparison within a single collection. The children at a less advanced level proved incapable of making the comparisons between two collections even though in the first part of the training procedure, they managed to make up equivalent collections with different numbers of elements in the subclasses—in this situation the child could adjust the number of elements of the subclasses progressively, which facilitates the solution. However, once the child had made up a correct collection (e.g., experimenter's collection: LLPPPP; child's collection: LLLLPP), he was perplexed when the experimenter asked him questions calling for a comparison, first, between a subclass of one of the collections and the total class of the other and then between the two total classes. In this situation, two complementary types of responses were noted which recalled certain answers to questions of elementary conservation of number. Some children maintained that the two dolls had the same number of *fruits* and correctly counted six *fruits* in the experimenter's collection, but when the experimenter hid the child's collection and asked how many *fruits* it contained, the child answered: "Eight, I put two extra apples." Here, the two collections had "just as many," but one had six and the other eight *fruits*!

Other children correctly counted six *fruits* in the two collections—"There, there are six and there, there are also six," but they maintained that in one there were more than in the other. This type of response is exactly parallel to that associated with the concept of quotity, in the sense that, while admitting that both collections contain six elements, the child still judges that there are more elements in one than in the other. In the elementary number conservation problem, it is the change in the position of the elements resulting in a "longer" line that causes the difficulty. Although no such spatial modification intervenes in class inclusion, it, like number conservation, demands a grasp of *reversibility*. In the first part of the procedure, the child can proceed step by step, first thinking of the criteria of the subclass and then adjusting the number of elements in his collection to that in the experimenter's. He does not need to coordinate the criteria of the classes and the number of elements contained in them. When, however, the two collections are present simultaneously and the experimenter asks first, "Does someone have more apples?" and then immediately afterward, "Does someone have more *fruits*?" children of this less advanced level cannot adjust to the change from subclass to total class. Such a change requires a reasoning based on compensation, i.e., an understanding of the fact that the class which is defined by a greater number of criteria contains a smaller number of elements. The action of building up the collection may reflect only the operation $A + A' = B$, whereas in order to solve the quantification problem this operation must be combined with the inverse operation $B - A' = A$ or $B - A = A'$.

Children of a still lower level find it difficult to build up numerically equal collections step by step. They make mistakes which seem to reflect the same difficulties as those encountered by the more advanced group. Even the elementary decentration necessary for a switch in focus from a subclass to a total class is beyond their capacity.

The development of the concept of class inclusion is similar to that of other concepts, in that the initial changes in focus have to be followed by coordinations between the different foci of attention. However, the appearance of conflicts as a result of decentrations is much less evident in the class inclusion experiment than in the conservation studies. The only types of responses that are comparable to the compromise solutions of the problems of length, for example, are those where the children maintain that there are the same number of fruits in both collections but that one has eight and the other six, or, on the contrary, that the two collections contain six fruits but that there are more in one than in the other. The compromise solutions found in other studies derive from a conflict between two schemes based on different aspects of the same problem. No such conflict seems to exist in the class inclusion problem: the schemes of partition and union may be in contradiction and lead to errors, but they do not combine and lead to compromise solutions. Furthermore, in the conservation studies the compromise solutions are intermediate responses and generally announce a more advanced solution. By contrast, the contradictory responses in the problems of class inclusion, even when the children are clearly not satisfied with their answers, do not lead to the correct solution, at least not with the training procedure used. The contradictory answers were given almost exclusively by children who made little or no progress. This difference in modes of transition may be due to the very nature of logical-mathematical knowledge.

A number of investigators have carried out experiments on the acquisition of quantification of inclusion relationships (Morf, 1959; Lasry, 1965; Kohnstamm, 1967; Wohlwill, 1968; and others). Morf's research at the Center of Genetic Epistemology in Geneva showed that empirical observations, such as the comparison between the length of a line of plastic cars and that of a line of blue plastic cars, are inadequate to foster the growth of the requisite logical structures for the solution of problems of quantification of inclusion. As Morf says, ". . . It is difficult to imagine by what mechanism empirical observation could have an effect on the reasoning of subjects who do not yet possess the intellectual instruments necessary to apprehend it." Indeed, it is most unlikely that counting or measuring will lead to the acquisition of a logical structure when this logical structure is itself necessary to know what to count or measure. In our study, counting, even when carried out correctly, was the least successful method.

Other researchers, using a variety of methods, found that their subjects progressed to a greater or lesser extent. Without going into a detailed discussion of such results (see Pascual-Leone and Bovet, 1966 and 1967; Lasry, 1965; Kohnstamm, 1967), we would like to refer briefly to some of the arguments used by these researchers to explain why children have difficulties with the original questions of quantification of inclusion.

In general, two types of factors are considered to explain failures in the class inclusion task (e.g., Kohnstamm, 1967): (1) socioeconomic factors, mainly associated with language; and (2) memory factors, especially verbal memory.

Language

No systematic study was carried out in Geneva on the language used by children in their arguments during the experiments. However, a few comments should be made on the findings of several researchers (e.g., Kohnstamm), to the effect that children from a privileged socioeconomic background generally do slightly better at the inclusion task than others. The suggestion is that this better performance is mainly due to differences in language (both in comprehension and production). Although our studies did not usually control for environmental differences, the parents' occupation was noted for every subject. On the basis of this information a broad distinction can be made between children whose parents are engaged in intellectual professions, and those whose parents are engaged in manual employment. The former group of children did somewhat better at the inclusion task than the latter. Our feeling was that these middle-class children had a different "attitude" toward the questions, and we suggest that the role of the environment might be reflected in the amount of attention the children pay to the questions and the degree to which they are expecting to be "tricked" by the experimenter. One noteworthy difference was that those from a more privileged environment repeated the questions correctly and thought for a while before giving their answers, whereas those from a less privileged background had a marked tendency to modify the questions and make them more "natural." This difference in "attitude" toward the questions is confirmed by two findings.

First, Kohnstamm notes that there appears to be a difference between children who immediately give the correct solution and those who do so only after they have been given a series of equivalent problems. There are many more subjects in a higher socioeconomic situation who give correct answers immediately, and more subjects with an average or low sociocultural level who give correct answers only at a second series of problems (findings based on a collective test given to a group of eight-year-old subjects).

Second, a considerable difference was noted in Geneva (nonsystematic observation) between the performance of subjects with a lower sociocultural level in the first part of the training procedure (where the instructions are "natural") and in the later parts, where verbal questioning is used. Collections are made up correctly, but incorrect responses are given to the verbal problems, even when these involve two collections. The subjects with a higher socioeconomic but equivalent developmental level, on the other hand, usually give correct responses to both types of situations and have difficulties only in the problems where a single collection is involved. This discrepancy in performance between the children in different socioeconomic situations is noted neither in the final training sessions nor at the posttests.

The correspondence between performance in the inclusion problems and the level of the child's language does not seem to be due to knowledge of the specific or generic terms, nor to familiarity with objects used in the task (except in the case of certain classifications which have to be "learned"—for instance, many adults would include whales in the class of fish). It seems rather that this correspondence, to the extent that those who understand inclusion also have a certain facility with and grasp of language, is related to the use and comprehension of syntactic rules which govern word order and the use of *"les"* ("the") and *"des"* ("some"). In French, both word order and the contrasting use of *"les"* and *"des"* indicate a relation of class to subclass. In other languages, word order alone conveys this difference: in English, e.g., one says "dogs are animals" and not "animals are dogs." Incorrect word order and wrong use of *"les"* and *"des"* was observed in the justifications given by children who had not acquired the concept of class inclusion (e.g., "Fruit, that's the peaches"). Such mistakes were not made by those who carried out all the instructions correctly. By contrast, no difference in performance in the inclusion tasks was noted between children who could and those who could not initially answer the question: "And all these things together, what would you call them?"

Kohnstamm suggests that in problems where the subject has to deal with subclasses and total classes which are verbally distinguishable only by predicates (e.g., black pencils and pencils, in contrast with dogs and animals) the problem is facilitated because of early experience with qualifying adjectives. However, in the study of the use of adjectives such as "long" and "short," "wide" and "thin," many subjects could correctly describe objects with such qualities, but remained incapable of describing contrasts such as "long but thin" or "short but thick" if they had not yet acquired the notion of conservation. Lack of lexical knowledge can no more explain such behavior than lack of perceptual discrimination. The real difficulty lies in the mental operations necessary to establish compensatory or inclusive relationships.

Retention of Instructions

Insufficient memory span has often been mentioned as another factor that might be responsible for the young children's lack of success in the class inclusion problems. Kohnstamm (*passim* and p. 25) refers to this factor, in relation to both the experimenter's questions and the characteristics of the objects presented. He says that in answer to the quesion "Are there more black bricks or more little bricks?" (four black bricks, only one of which is large), even adults tend to say, "More little ones," but the question continues to reverberate in their ears and they subsequently correct themselves, realizing that "black" refers to all the bricks. It is quite true that children, when asked to repeat the experimenter's question, very often distort it, and some will continue to do so even if the question is repeated slowly. Some recent studies (Piaget, Inhelder, and Sinclair, 1968) show that memory distortion is neither random nor due to a gradual fading of the recollection, but closely associated with the subject's level of reasoning: distortions are systematic and reflect the level of the child's logical schemes and the conflicts beween these schemes. Memory of sentences is also affected by such distortions and transformations. In an experiment on sentences in the passive voice (Ferreiro and Sinclair, 1971), it was found that at a certain stage of development children who are able to act out the sentence "Mary is knocked over by Peter" correctly cannot repeat the sentence in this form when asked to do so. They respond by saying: "Peter knocks over Mary," and are convinced that this is what they heard. Less advanced children who are not yet able to carry out the instruction correctly say, "Mary knocks over Peter," and distort the sentence to correspond to their incorrect action. However, some of the even younger children, even though they are utterly incapable of acting out the sentence correctly, do repeat the sentence accurately in a parrot-like fashion. In the case of the concept of class inclusion, the distortion or lack of retention of the question despite several repetitions appears more likely to be a symptom of a prelogical approach to the problem than a possible reason for the lack of understanding. In fact, children who are still far from acquiring the concept can learn to repeat the instructions and questions correctly, but this does not necessarily lead to a change in their action responses.

LEARNING OF QUANTIFICATION OF INCLUSION AND ITS POSSIBLE EFFECTS ON CONSERVATION CONCEPTS

TRAINING PROCEDURE, TESTS, AND SELECTION OF SUBJECTS

The training procedure described above was used, and the same types of responses were observed. The children selected were all given six training sessions, each lasting approximately half an hour. The pre-test and post-tests included conservation tasks, but training was given only in inclusion.

Pre-test. Three tests were used: (1) elementary number conservation (see Appendix); (2) conservation of quantities (modeling clay and liquids, pouring of liquids into glasses of different shapes; see Appendix); (3) quantification of inclusion (flower task; see Appendix). All the subjects selected failed in the quantification of inclusion test and had at least reached the level of quotity in that of conservation of number.

Post-tests. The same tasks as for the pre-test were used, with the addition of: (1) conservation of weight task (see Appendix); (2) all the post-tests for the quantification of inclusion described on pp. 177–178; (3) an intersection problem which also included an inclusion problem (see Appendix).

Subjects. Nineteen children aged between 5;6 and 6;8 years from the second year of nursery school and first year of primary school were selected.

RESULTS OF THE INCLUSION TASK

Comparison of Pre-Test and Post-Tests

As in the learning experiment on inclusion, the subjects were divided into two groups (advanced and less advanced) according to their initial level in the inclusion task and regardless of their level in other tasks. Already at the pre-test three of these children gave intermediate-type answers to the inclusion problems. During the first training session, nine others gave correct answers of types IV or V to the problems, but none answered correctly without first making a mistake (i.e., types I.a, II, or III). Subsequently, these children gave only

199

TABLE 7.3

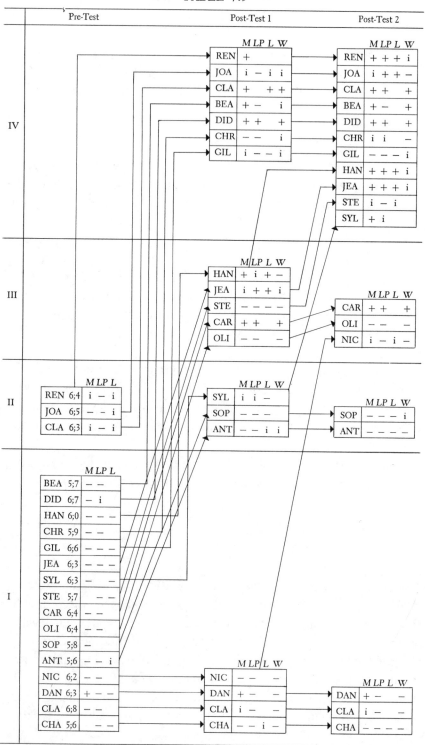

	Pre-Test	Post-Test 1	Post-Test 2

Group IV

Post-Test 1 (M LP L W):

	M	LP	L	W
REN	+			
JOA	i	–	i	i
CLA	+		+	+
BEA	+	–		i
DID	+	+		+
CHR	–	–		i
GIL	i	–	–	i

Post-Test 2 (M LP L W):

	M	LP	L	W
REN	+	+	+	i
JOA	i	+	+	–
CLA	+	+		+
BEA	+	–		+
DID	+	+		+
CHR	i	i		–
GIL	–	–	–	i
HAN	+	+	+	i
JEA	+	+	+	i
STE	i	–	i	
SYL	+	i		

Group III

Post-Test 1 (M LP L W):

	M	LP	L	W
HAN	+	i	+	–
JEA	i	+	+	i
STE	–	–	–	–
CAR	+	+		+
OLI	–	–		–

Post-Test 2 (M LP L W):

	M	LP	L	W
CAR	+	+		+
OLI	–	–		–
NIC	i	–	i	–

Group II

Pre-Test (M LP L):

		M	LP	L
REN	6;4	i	–	i
JOA	6;5	–	–	i
CLA	6;3	i	–	i

Post-Test 1 (M LP L W):

	M	LP	L	W
SYL	i	i	–	
SOP	–	–	–	
ANT	–	–	i	i

Post-Test 2 (M LP L W):

	M	LP	L	W
SOP	–	–	–	i
ANT	–	–	–	–

Group I

Pre-Test (M LP L):

		M	LP	L
BEA	5;7	–	–	
DID	6;7	–	i	
HAN	6;0	–	–	–
CHR	5;9	–	–	
GIL	6;6	–	–	–
JEA	6;3	–	–	–
SYL	6;3	–		–
STE	5;7		–	–
CAR	6;4	–	–	
OLI	6;4	–	–	
SOP	5;8	–		
ANT	5;6	–	–	i
NIC	6;2	–	–	
DAN	6;3	+	–	–
CLA	6;8	–	–	
CHA	5;6	–	–	

Post-Test 1 (M LP L W):

	M	LP	L	W
NIC	–	–		–
DAN	+	–		–
CLA	i	–		–
CHA	–	–	i	–

Post-Test 2 (M LP L W):

	M	LP	L	W
DAN	+	–		–
CLA	i	–		–
CHA	–	–	–	–

Note: M = modeling clay task; LP = liquid pouring task; L = liquid conservation task; W = weight conservation task; – = NC response; i = Int response; + = C response.

correct answers, except in the situations where the collections contained many elements, when they gave type III responses at first but rapidly corrected them. By contrast, the seven initially less advanced children made many mistakes and required several training sessions before they could produce type IV or V solutions for the items where they themselves had to make up collections.

The pre-test results for the conservation tasks, although not used to categorize the subjects, are also shown in Table 7.3 (*M*: conservation of matter: modeling clay; *LP*: liquid pouring; *L*: liquid conservation) (see Appendix).

The post-test results are categorized according to the level obtained for the inclusion task (categories I to IV). Table 7.3 gives details of the responses. At the first post-test, the most advanced group (seven children, category IV) correctly solve all the problems, including those which were not touched upon during the training sessions; these seven subjects are considered to have acquired the concept. A second group of five children (category III) make considerable progress but remain unsuccessful in the situations $A = A'$, $A = B$, or when asked, "How many more?" A third group consists of three children who not only fail to solve some of the more difficult problems, but also make mistakes in other situations (category II). One of these children (Syl) seems to progress during the first post-test and manages to give correct responses to the last two problems, which are the most difficult ones. Her responses at the second post-test show that this progress is maintained and the concept completely acquired. A final group of four children (category I) make many errors and give very few correct answers; in fact, they change their minds so often that they give the impression of answering haphazardly.

Justifications. See Table 7.4. The best group (with the exception of Dip) again gives what is considered the most advanced argument: "More of B, because there isn't only some of A, there's also some of A'."

The second type of argument, "More B's because they'll all B's," is sometimes completed by "and the A's are only those," accompanied by a gesture. This argument has a "spatial" character, but it collapses when the number of objects in the collection is increased (see excerpt from Syl's protocol, below).

TABLE 7.4

Symbols used
+   Correct answer   —   wrong answer
0   no answer   —, +   child spontaneously corrects his answer
— × +   experimenter's intervention: he either says, "Show me the B's," or reduces the number of elements

Subjects			Fruits	Flowers	Dogs	Animals	How Many?	A = A'	A = B
REN	6;4	(1)	+	+	+	+	+	+	+
		(2)	+	+	+	+	+	+	+
JOA	6;5	(1)	+	+	+	+	+	+	+
		(2)	+	+	+	+	+	+	+
CLA	6;3	(1)	+	+	+	+	+	+	+
		(2)	+	+	+	+	+	+	+
BEA	5;7	(1)	+	+	+	+	+	+	+
		(2)	+	+	+	+	+	+	+
DID	6;7	(1)	+	+	+	+	+	+	+
		(2)	+	+	+	+	+	+	+
CHR	5;9	(1)	+	+	+	+	+	+	+
		(2)	+	+	+	+	+	+	+
GIL	6;6	(1)	+	+	+	+	+	0	—
		(2)	+	+	+	+	+	+	—, +
HAN	6;0	(1)	+	+	+	+	0	+	+
		(2)	+	+	+	+	+	+	+
JEA	6;3	(1)	+	+	+	+	—	+	—
		(2)	+	+	+	+	+	+	—, +
STE	5;7	(1)	+	+	0	0	—	+	+
		(2)	+	+	+	+	0	+	+
SYL	6;3	(1)	—, +	+	—, +	+	—	+	+
		(2)	+	+	+	+	+	+	+
CAR	6;4	(1)	+	+	+	+	+	+	—
		(2)	+	+	+	+	+	—	—, +
OLI	6;4	(1)	+	+	+	+	+	—	—, +
		(2)	+	+	+	+	+	—	—, +
NIC	6;2	(1)	—, +	—	0	0	—	—	—
		(2)	+	+	+	+	—	+	—
ANT	5;6	(1)	+	+	+	+	—	+	—
		(2)	+	+	+	+	—	+	—
SOP	5;8	(1)	+	+	+	—	—	+	—
		(2)	+, —	—, +	—, +	0	— × +	—	—
DAN	6;3	(1)	—	— × +	—	—	—	—	—
		(2)	—	—, +	—	—	—	—	—
MAR	6;8	(1)	— × +	+, —	— × +, —	—	—	—	—
		(2)	— × +	—, +, —	—, +, —	— × +	—	—	—
CHA	5;6	(1)	— × +	—, +	— × +	—	—	0	—
		(2)	— × +	— × +	—, +	—	—	—	—

Justifications

The roses (A') are flowers as well; with the roses, that makes more flowers.	REN
Counting.	JOA
More flowers, because there aren't just daisies (A) but other flowers as well.	CLA
More flowers, because there are other ones than daisies (A).	BEA
The flowers are all those; the daisies (A) are only those (gestures).	DID
There are the others as well, there are more flowers.	CHR
The flowers, there are more than the daisies (A). More flowers because there are daisies and roses.	GIL
Those are the roses (A'); those are the flowers (gestures).	HAN
All those are flowers.	JEA
That makes more than that (gestures). More flowers because the roses aren't there (A').	STE
The flowers, they are all the ones with a name. More flowers, because that's the whole bunch.	SYL
With the two poppies (A'), that makes more flowers.	CAR
All those are flowers, there, there are only daisies (A).	OLI
No reason.	NIC
They are all flowers.	ANT
Because the roses and the daisies are flowers.	SOP
There are a lot of them (incorrect counting).	DAN
There are a lot of them, they smell nicer.	MAR
No reason.	CHA

The third type of argument, "More B's, because the A's are also B's," is no longer given at the post-test, but is given fairly frequently during the training sessions, which would seem to confirm our view that it indicates that the child is arguing with himself. The excerpt from SYL's protocol, below, is an illustration of this type of argument.

Finally, some children count the apples, peaches, etc., and base their answers on the result: "More apples, there are four." This response occurs frequently during the training sessions, but as the children make progress, it is gradually replaced, either by "all those are fruit" or by the more advanced type of argument, and it is given at the post-test only by children who make no progress.

Five subjects progressed between the two post-tests. SYL reached complete acquisition (at the first post-test she had already been successful in the final problems). In the second post-test she gave correct answers to all the questions and improved her justifications. Four others progressed, but not to category IV. For the other children the results of the second post-test were the same as those of the first.

Analysis of the Responses during the Training Sessions

In situations where the child has to make up a collection containing the same number of *fruits* as that of the experimenter, the same five types of responses are found as those that have already been discussed at length in the Results section of the preliminary learning experiment. Some children continued to give the less advanced types of responses (particularly type II in the case of NIC and OLI, and type I in that of MAR) throughout the entire duration of the training sessions, even though they gave correct answers when the experimenter reduced the number of elements in the mode' collection to three. Here again, as soon as the children were able to make up collections correctly, they could also give correct answers to questions about two collections; it was only when one of the collections was removed that they had difficulty. Some of the initially less advanced children did not give any correct answers to the questions involving a single collection throughout the training sessions. As in the previous experiment, the phrasing of the question had an effect on the response. The question "What would he say to eat the most: I'm going to eat all my apples or I'm going to eat all my *fruits*?" was easier than "When does he eat the most, when he eats all his *fruits* or when he eats all his apples?" This latter question sometimes led to a pseudo-success, since in this formulation class B is mentioned before subclass A, e.g., OLI: "He eats more when he eats all his *fruits* because afterward when he wants to eat all his apples, they're already eaten."

Some of the responses given during training clarify the ways children try to solve the problems and highlight their difficulties. The following strategies will be discussed: *counting*, which can lead to responses which are reminiscent of the quotity answers to number conservation problems; *evaluation of the space occupied* by the objects; and, finally, *substitution* of objects belonging to one subclass by those of another.

The *counting method* was used by almost all the subjects at one time or another, although the more advanced children used it to check that their collection had the correct number of elements and not to justify their answers to questions concerning either one or two collections. The subjects who made the least progress used counting to justify their (sometimes correct) answers. For some children, however (e.g., CLA), counting resulted in quotity-type answers.

CLA (6;3)

CLA still hesitates a little in the elementary number conservation task (see Appendix), but this may be because of inattention, since these hesitations occur when the experimenter adds or takes away some of the counters. In the situation where six red counters are compared with six blue ones that have been spread out, she answers correctly: *"It's the same."* —"How do you know?"—*"There are still six and six."* When the experimenter suggests that there must be more blue counters because the blue line goes beyond the red one, she answers: *"No, you've spread them out, it's the same."* It seems therefore that in this task she has gone beyond the level of quotity, but as soon as she is faced with problems concerning the number of elements in the class and subclasses, she gives the following response.

The experimenter gives the boy doll LLLLOO and asks for the girl doll to have less apples but as many *fruits* as the boy. The correct answer is given: LLOOOO. "How did you work that out?"—*"There are six."*—"Six what?"—*"Six apples . . . no, six fruits."*—"Alright. How many has the boy got?"—*"Six."*—"And the girl?"—*"Six."*—"Six what?"—*"Six fruits."*— "Yes, that's right. Tell me, does one of them have more *fruits*?"—*"Yes, the boy."*—"You're quite sure? Because, remember that when you gave the fruit you made sure that they both had just as much, so that they'd both be happy! Show me the boy's *fruits*."—(She answers correctly.)—"Good. And now the girl's fruits."—(She answers correctly.)—"Then, one of them has more *fruits*?"—*"Yes, the girl."*—"How many has she got?"—*"Six."*— "And the boy?"—*"Six."*—"One of them has more?"—*"Yes, the girl."*—"Six is more than six?"—*"Yes."*—"You're sure? One of them has more things to eat?"—*"The boy got more, he's got a lot of apples."*—"Yes, but we're not talking about apples, we're talking about things to eat. How many things

has the boy got to eat?"—"*Two.*" (She points to the two "nonapples.")—
"But he can also eat those (apples)! In all, I mean."—"*Six, then.*"—"And
the girl?"—"*Six.*"—"Does one of them have more to eat?"—"*No.*"—"What
do they both have?"—"*They've got the same.*"

Here the session ends, but subsequently the same difficulties arise. It is
not surprising that CLA does not show much progress at the post-test, even
though she gives a few correct answers when counting on her fingers.

Spatial evaluation, like counting, leads to correct answers only in
simple situations; when the experimenter progressively increases the
number of elements this strategy collapses. SYL's protocol is an example.

SYL (6;3)

SYL has no difficulty with the questions "What must we say to eat the
most?" and "When does he eat the most?" She also gives a correct answer
to the question "In the basket (seven apples and three other *fruits*), are
there more *fruits* or more apples?"; but when the number of apples is increased to ten while two other fruits are removed, there comes a moment
when she begins to have doubts. With the collection LLLLLLLLLLO, she
responds as follows: "And now?"—"*More fruits . . . no, more apples.*"—
"How come?"—"*More apples, apples are also . . . they're also fruits . . .
It's the same.*"—"And that?" (Experimenter points to the apricot.)—"*It's
a fruit, it's the same thing.*"—(Experimenter adds two other *fruits*, nonapples.) "And now?"—"*There are more fruits . . . or else the same
thing?*"—"What do you think?"—"*. . . More fruit*" (apparently convinced)—"How do you know?"—"*The fruits are all that and the apples
only that*" (she points to the fruit and the apples). At this point, the session is brought to a close; the difficulty seems to have been overcome, but
in subsequent sessions SYL's doubts return and again she gives incorrect
answers.

This protocol illustrates the different status of the various justifications. It is quite clear that the argument "the A's (larger subclass) are
also B's" is one which the child uses against himself and, what is
more, that it generally leads him to maintain temporarily that since
the apples are also fruits, there must be the same number of A's as
B's (frequent answer at the intermediate stage). The argument "more
fruit because all those are fruit and only these are apples" (accompanied by the appropriate gestures) is clearly based on spatial criteria.

The *substitution* strategy yields better results than counting. Almost all the children at the more advanced level use it at one time or another. Dɪᴅ uses it to justify his correct answers during the training sessions.

Dɪᴅ (6;7)

The experimenter's collection is LLOOO; the instruction is, "Give the boy more apples but just as much fruit as the girl. Dɪᴅ gives the girl doll LLLOO and says: *"The boy's got more apples than the girl."*—"And the two? . . ."—". . . *have got the same."*—"Can you tell me how you worked that out?"—*"It's easy, because those (the three apples) take the place of those (the three nonapples in the other collection) and those (the two nonapples) take the place of those (the two apples in the other collection).* Initially, this process seems to result in a symmetrical solution with two subclasses containing the same number of elements, but Dɪᴅ is also able to find a different solution: when one doll has the only three tangerines available and two apples, and Dɪᴅ has to give the other one more apples but the same amount of fruit, he says first, *"That won't work, I haven't got any tangerines,"* but then realizes his error and says, *"It doesn't matter what fruits I give."* (LLLLO.)

RESULTS OF THE CONSERVATION TASKS

Table 7.3 gives a summary of the results for the conservation tasks, for which no training had been given. The subjects are grouped into four categories.

Marked progress. This category includes all subjects who were completely successful at one of the conservation tasks and gave explicit arguments, although at the pre-test they had not even been at an intermediate level for any of the tasks. As may be seen from Table 7.3, in most cases the children succeeded in two or even three of the tasks. This category also includes children who were at an intermediate level for any of the tasks of the pre-test and succeeded in two of them during the post-tests.

Average progress. This category includes children who were at an intermediate level for at least two of the tasks of the post-tests, although they were not completely successful at any of them. It also includes children who were at an intermediate level (Int) for any task at the pre-test and who were completely successful at one of them during the post-tests.

Slight progress. This category includes children who started by giving completely incorrect responses in all the tasks of the pre-test and managed to reach an intermediate level for one of them during the post-tests.

No progress. This category includes all subjects who were at the same level at both the pre-test and the post-tests.

As may be seen from Table 7.3, the children made considerable progress in the conservation problems. No conservation training was given to these subjects, although the first part of the inclusion training must have helped them comprehend that the whole remains conserved despite the changes in the number of the component parts. However, in this situation, the whole was made up of units and, moreover, all the children had already been successful in the conservation of number problem (counters) during the pre-test.

Pre-Test

Of the children who progressed in the conservation problems, only DID (6;7) was at the intermediate stage in the pre-test for the liquids pouring task (having poured the liquid to the same level in glasses of different diameters, he then put a little more liquid into the thin glass and said: "I'm putting a bit more there, it's higher").

Two children who were given the usual liquids conservation task (see Appendix) wavered between "more to drink because it's higher" and "the same to drink because where it's low it's fat." Two other children were at the intermediate level for both the modeling clay and liquids conservation tasks. All the others were clearly at the preoperatory level as regards matter, weight, and liquids, and maintained that "there is more in the sausage because it's bigger, less in the biscuit because it is very thin," etc., with no correct answers, or even any hesitations that might indicate the presence of a conflict.

One of the two children who made no progress, either in inclusion or in conservation, DAN (6;3), had given correct answers in the pre-test for the modeling clay and liquids tasks with rather vague justifications, such as, "It's the same, because before it was the same."

Post-Test 1

In the first post-test, twelve out of the nineteen subjects showed progress for both the inclusion and conservation problems; two children progressed only in conservation and three only in inclusion. Apart from these three, all those who made progress in inclusion also improved in conservation and, as a general rule, the clearer their progress in inclusion, the more marked their progress in conservation.

It must be emphasized that the children who made progress in conservation justified their correct answers with the same types of arguments that were observed in the original experiments. Those who acquired conservation of matter and of weight explained this way: DID (6;7), modeling clay task: "If you make the ball again, it's the same, you haven't taken anything away"; CLA (6;3), weight task: "It's thin, but it's still the same, when it was in a ball, it weighed the same." Some children gave less explicit arguments for the conservation of matter ("Before it was in a ball and was the same, now it's no longer in a ball, but you've still got the same to eat"), but remained at an intermediate stage for weight, affirming conservation for the sausage and the small pieces, but judging the biscuit shape to weigh less ("It's very thin").

Different levels of conservation responses were given by the children who did not quite achieve the concept of inclusion (category III). One of the five subjects (CAR, 6;4) was completely successful in the conservation of matter and of weight tasks, as well as in the liquid pouring one: "I'm putting a bit more, because this glass is wide open and the other's closed." He justified his conservation of weight answer by saying: "You haven't taken away any modeling clay and you haven't put in any more; before it was the same, now it's also the same." Another child (HAN, 6;0) had already acquired conservation of liquids and matter and made even more progress at the second posttest. By contrast, a third child (OLI, 6;4) made no progress in conservation and remained at a clear preoperatory stage. The question then arises as to what is responsible for the difference between two subjects whose results at the inclusion tasks of the post-tests were identical, except that CAR gives the most advanced justification for B being more numerous than A: "More fruit, because there aren't only apples, there are also peaches"; whereas OLI only gives what has been called the "spatial" argument: "All those are flowers, only these are roses." There is a greater difference between their reactions during the training sessions: CAR learned thoroughly; even in the first training session he gave type IV.b solutions (symmetrical) and by the third session had started giving type IV.c answers. From this point onward, he had no more difficulty in making up the collections or in answering the questions involving one or two collections. OLI, by contrast, continued to make mistakes when making up a collection, even at the fifth session (type II responses) and his excellent results for the inclusion task at the post-test were somewhat surprising. In a way, he was similar to CHR in that, for both children, the progress in the area of inclusion seemed too recent for them to be able to apply it to other types of problems.

Two children of the group that made partial progress in inclusion showed a slight improvement in the conservation problems, e.g., SYL (6;3) on one occasion used the argument of reversibility (biscuit situation: "If you make the ball again, it's the same").

The group that made little or no progress in inclusion also made little or no progress in conservation.

The results of the intersection problem are more or less in line with those of the inclusion problem. Some children solved the intersection problem before that of inclusion, but with two subjects it was the other way round. It seems that this problem was easier for subjects who use counting than for those who use the "spatial" type of argument. In fact, in the situation where the experimenter added or took away an element from the common class, the latter subjects considered that the equality no longer existed because "you've taken away a round one" (forgetting that since the round counter was blue, a blue one was also removed), whereas the subjects who counted took longer to solve the problem, but eventually gave a correct answer, which they reached by carefully counting the relevant elements.

Post-Test 2

The second post-test shows that the children's progress for the concept of inclusion is stable; five children made even further progress, either acquiring the concept completely, or giving responses indicating that they were on the verge of acquiring it. Thus, five subjects made delayed progress (three of them progressed only slightly).

As regards conservation, nine children made delayed progress at the second post-test, whereas three regressed, giving both correct and incorrect answers.

The five children who made further progress in inclusion problems between the first and second post-tests did the same for conservation, sometimes in a very clear fashion, as illustrated by SYL, who at the second post-test (modeling clay, sausage) maintained, in answer to a counter-suggestion: "Yes, you'd think it's more because it's longer, but it's still the same, it's much longer but it's much thinner."

In certain cases, the acquisition of the quantification of inclusion seemed to have a delayed effect on conservation, but the opposite did not occur. CLA and DAN, who at the pre-test were more advanced in conservation than in inclusion, made no progress whatsoever in the inclusion problems or in those of intersection.

CONCLUDING REMARKS

1. Progress in problems of logic and conservation through training is clearly conditioned by the child's initial level of reasoning. It is also related to the types of responses that the child gives during the training sessions.

2. Many children progress simultaneously in both types of problems (quantification of inclusion and conservation), despite the fact that the situations presented during the training sessions dealt only with problems of inclusion. Some children make only delayed progress in the conservation problems (apparent in the second post-test). It seems therefore that what is learned in the area of inclusion can generally be applied to conservation. This finding supports the postulate of the existence of very general organizational structures.

3. Some children show progress in the inclusion problems as early as the first session; others advance more slowly but still have acquired the concept at the post-test. It seems that the less rapid the progress in inclusion during the training sessions, the less it affects the conservation tasks. However, during the interval between the two post-tests, progress in inclusion appears sometimes to become consolidated and to have a delayed effect on the conservation tasks of the second post-test.

4. The children who acquire conservation resist counter-suggestions and justify their answers with the same arguments as those found in the original conservation experiments. These arguments are based on identity, reversibility, and, less frequently, compensation. Familiarization with the tasks, owing to the fact that they are presented three times (one pre-test and two post-tests), can be discounted as a cause of progress, since a control group of eight subjects, who were not given any training but only the three tests at the same intervals, made no progress in either area.

5. There remains the question of how experience in problems of inclusion affects understanding of conservation concepts. It seems clear from the above findings that this influence is indirect. The only exercises which could have a direct effect on conservation are those where the children have to make up collections equivalent to those of the experimenter. This situation could be regarded as an exercise in additivity. In the first place, however, only discontinuous elements are involved and not continuous quantities and, in the second place, the children who give some correct answers in the conservation problems do not usually do so in the situation where the modeling clay is broken into a number of smaller pieces, but rather in those where the experimenter makes a sausage or a biscuit. This finding is similar to that of previous cross-sectional research. Had the opposite occurred, it might have been supposed that the exercises of the training sessions were indeed directly responsible for the progress, since when the modeling clay is broken into pieces the part-whole relationship is of major importance, and it is precisely this relationship that was emphasized during the inclusion training procedure, even though the material consisted of discontinuous elements.

In general, then, it seems that operatory exercises in logic can lead to the active elaboration of certain structures which allow the child to progress in conservation problems. In the training sessions no attempt was made to force the children to adopt a particular strategy. They chose their own method for solving the problems, adopting several different strategies (counting, substitution, compensation), and neither the experimenter nor the characteristics of the experimental situations favored any particular one. Although the experimenter attempted to make those children who gave incorrect solutions to the problem realize their mistakes, he accepted all the correct answers and justifications without suggesting any particular arguments. The important advances made by the subjects in two different areas of concept formation can hardly be explained otherwise than in the sense of a new structuration of their reasoning.

8 / Conservation Learning and Its Influence on Class Inclusion

The training procedure for conservation concepts was elaborated from the situations already used in Chapter 2. At first it was planned to include conservation of weight in the training procedure, but the final version of the experiment aimed only at the conservation of quantities, thus permitting a more leisurely pace in the training procedure.

The two main features of the final procedure are the following. First, the training situations at first use clearly discontinuous material, in fact countable collections of objects, then collections that are only theoretically countable (small beads in glasses), and finally continuous quantities (water). Second, the exercises bear on the operations that are implied in the conservation notions to be acquired. For the countables, an iterative method is used in one-to-one correspondence exercises; for the continuous quantities a pouring procedure is used in which the subjects have to pour equal or different amounts of liquid into glasses of various dimensions—this calls for an understanding of additive part-whole relationships and of the covariation between the height of the liquid and the diameter of the glass.

TRAINING PROCEDURE, TESTS, AND SELECTION OF SUBJECTS

DISCONTINUOUS QUANTITIES

During the first part of the training procedure the iterative method is used: the experimenter and the subject each put down objects one by one on the table, and arrive at equal or unequal collections according to whether or not the one-to-one correspondence has been maintained.

The experimenter may, for example, put down toy houses to make a village, while the child simultaneously puts down toy trees to make a forest. The experimenter takes care that the spacing of his objects is different from that of the child; e.g., he may make "a big village" while the child is making "a small wood." Sometimes the experimenter adds an extra object to his collection, interrupting the repeated one-to-one correspondences.

There are many possible variations of this type of situation. For example, two matchstick roads can be built; these may be of the same or different lengths and can be laid out in a straight or zigzag line, etc.

When the collections made up by this iterative procedure each contain about nine units, the experimenter interrupts the game and questions the child as to the numerical equality of the two collections: "Are there as many houses in my village as there are trees in your forest, or are there more houses or more trees? How do you know?" If the child cannot answer or judges according to the total area covered by the collections (e.g., "More trees—there's a big forest and just a little village"), the experimenter asks him, "Don't you remember how we are playing?" and, if necessary, helps him to recapitulate: "You put a tree at the same time that I put a house . . . and then . . . ?" The experimenter then asks about the correspondence between the units in the two collections: "If you wanted to put a tree next to each house, would there be enough houses, or too many, or would some trees be on their own?" In addition, the experimenter can make the child count the units in one collection and then ask him to say, without counting, how many there are in the other. After these questions, the answers the subject has given (regardless of whether or not they are correct) are checked: either a tree is actually put next to each house or the child is asked to count the units in both collections and to explain the result (which astonishes or satisfies him depending on whether or not his original answer was right).

After several such exercises (village, forest, herd of cattle, etc.) more difficult situations are presented in which, once the two collections have been constituted, it is impossible to perceive the one-to-one correspondence between the individual units; the initial correspondence has to be recalled through a recapitulation of how the collections were formed. For these exercises, little balls or beads are used, which the experimenter and the child simultaneously drop into glasses, using the same iterative procedure as above. Sometimes the beads are identical in size and the two glasses are not, and sometimes the glasses are identical and the beads differ in size.

The change from the easily countable objects to the small beads was not always easy. Even in the simple situations the children often tried either to count the units or to pair them off visually (they were not allowed to move them), although they had just correctly described how the collections had been constituted. The differences in area covered or in the size of the glasses appeared to them to be in contradiction with the judgments about equality (or inequality) derived from the iterative method of constitution.

CONTINUOUS QUANTITIES

Additive Relationships

The experimenter places two glasses, A' and B', which the subject has agreed are identical, behind a screen. He then puts two more identical glasses, A and B, in front of the screen and, guided by the child, pours an equal quantity of liquid into each. Next, he transfers all or part of the liquid from A into A', which remains hidden behind the screen, and asks the child to pour the same quantity of liquid from B to B' (A' and B' cannot be compared visually). When only part of the liquid in A has been poured, it is necessary to understand part-whole relationships (and addition and subtraction) to make the quantities in A' and B' equal.

Multiplicative Relationships

The glasses A' and B' are replaced by a narrower one, N, and a wider one, W, and the same problem is presented. Here, multiplicative relationships between the diameter of the glasses and the height of the level of the liquid have to be taken into account.

216

Additive and Multiplicative Relationships

The experimenter first pours the same quantity of liquid into each of two identical glasses, A and B, and then transfers that in A, or half that in A, into W and asks the child to pour into N a quantity of B equal to that which has just been poured into W. In that situation, both additive relationships (e.g., leaving identical amounts in A and B) and multiplicative relationships (understanding that the dimension of the diameter of W is compensated for by a higher level in N) have to be mastered.

Any one of these three types of exercise could be repeated if a subject had difficulty in solving the problems. Generally, each subject was given six sessions (in some cases five; however, each child was allowed the same total time for the whole procedure). The principle of not going on to the next exercise before a subject had correctly solved the previous problem was followed.

SELECTION

Subjects and selection criteria. Subjects were selected if they gave quotity responses to the counters test, but failed the conservation of quantity test (see Appendix). Twenty children, from the second year of kindergarten and the first year of primary school, aged 5;1 to 6;10 years, were selected.

Pre-tests. The same pre-tests were used as those described in Chapter 7: (1) elementary conservation of number (counters test, see Appendix); (2) conservation of continuous quantities (modeling clay and liquid pouring problems, see Appendix); (3) quantification of inclusion (flowers test, see Appendix).

Post-tests. The post-tests comprised: (1) the three pre-tests; (2) a weight conservation test; and (3) an intersection problem (see Appendix).

RESULTS

On the basis of their responses to the conservation of quantities tasks (modeling clay and liquids) and to the liquid pouring problems, the subjects were grouped into four categories. (The results of the

217

TABLE 8.1

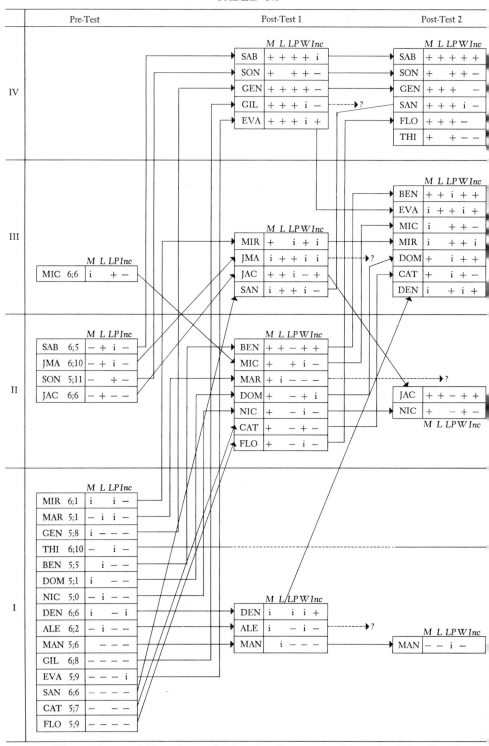

Note: M = modeling clay task; L = liquid conservation task; LP = liquid pouring task; *Inc* = inclusion task; W = weight conservation task; — = NC response; i = Int response; + = C response.

weight conservation test are also given in Table 8.1, but these did not serve as a basis for the categorization.)

I. The children in the first category solved none of the problems although some of them gave one or two correct answers to individual questions (− and Int).

II. Those in the second category found at least one of the problems too difficult, but correctly solved one or both of the others (1 + and 1 − or 2 −).

III. Those in the third category solved at least one problem, if not two, correctly and gave some correct answers in the case of the other one or two (at least 1 + and no −).

IV. Finally, those in the fourth category solved all three problems correctly (3 +).

Having established these categories, we then evaluated the children's responses to the problem of the quantification of inclusion and intersection as follows:

+ for those children who gave only correct answers;

Int for those who gave some wrong and some correct answers;

− for those who gave no correct answers.

DIVISION OF SUBJECTS ACCORDING TO THE CATEGORIES

Conservation Tests

Table 8.2 shows the 20 subjects classified in categories at the pre-test and post-tests. Categories III and IV indicate *clear progress*; category II indicates *partial progress*; category I marks no or virtually *no progress*. At post-test 1, we thus obtained 9/20 *clear progress* re-

TABLE 8.2

Categories	Pre-Test	Post-Test 1[a]	Post-Test 2[b]
IV	—	5	6 (1)
III	—	4	7 (1)
II	4	7	2 (1)
I	16	3	1 (1)

a. One subject was absent at the time of the first post-test.

b. Four children were not given a second post-test; their first post-test results are shown in parentheses.

219

sults, i.e., only three subjects made no progress and 7/20 made partial progress. At post-test 2, we noted further advances: 15/20 subjects reached the two top categories (III and IV), with only three remaining in category II and two in I.

Generally speaking, half the subjects made clear progress at the first post-tests, while half of the others reached the same high level at the second. The fact that some subjects progressed immediately, while others seemed to require more time for what they had learned to become internalized, is discussed at greater length when we consider the children's reactions to the training procedure.

Quantification of Inclusion Problems

Table 8.3 shows the 20 subjects classified as +, Int, or − at the pre-test and post-tests. Eight subjects progressed between the pre-test

TABLE 8.3

	Pre-Test	Post-Test 1[a]	Post-Test 2[b]
+	0	4	6
Int	2	4	1 (+1)
−	18	11	7 (+5)

a. One subject was absent at the time of the first post-test.
b. The first post-test results of those who were not given the second post-test are given in parentheses.

and the first post-test, four reaching + (of whom two, DEN and EVA, had been classified Int at the pre-test) and four (DOM, MIR, JMA, SAB, all initially classified as −) reaching Int. Further progress was observed at the second post-test, where six children were classified + and two Int. However, two children remained at their first post-test level and so, generally speaking, progress in the quantification of inclusion became apparent at the first and not the second post-test.

The conservation exercises do therefore seem to help the children with this inclusion problem. A simple comparison of the number of children finally reaching the top category for each of the two types of problem shows that out of a possible twenty, six children reached category + for inclusion and seven category IV for conservation. However, if the two top categories in each case are taken together, then we see that eight children reached categories + and Int for inclusion, while fifteen were finally classified III or IV for conservation. So, not surprisingly, although good progress was made in inclusion, it occurred twice as frequently for the conservation problems, which had been dealt with in the training procedure. Moreover, it seems that the children either made good progress or no progress at all with the inclusion problem (six reached category + and two Int, while twelve were finally classified −). This "all or nothing" aspect of the class inclusion results will be discussed when these findings are compared with those of the parallel learning experiment in which the procedure concerned quantification of inclusion problems.

Consider now Table 8.1.

1. Four of the nine children who made clear progress in conservation at the first post-test (Jma, Jac, Son, Sab) had been in category II at the pre-test, while the other five (Gil, Gen, San, Eva, and Mir) had started off in I. Some children who in the pre-test had only just satisfied the selection criteria gave responses in the first training session that were fairly close to an operatory solution of the problems. This shows just how difficult it is to give an accurate assessment of a child's level through a pre-test, even if this includes several problems of the same type. Examples will be given in the discussion of the children's responses during the procedure.

2. As has been pointed out, when children advance in conservation from post-test 1 to post-test 2, their progress is generally from category II to III; only two children (San and Flo) reached category IV by delayed progress, which seems to suggest that if the exercises are to result in a child's complete acquisition of conservation, then he achieves this at the first post-test. In the interval between the two post-tests only partial progress took place and this does not result in a complete mastery of the different problems.

3. In the first inclusion post-test (i.e., the problems not dealt with in the procedure), eight subjects gave all or at least some correct answers (four Int: Sab, Jma, Dom, Mir; four +: Eva, Jac, Ben, and Den), while in the second, two gave at least some and six all correct answers; these are the same eight subjects of whom two progressed from Int to + at the second post-test. No new top category answers

appeared at the second post-test. The eight children who made progress in the quantification of inclusion problems were nearly all in categories III and IV at the second conservation post-test. It is, however, surprising that most of them did not completely acquire the concept, although they were not far from doing so. Apparently, the fact that a child has become able, as a result of learning, to give stable operatory responses to conservation problems does not necessarily mean that he will make progress in class inclusion. All we can say is that considerable progress in conservation leads some children to a corresponding advance in their operatory understanding of class inclusion problems.

ANALYSIS OF THE RESPONSES TO THE TRAINING SESSIONS

During the training sessions two types of responses appear, both resulting in correct "answers" to the problems, but based on reasoning of two clearly different levels.

In the exercises on discontinuous quantities, the children with the less advanced reasoning learn to use their understanding of the repeated one-to-one correspondences to determine whether the completed collections are equal in quantity; however, in the process, they simply come to disregard the differences in the final appearance of the collections. The fact that these children are able to give this type of solution means that they are able to understand that, if the units in two collections have been laid out in strict one-to-one correspondence, then there must be an equal number in each, and they check this either by counting all the units or by visually pairing them off. This solution constitutes an advance compared with their initial responses in which, although they could already verbally recapitulate the one-to-one method of constitution, they judged the quantity by looking at the area covered by each of the final collections. The connection between the method of constitution and its final outcome is not yet understood.

The following excerpt illustrates this type of response.

MAN (5;6)

For each toy animal the experimenter puts on the table the child puts down a toy tree; at one point the experimenter ostentatiously puts down an extra animal and then the one-to-one procedure is continued. After putting down nine animals, the experimenter stops and asks the child whether there are as many trees as animals.

MAN says that there are more trees (in fact there is one fewer tree, but they are spread over a wider surface area than the animals) even though he correctly describes the one-to-one procedure and the fact that he stopped while the experimenter placed an extra animal: clearly, he sees no connection between the one-to-one procedure and the resulting collections of animals and trees. He is puzzled when the two collections are laid out in visual correspondence and can give no explanation. After several exercises he begins to understand the implications of the iterative method: e.g., after an incorrect answer based on the final appearance of the collections, when he sees the paired units (which contradict his answer) he comments: "There's one house missing because I didn't put another when we stopped."

Subsequently, when he has given another wrong answer, he spontaneously corrects it and, referring to the one-to-one procedure, firmly rejects all the experimenter's counter-arguments. The problems concerning lengths raise new difficulties, as was the case with most of the subjects. When the children were asked to lay down matchsticks, whether of uniform or different lengths, in the form of a "road" as long as one laid down by the experimenter, most of them found it difficult to break away from the idea that the road that went further to the right was the longer, i.e., they judged length by the order of the end points. However, after many repetitions of such problems where MAN was able to check his answers either by counting or by pairing off the units, he finally manages to give a correct answer based on the one-to-one procedure. Despite the correct answers, however, it is clear that MAN does not understand the difference in appearance between the two "roads"—he learns only to disregard it. Finally, in explanation of a correct answer, he says, "Before, we made crosses and it was the same," referring to the fact that to check the correspondence, the experimenter and the child had in turn taken one match from their respective collections and laid them one on top of the other in the form of a cross.

By contrast, other children gave a clearly more advanced type of answer to these same questions: they do not ignore the final appearance of the collections, since although they judge by correspondence, they also refer to the respective sizes of the units (where, for example, the matches in one collection are longer than those of the other, so that the lengths of the final roads are different, despite the equal number of matches in each), or the relative densities of the two collections (where, for example, a greater number of houses covers a smaller area than a smaller number of more spaced-out trees). These children also understand that where two continuous lines are made up of the same number of matches of uniform length, then however the lines are laid out (e.g., zigzag), the number of matches remains the same.

The following excerpt illustrates this type of response.

SON (5;11)

The child lays out all her matches in a straight line while the experimenter arranges his in a zigzag, such that the two roads contain an equal number of matches of uniform length. When SON is asked if there are the same number of matches in the two collections, she answers correctly, referring to the one-to-one procedure, and adds: "They are arranged differently; if we put them both straight out, then they'd be the same."

However, children do not usually give this more advanced type of response; often they start off with an incorrect answer based directly on the final appearance of the collections, then correct it by reference to the one-to-one procedure, before finally coordinating the pertinent aspects of the problem.

We were not at first aware of the existence of these two levels of reasoning, both leading to correct answers to the problems, although some children were more explicit than others. During the training procedure, the experimenter went on to the next exercise as soon as the child had given a correct answer to the preceding problem. That this could be given without complete understanding of the problem was really discovered only at the post-tests, where clear differences appeared among subjects who were all thought to have successfully completed the training procedure.

The same two levels of reasoning govern the subjects' reactions to the exercises on discontinuous quantities, where the one-to-one correspondence does not remain visible: e.g., small beads in two glasses of different sizes. Again, some children give correct answers, referring to the one-to-one procedure, but can give no explanation of the final appearance of the beads in the glasses. The following excerpt from a protocol illustrates this point.

EVA (5;9)

When asked whether there are as many small beads in the experimenter's glass as there are big ones in her own (more small ones) EVA correctly answers: "It's not the same, because I had to stop a bit . . . and you went on." She resists the experimenter's counter-argument stressing the difference in the fullness of the two glasses, saying: "It doesn't matter, there are still more here (correct)." Apparently considering this irrelevant to the problem in hand, she makes no attempt to explain it.

By contrast, in these situations, subjects at the more advanced level clearly take account of the final appearance of the collections as well as of the correspondence. The following excerpt from a protocol illustrates this response.

GEN (5;8)

When questioned about the quantities of beads in a narrow glass, N, and a wide glass, W (same number in each), GEN immediately gives the right answer, referring to the one-to-one procedure. However, his explanation of their final appearance is still rather clumsy: "It's like that (pointing to the height of N), it's higher because it's got a smaller circle . . . there's only room for one, so the beads come right up to here (pointing to the level in N) and only to here (pointing to the level in W), because here there's a big circle."

Similarly, different levels of reasoning also exist in reactions to the exercises on the pouring of liquids. As has been described, these exercises take place first with the child pouring into a glass behind a screen so that he cannot see the outcome of his action; then the screen is taken away and he can actually see what has happened. At this point, the visual appearance of the result has an importance for the subject. In the children's reactions to this possibility of looking at the result, the same difference in types of reasoning can be distinguished, i.e., some subjects become progressively able to adjust their actions in relation to the dimensions of the glasses and can explain their initial mistakes, whereas others appear simply to disregard the figural features of the end result. Several examples of superior and inferior types of reasoning will be given, first reasoning shown only in the training procedure, and then reasoning linked with the subjects' post-test behavior.

In the exercises with identical glasses and initial identical quantities, some children who start off by guessing how much to pour into the glass behind the screen correct the amount they have poured when the screen is taken away. This apparently leads them to become aware that, as long as the screen is present, the only way to succeed is carefully to compare the liquid remaining in the initial glasses. When the initial quantities in the identical glasses are unequal and the experimenter has emptied his glass into one of those behind the screen, the children often empty all of the larger amount contained in their glass into the other glass behind the screen. As soon as the screen is removed, they see that the quantities are not the same, realize their mistake, and correct it by pouring back the right amount into their initial glass. In these situations with identical glasses, the taking away of the screen generally leads to these types of corrections.

The situations with glasses of different sizes are far more difficult than those with identical glasses. The removal of the screen does not usually have the same propitious effect. The multiplicative problems, and to a greater extent those that combine addition and multiplication, reveal an inferior and a superior level of reasoning. For example, starting with equal quantities, the experimenter pours some of the liquid in his glass into a wider glass, W, and the child is asked to pour some of his liquid into a narrower glass, N, such that the quantities in W and N are equal; instead of correctly equalizing the remainders as he has done in the problems with identical glasses, he simply makes the levels in W and N the same. Even when the experimenter then returns to the straightforward additive problem (i.e., with two pairs of identical glasses) several children appear not to see the analogy between the two problems: they maintain that the experimenter's solution of equalizing the remainders in the multiplicative problem is incorrect, since they consider the quantities in N and W unequal. Some children, however, continue to hesitate between making the levels equal and respecting the relationship between the whole and its parts. Sometimes, they finally accept the unequal levels in W and N, arguing only that if the two initial glasses had contained the same amount of liquid, the amounts remaining in them must be made equal. This is reminiscent of some of the children's responses to problems involving discontinuous quantities: they answer correctly, judging by the number of units in each collection, while disregarding the misleading final appearance. The following extract from a protocol illustrates this point.

BEN (5;5)

BEN gives correct solutions to the additive problems with identical glasses. By contrast, when the liquid is poured into glasses of different diameters (multiplicative problem) he answers incorrectly, judging the quantities solely by the height of the levels, despite numerous attempts by the experimenter to make him consider the difference in the diameters of N and W. In the combined additive and multiplicative problems, he gives the right solution by making the remainders in A and B equal "because before we had the same." He even resists the suggestion of making the levels in N and W equal: "I don't think we'd have the same to drink because you've poured a tiny bit there (from B into N)"; however, in explanation, he simply says, "Because it's bigger (pointing to the height in N) and it's smaller (lower in W) but it's still the same thing." Here, therefore, although he gives the right solution, he does not seem to be aware of the relationship between the heights of the liquids and the diameters of the glasses.

Other children, concerned by the difference in the solutions obtained by what they consider two legitimate ways of solving the problem, eventually decide to ignore the remainders in the initial glasses and make the levels in N and W equal. JAC (6;6), after changing his mind several times and even attempting to take account of both the height of the liquid and the diameters of the glasses, finally gives up, saying: "You've just got to look at the levels, there's no way of fiddling it."

In contrast with these inferior types of solution, a child who has completely mastered the multiplicative relationship understands that the difference in diameter is compensated for by that in the liquid levels of the two glasses. After removal of the screen, this explanation is sometimes given straightaway. In the multiplicative problems, some children first want to correct the levels so that they are only slightly different—however, they never suggest making the levels exactly the same. In the problems where addition and multiplication are combined, some children start off by pouring the liquid to a higher level in N than in W, but without making the remainders in the initial glasses equal. When this occurs, the experimenter returns to the problem with identical glasses, which the child has correctly solved, hoping to trigger an awareness of the need to use the same reasoning in the new problem. The superior level of reasoning in the multiplicative-additive problems is illustrated by the following example.

SAB (6;5)

SAB gives correct answers to the multiplicative and multiplicative-additive problems. She makes the remainders in the initial glasses equal, but justifies her answers only by relating the different dimensions of N and W: "Because there (N) it's thinner and there (W) it's wider." When the experimenter tries to get her to give a more complete explanation, she clearly describes the relationships between the parts and the whole: "There has to be the same left over (in the initial glasses) because before we both had the same."

As was the case with the discontinuous quantities, the difference between the two levels of behavior was particularly clear at the post-tests. Again, generally speaking, the subjects who during the training procedure displayed the inferior type of reasoning were found at the post-tests to be in categories I or II, while those who displayed the superior type of reasoning reached level IV. However, in several cases, the subjects' reasoning was intermediate between the inferior and superior levels, and they reached category III in the first post-test and sometimes IV in the second.

To illustrate the link between responses to the training procedure and results in the post-tests, three protocols are given below. The first is a typical example of a subject who has great difficulty with the training problems and who makes little or no progress at the post-tests.

MAN (5;6)

At the pre-test, MAN was among the least advanced of the subjects: he gave wrong answers to all the problems and was selected as a subject only because of his semioperatory response (quotity level) to the elementary number test.

During the training procedure, MAN incorrectly judges the discontinuous quantities according to the area occupied by the final collections, even though he correctly describes how these were formed. He cannot explain what he sees when the experimenter shows his answer is wrong by pairing off the units. However, after several such situations, and after yet another verification disproving his answer, he admits: "There's one house missing because I didn't put another one when we stopped." After two more exercises, he finally solves the problem without the experimenter's help: "Because you've put two more and I haven't." In the first length problem, however, he reverts to an answer based on the final appearance, i.e., the position of the end points of the two "roads," and it is only after several such situations that he disregards this and answers correctly, considering only the one-to-one correspondence.

When the experimenter goes on to the problems with the beads, he immediately gives correct answers based on the one-to-one correspondence, but he clearly has no idea of relating the number of the beads to their size or to the dimensions of the glasses.

Thus three laborious training sessions have led MAN to judge the quantities solely by reference to the one-to-one procedure, to which his attention was drawn on several occasions when the experimenter paired off the units to check his answers.

In the exercises on continuous quantities, MAN has no difficulty with the additive problems: for instance, when the experimenter pours half of his liquid into one of the identical glasses behind the screen, MAN refuses to pour all the contents of his glass into the other one: "It's the same thing here as in there (remaining amounts) because that's got to be the same (the two new glasses)." However, in the additive-multiplicative problems, he encounters the obstacle of the levels: he thinks that to have equal quantities in N and W, the levels must be the same. He no longer pays attention to what remains in the initial glasses and when this is pointed out to him, says: "I ought to have poured a bit, but then that (W) wouldn't have been the same (as N)." After several situations, where (after the experimenter has poured all his liquid into W) MAN is asked to pour his liquid into N such that N = W, he becomes confused: "I've got to pour all mine to make the same as here (empty experimenter's glass) . . . but if I pour it all, it goes further here (level N)." Equalization of the levels in N and W thus no longer completely satisfies him and he cannot decide whether to make the remainders the same or to make the levels in N and W equal. Finally, however, MAN decides on the latter solution.

The effects of the exercises are almost nonexistent: as at the pre-test, MAN's answers at the first post-test are incorrect, except for the conservation of liquids problem, where he now gives several correct answers with no, or virtually no, explanation. At the second post-test, however, the fragility of his progress during the training procedure becomes apparent when he reverts in the same liquids problem to judging the quantities according to the final appearance of the liquid in the glasses.

Although the post-tests showed no progress, during the exercises, MAN did realize the need to consider the one-to-one procedure (discontinuous quantities problems) and the need to make the amounts remaining in the initial glasses equal (continuous quantities). Since this did not trigger an understanding of the multiplicative relationship, which was not absolutely necessary for the solution of the training problems, it is not surprising that MAN failed to give truly operatory answers at the post-tests where such an understanding was vital.

Understanding of numerical correspondence may be acquired at a level corresponding to that of quotity, which Gréco (1962) describes as constituting a semioperatory scheme still quite distinct from the concept of numerical quantity, but more advanced than the total irreversibility that precedes it. Similarly, a semioperatory understanding of continuous quantities can be acquired before an understanding of the multiplicative relationships between the dimensions of a container and the level of the liquid.

The following protocol is a typical example of a subject who profits from the training procedure and reaches category IV at the second post-test.

FLO (5;9)

When the two collections are arranged to cover two very different surface areas (one spaced out and one packed tightly together), FLO immediately gives correct answers, but can give no reasons for them and hesitates to predict the outcome of the verification by pairing of the units: "Because when you put one, I stopped a bit, I didn't put one down and after, we went on . . . there'll be one dog which won't have a tree (correct) . . . we've got to try it out."

Later, when she is questioned on the numerical equality of the two collections, she begins to count the units, saying that she cannot guess the answer without counting. However, in the following exercises, she refers to the one-to-one procedure "because we both did the same all the time, right from the beginning." From then on, whenever faced with this type of situation, she answers and explains correctly.

The length problems cause her a little trouble, but she corrects her wrong answers and her argument takes account not only of the established numerical correspondence, but also of the lengths of the individual matches (collection B has more matches although it forms a shorter "road" than A): "B's got more . . . because my matches are bigger (A) and yours are smaller." She can also picture the two collections laid out in the same way, so that the numerical equality would be obvious (one of the collections forms a straight line, the other a zigzag): "There are the same number (correct) because you've turned (zigzags) and I didn't turn. If I turned, it would have been the same (pointing to the lengths)."

In the problems where the correspondence does not remain visible (beads in glasses of different diameters), FLO backs up her correct answers by the compensation argument. In the situation where the big beads have been placed in the narrow glass, N, and the small ones in the wide glass, W, she says: "Because there isn't enough room at the bottom (in N) and these beads are smaller than the others."

In the exercises on continuous quantities, she quickly overcomes the difficulties and responds correctly: e.g., when the experimenter empties his glass, which had originally contained less liquid than FLO's, into one of the identical glasses behind the screen, she pours only a part of her liquid into the other glass and says: "We've both got to have the same . . . because you started with less . . . yes, we've both got the same behind (the screen)."

By contrast, FLO has difficulty when the problems involve both addition and multiplication. She changes her correct solution to obtain equal levels, saying: "You poured it all to get this level (in W) and I've got to pour only a little bit to get the same height (in N) . . . I think I've got to have a big glass like you (W) to get the same." However, after three exercises, FLO maintains and explains a correct solution: "The water's got more room (in W) because it's bigger than there (N), because that's little." This insight is only momentary, however, since she later responds to a similar problem by making the levels equal.

At the first post-test, FLO reaches only category II: she has no trouble with the conservation of matter problems, but makes the levels the same in the liquid pouring problem; she gives incorrect answers to the problems on the quantification of inclusion and intersection.

At the second post-test, FLO reaches category IV: she again correctly solves the conservation of matter problem and this time not only gets the level right in the liquid pouring problem, but also justifies this correct solution by an argument which clearly indicates her understanding of the relationship involved.

FLO's responses contrast strikingly with those of MAN, who remained at a clearly less advanced level. Nevertheless, FLO seems to encounter numerous difficulties during the training procedure, particularly with the exercises on continuous quantities. At the first post-test, which follows immediately after the exercises, she has not made much progress. Several weeks later, however, at the second post-test, her responses reveal that she has reached a considerably higher level—in fact, she is the only subject who makes so much delayed progress (from category II to IV).

The next protocol illustrates the responses of those subjects who make only partial progress.

BEN (5;5)

BEN starts off by giving correct answers in the exercises on discontinuous quantities, but can justify them only by saying: "I thought." In the third exercise, however, he backs up his answers by referring to the one-to-one procedure and has no trouble with the length problems that perplexed so many of the other subjects. Nothing appears to shake his faith in the value of the one-to-one correspondence, although he clearly has not grasped the multiplicative relationship between the dimensions. It is only in the sixth exercise that he begins to take account of the dimensions, but even then only those of the individual units and not those of the whole collections: he correctly judges the numerical equality of two collections of matches making up two "roads" of very different lengths "because the green matches are longer." When it comes to the problems involving beads in glasses, BEN refers to the compensatory dimensions of the beads, but not to those of the glasses: "That makes no difference (if the level in N is higher than in W) because those (beads in W) are smaller."

BEN has trouble with the additive problems in the exercises on continuous quantities where the quantities are not initially equal. After several of these problems, he answers them correctly.

So, BEN manages to solve these first problems, but does not explain his answers as clearly as FLO.

In the multiplicative problems he encounters great difficulties and all his solutions are based on the final levels of the liquids.

Rather surprisingly, he correctly solves the problems combining addition and multiplication. He justifies his correct solutions by saying: "Because before we had the same." He is not swayed by mention of the difference in the levels, but his arguments do not prove that he understands the compensatory covariance, since he refers only to the height: "Because it's bigger (N) and it's smaller (W), but it's still the same."

When the experimenter returns to a multiplicative problem, BEN again makes the levels in N and W the same: "It's right like that because they're the same height." When presented with another problem combining addition and multiplication, he admits that the levels can be different in N and W and that there is still "the same to drink . . . but there (N) it goes up higher."

In the first post-test BEN reaches category II. He has attained conservation of quantity of matter and continuous quantities (at the pre-test he had been classified Int for liquid conservation and NC for the modeling clay task). However, he still responds to the liquid pouring problem by making the levels the same. At the second post-test, he reaches category III, but only just: BEN attempts to relate the liquid levels with the diameters of the glasses, but he still opts for making the levels the same. His second post-test results show very little progress compared to the first.

A brief comparison of the responses of MAN, FLO, and BEN to the exercises and of their post-test results provides an illustration of the difference between the inferior and superior types of reasoning and also gives an insight into the full range of developmental processes underlying the post-test results.

When MAN is finally able to use the one-to-one procedure to judge numerical equality or inequality, he can do so only by disregarding the various differences in dimensions. BEN reaches a slightly more advanced stage than MAN since he takes account of the dimensions of the units (length of the matches, size of the beads) and so clearly has some idea of a relationship between dimensions, although he cannot apply this to the dimensions of the collections formed by the units. FLO, even more advanced, takes account of the zigzags in determining the length of the "roads" and relates the height of the beads in the glasses to the diameters of the glasses.

In the exercises on continuous quantities, MAN cannot at first conserve the initial part-whole relationship. Although he gradually learns to do this, he remains clearly less advanced than BEN, since a grasp of this first quantitative relationship enables the latter, unlike MAN, to disregard the difference in the liquid levels and give correct answers to the additive-multiplicative problem. Like BEN, FLO starts off by disregarding the difference in the liquid levels, but she attempts to relate the dimensions and, although she is still a little unsure, has obviously begun to grasp a genuine quantitative concept.

There is thus a striking difference between these three children: both MAN and BEN understand the part-whole relationship, but BEN, unlike MAN, is able to apply it to every appropriate situation. FLO has a grasp of the compensatory relationship between different dimensions, although she is not yet fully confident.

Since all these three children make gradual progress during the training procedure, their reactions clarify the process by which quantitative concepts are elaborated.

At the post-tests, MAN makes no further progress and remains in category I, FLO reaches category II at the first post-test and, as has been said, shows remarkable progress at the second (category IV). This result can be related to her responses during the exercises, when she does indeed envisage all the aspects of the problem, but cannot yet coordinate them. In the first post-test, she was probably still troubled by the conflicts experienced during the exercises. During the interval between the two post-tests, she seems to have resolved these conflicts. Similar cases of delayed progress were observed in several other experiments (see Chapters 2 and 6).

BEN's results at post-test 2 are practically the same as at post-test 1. He had given fairly satisfactory answers to the exercises, because he had become able to apply the part-whole relationship wherever appropriate, but, as he clearly did not understand the multiplicative relationship, his post-test results (he just reached category III in the second post-test) correspond well to his level during the procedure; in every respect, he appears to be at a level midway between those of MAN and FLO.

Two cautionary remarks have to be made. Although the pre-test indicated only two slightly different levels of reasoning, consideration of the subjects' reactions to the training procedure allows finer distinctions, which were confirmed in the post-test results. These finer distinctions showed up the difficulty of deciding when to go on to the next series of exercises, since a child could give correct answers to the problems without in fact grasping their full implications. It would perhaps have been wiser with children like MAN and BEN not to go on to the more complex problems, but rather to present them with a greater variety of simpler situations.

CONCLUDING REMARKS

The salient points of this training procedure may be summarized as follows.

There is a first series of exercises in which the child and the experimenter each simultaneously make up a collection of "countables." Where the iterative one-to-one procedure is adhered to strictly, the two collections end up numerically equal, where it is broken (deliberately, by the experimenter's adding extra units) they do not.

The first exercises in a second series involve discontinuous, but no longer countable, quantities, while in subsequent ones the experimenter introduces liquids, i.e., continuous quantities.

The degree of difficulty of the problems is gradually increased and the child is required to allow for differences in more and more aspects (e.g., number and size, height of liquid and diameter of glass).

The exercises are not always presented in exactly the same order, but, according to the child's responses, the experimenter repeats certain problems and generally suggests comparisons between different solutions to problems of the same type.

The results of this study allow, to a certain extent, the reconstruction of the developmental stages leading up to the acquisition of the concept of conservation of continuous quantities.

1. The exercises on discontinuous quantities brought to light a first stage (noted only in the first training session): some children were able to recapitulate the way the collections had been formed (e.g., "We both put them at the same time and then you put another one"); however, they appeared not to realize the relevance of this to the questions concerning the quantities of beads in glasses and so, for instance, continued to think that a higher level in one of the glasses denoted the greater quantity. Such responses are reminiscent of those given in other experiments: in the class inclusion experiment (Chapter 7), although they had counted the units correctly, some children could not solve the problem; in the length experiment (Chapter 6), although they had clearly acquired the

number scheme, some children could not solve the problems because they took no notice of the different lengths of the units.

2. These same exercises (discontinuous quantities) revealed a second stage: some children gave correct answers to the questions on the quantities solely because they remembered how the collections were formed; they paid no attention whatsoever to their actual appearance. Here again, such responses are reminiscent of those given in the length experiment, where some children based their answers solely on the number of units without reference to their individual sizes.

3. Children at a third stage (still regarding discontinuous quantities) fully understood the significance of the iterative one-to-one procedure and were beginning to combine this with an understanding of the covariance between the different aspects: first between the size of the units and the length of the total line and then, later, between the height of the beads in the glasses and the diameter of the glasses.

4. A parallel development, although the stages were reached a little later, took place with regard to continuous quantities. At first, the children concentrated on the part-whole relationship and disregarded the final appearance of the liquid in the glasses. This led to correct solutions in certain problems, but to wrong ones in others.

5. A new stage was reached in the more difficult situations (additive-multiplicative exercises), when the children began to try to take both the remainders and the newly constituted quantities into consideration, while still attempting to reconcile these with their feeling that the final levels should be the same; they tried to compromise by making the remainders and the final levels more or less the same, and thereby, inevitably, failed to solve the problem.

6. Finally, the children mastered all these difficulties and could give full explanations of their now correct solutions.

These results thus reveal a developmental pattern similar to that encountered in other experiments.

From the children's responses to the training problems in each experiment, it was possible to determine the following developmental levels.

First level. The child's attention is fixed on one particular feature of the situation or problem, each of which activates a distinct conceptual scheme; he is unaware of any discrepancies in his answers, since each type of situation is apprehended separately with no reference to previous solutions to other problems.

Second level. One of the schemes—and in most cases it seems to be the one most firmly established in the child's thoughts—dominates in all situations.

Third level. This is an extremely interesting level, at which conflicts arise between the various schemes; these are revealed by the child's confusion, hesitation, and, above all, attempts to reconcile two contradictory arguments (compromise responses).

Final level. The various conceptual schemes combine and become coordinated through differentiation and generalization; a new structuration of a more advanced developmental level has taken place, derived from already existing, but uncoordinated, patterns of thought.

COMPARISON BETWEEN THE RESULTS OF THE INCLUSION CONSERVATION AND CONSERVATION INCLUSION LEARNING EXPERIMENTS

In both experiments, important and genuine progress was obtained. After the training sessions, progress was noted not only in the subjects' responses to the type of problems covered in the procedure (procedure-covered problems), but also to those for which they had received no help at all (no-help problems). A first question concerns the comparability of the results in the procedure-covered problems. Although no strict comparison between the results obtained by the two groups is possible because of the inevitable differences in the two training procedures, Tables 8.4 and 8.5 do give an indication of their relative efficacy. In both experiments, the subjects are divided into four post-test categories, according to criteria already described: (I) those who make no progress; (II) those who make slight progress; (III) those who make average progress; (IV) those who make marked progress.

It is perhaps useful to repeat the relevant category descriptions.

Quantification of Inclusion Tasks

I. Subjects who make mistakes in all the problems and, although they may change their answers, make no real corrections after the experimenter's intervention.

II. Subjects who make several mistakes in different problems, but correct them either spontaneously or after the experimenter's intervention—they fail to solve the problem where $A = B$.

III. Subjects who make no mistakes for the questions about the quantification of inclusion for the fruit, flowers, and animal situations (two-level inclusion) and for the situation where $A = A'$, but give incorrect responses to the question "How many more?" and/or to the problem where $A = B$.

IV. Subjects who give correct solutions to all the problems.

Conservation Problems

I. Subjects who solve none of the problems although some of them give one or two correct answers to individual questions ($-$ and Int).

II. Subjects who find at least one of the problems too difficult, but correctly solve one or both of the others ($1 +$ and $1 -$ or $2 -$).

III. Subjects who solve at least one problem, if not two, correctly and give some correct answers in the case of the other one or two (at least $1 +$ and no $-$).

IV. Subjects who solve all three problems correctly ($3 +$).

Table 8.4 shows the relative efficacy of the two procedures as regards the procedure-covered problems. From these figures it does appear that the children obtained about the same amount of help from the two procedures as regards the problems directly concerned: after the exercises on inclusion, 14 out of 19 subjects were classified in

TABLE 8.4

	Post-Test 1				Post-Test 2			
	I	II	III	IV	I	II	III	IV
Inclusion	4	3	5	7	3	2	3	11
Conservation	3	7	4	5 (+1)	1(+1)	2(+1)	7(+1)	6(+1)

Note: The figures show the number of subjects. Where it was not possible to give a subject one of the post-tests, his result in the other is given in parentheses.

categories III and IV, and after those on conservation, 15 out of 20 subjects reached those levels at the second post-test. Furthermore, there is a similarity between the subjects' responses to the two sets of exercises, in that in both cases there are two levels ("inferior" and "superior") in the types of reasoning which enabled the subjects to give correct answers to the problems. This, in fact, we found reassuring, as we were anxious to avoid directing the children toward one particular strategy. The effects of the two training procedures on the responses to the second post-test are shown in Table 8.5, in which

TABLE 8.5

		PC+	PC−			PC+	PC−
Inclusion Group	NH+	13[a]	1	Conservation Group	NH+	8[b]	0
	NH−	3	2		NH−	10	2

a. Of whom 2 make only very little progress in NH.
b. Of whom 3 make only very little progress in PC.

progress (i.e., categories II, III, and IV) in the two types of problem is shown by PC+ and NH+, progress in either the procedure-covered problems *or* the no-help problems by PC+ and NH− *or* PC− and NH+, and no progress at all (category I) by PC− and NH−.

In both experiments, progress in the no-help problems was considerable. However, the children who had been given help with inclusion made more progress with conservation than those who had taken part in the conservation procedure made with inclusion (after the inclusion procedure there were 13 subjects PC+ and NH+ compared with 8 in these categories after the conservation procedure). However, the difference between the two sets of post-tests has to be kept in mind. In the case of the class inclusion problems, the subjects were given one test, completed by questions bearing either on different material or on a double inclusion. The conservation tasks involved both conservation of liquids and modeling clay and that of weight—concepts which, without specific training, are only acquired in the course of several years of development.

Nevertheless, the number of subjects given the conservation procedure who made progress only in the procedure-covered problems is much higher than that of those who were given the inclusion exercises (10 PC+ and NH− in the conservation procedure group against 3 in the other). This seems to call for the following interpretation of the comparative results: exercises in inclusion, if successful, have a more marked effect on conservation than vice versa. This led us to envisage some hypotheses as to the possible reasons for such a difference.

The conservation problems (particularly that of conservation of continuous quantities) have causal and temporal aspects not present in the quantification of inclusion. The exercises on the latter were aimed at helping the children make a "synchronic" judgment: the members of subclasses A and A' are at the same time and not alternatively members of the total class, B; the criteria of the subclasses A and A' include all those of class B, plus some more specific ones. It is psychologically conceivable that the atemporal reasoning necessary for the solution of problems of quantification of inclusion reflects more directly the logical structure of the grouping. Thus learning aimed at this type of reasoning could act more directly on the psychological structuration and result in an acquisition more immediately applicable to another type of problem.

By contrast, in the training procedure for conservation, which involves modifications of shape and therefore causal and temporal aspects, the exercises could not accentuate the atemporal aspect of the operations underlying the concept of conservation.

However, this immediately raises a second question: how then does the extemporaneous structure involved in the quantification of inclusion act on the temporal process involved in the conservation problems? One could perhaps argue that the latter also require a quantification independent of time (conservation of a quantitative property), while the passage of time involved in the changes of shape, etc., seems to imply a change in quantity. But since the conservation procedure was specifically aimed at dissociating the atemporal invariant from the change in shape, which is temporal, why does the understanding of this invariant have so little influence on the quantification of inclusion? There must be another reason, perhaps the following: in conservation, the quantification is reduced to a constant equality, $A = A$, while in inclusion problems, quantification has at least two principal values: B is greater than A with multiple values of B, and B remains equal to itself ($B = B$) regardless of how it is divided into A and A'. The dissymmetry of the results obtained in the no-help problems could thus be explained by the fact that conservation concepts constitute a less general quantificatory instrument than the quantification of inclusion.

Conclusions

The results of learning studies should be examined not only as to their significance for the problem of learning, but also as to their possible theoretical importance for those questions of developmental psychology still unanswered by the psychogenetic theory of thought structures.

The main goal of our learning studies was to get a better insight into the transition (or construction) mechanisms which enable children to attain certain concepts that are essential for scientific thought. In this first approach, different concepts of conservation (numerical, physical, and spatial) and their possible derivations were chosen for study, as well as the concept of quantification of class inclusion and its eventual links with conservation of quantity. The epistemological conviction that progress in human knowledge results from dynamic processes which imply self-regulatory mechanisms led us to pay close attention to clashes between the different patterns of thought that constitute a subject's competence at a certain level of his development, to the conflicts resulting from these clashes, and, especially, to the different ways these conflicts can be resolved. Two different types of conflict can be observed. First, different subsystems, each developing at its own developmental rate, can create a conflictual situation, since one system may already have reached a more advanced state than another. Second, the child's reasoning may be at a level where he becomes aware that experimental reality does not conform to his deductions or inferences.

The study of transition mechanisms is, in our opinion, essential if we want to find answers (even if only partial) to the following questions: What are the developmental links or derivations between the different key concepts? What are the dynamic processes that lead to new modes of thought? What are the role and nature of learning?

The mere fact that we chose training techniques to study transition mechanisms is sufficient to show that the Genevan school is not a proponent of a maturationist doctrine, as has often been thought. Only if training procedures are effective can one hope to observe acquisition processes at work in the individual child. The results bore out this assumption: in many cases, cognitive development was indeed speeded up, providing us with many opportunities for observing transitional behaviors that can only rarely, if ever, be apprehended in cross-sectional research. On the other hand, the design of the training procedures indicates our disagreement with classical learning theorists. The experimental situations were constructed to encourage the child's activity and to elicit the coordination and differentiation of thought patterns that are characteristic of the different levels of development. No attempt was made to lead the child through a series of preprogrammed steps toward the correct solution of a problem. The procedures provided the subjects with a series of situations which favored their apprehension of the experimental facts and which led to numerous comparisons and conflicts between the subjects' predictions and ideas and the actual outcome of certain manipulations. In this type of learning study, it is necessary to examine both the effects of learning in the strict sense and those of learning in the wide sense (according to Piaget's distinction). Before attempting to answer the three main questions mentioned above, we shall therefore discuss the general implications of the experimental results for the problem of the relation between learning and development.

LEARNING AND DEVELOPMENT: GENERAL IMPLICATIONS OF THE RESULTS

The overall effects of the training sessions are represented by the arrows in the progress tables which link each subject's results in the pre-test to his results in the two post-tests.

Many subjects, in the different experiments, made real progress—a fact that cannot be overemphasized, since without this result our analysis of the acquisition processes would be impossible. The training procedures mobilized the psychogenetic system, and acted as amplifiers of the subjects' activities. In general, progress followed the developmental line already known from cross-sectional research. Admittedly, this is hardly surprising, since no attempts were made to induce different acquisition modes. However, our aim was not to compare different training methods, but to study acquisition processes, and for this our procedures proved adequate: in many cases, development was clearly speeded up, and concepts were attained in a relatively short time.

The nature and extent of the subjects' progress was always, in fact strikingly so, dependent upon their initial developmental level; in other words, progress depends on the assimilatory instrument a subject already has at his disposal. Generally speaking, the hierarchical order of the subjects, first established according to their level of reasoning in the pre-test, remained the same in the two post-tests. In the results tables, most of the arrows remain parallel. However, the gaps between the achievement levels of certain subjects were considerably greater after training than before. The training situations and the dialogue with the experimenter tend to increase initial advances, even if they are only slight. To account for these effects, it would appear necessary to invoke internal mechanisms which adapt and transform external data according to certain developmentally determined organizational patterns.

Comparison of the results of the two post-tests brings to light an interesting phenomenon: in certain cases, the acquisitions observed at the first post-test showed perfect stability, and were confirmed at the second post-test; in other cases, there was no such stability and the second post-test showed either an improvement or a deterioration compared to the first. Once the subjects had shown a clear understanding of a conservation or class inclusion concept, no changes were observed in their way of reasoning; the concept attained showed the stability of a truly operatory construction. By contrast, many of the subjects who at the first post-test reached one of the intermediate levels either regressed or progressed at the second post-test. It seems that regressions occur when the subject only momentarily establishes certain coordinations suggested by a specific situation: his reasoning remains strictly local, cannot be generalized to other situations, and is probably not accompanied by the feeling of logical necessity that is another characteristic of a truly operatory construct. Delayed progress, on the other hand, is a more interesting effect of the disequilibrium created by partial acquisition. Some of the subjects progressed from an intermediate level at the first post-test to an operatory level at the second, while others made considerable advances, although not to the same level. In the interval between the two post-tests, progress started during training appears to continue, and new coordinations become established which cannot be observed but whose results suggest the intervention of organizational processes similar to those occurring with other subjects during actual training. The comparison of pre-tests and post-tests of all our experiments taken together leads to the conclusion that the findings fit the conception of learning as an integral part of the developmental mechanisms.

Turning from the results of the learning experiments to the different modes of progress observed, we would like to make the following general remarks. The analysis of the different types of behavior during the training sessions showed not only the various stages in the construction of the concepts that were already familiar to us, but also as yet unknown intermediate levels. This seems to provide additional evidence of the psychological reality of the operatory construction, which is sometimes questioned by psychologists for whom the stages only reflect the Genevan school's epistemological and logical tenets. Similarly, scrutiny of the difficulties individual subjects encountered during the training procedures contradicted the idea (particularly in favor with our Soviet colleagues of the Galperin school*) that inadequate modes of reasoning are, in the main, artifacts caused by insufficient and incorrect education. The tenacity of the preconservational modes of thinking, and their gradual replacement by intermediate conflictual reasoning in many children, seems to confirm the Genevan view that such semilogical constructs are inherent in the child's thought and necessary for his progress.

* Preface to the Russian translation of *The Developmental Psychology of Jean Piaget* by J. H. Flavell.

DERIVATION AND CHRONOLOGY OF
CONSERVATION CONCEPTS

The concepts of conservation are acquired in a constant chronological order. Genevan research (Piaget and Inhelder, 1941; Piaget, Inhelder, Szeminska, 1948; Piaget and Szeminska, 1941) has already shown that children acquire the conservation concepts studied in the learning experiments in the following order: discontinuous quantities, continuous quantities (liquids, solid matter [modeling clay], and then length). The standardization studies undertaken by Vinh Bang in Geneva and by other researchers in various countries confirm this order, although the actual ages at which children acquire these concepts may vary with differences in individual capacities, in educational standard, and in cultural environment.

All conservation concepts have certain characteristics in common: they are based on the same operatory systems characterized by transformational properties, and their acquisition is attested by the appearance of astonishingly similar arguments (identity, compensation by reciprocity, and cancellation through reversibility). The fact that these concepts are not all acquired at the same time poses a psychological problem, as Piaget himself has stressed (1968a). It seems that the child, in the process of structuring his thinking, encounters specific resistances from the physical reality. These resistances may be studied from two complementary angles: the child's apprehension of the properties of objects which we are beginning to understand better as a result of research on causality (Piaget and Garcia, 1971)—and the structure of his activity as he tries to come to grips with them. Learning studies provide one method of determining why these first notions of quantification, which precede and make possible the notion of measurement, are not all acquired simultaneously.

This problem is linked to that of the developmental relationships between concepts. What can be called "vertical" relationships have already been studied from the logical and psychological angles at the main stages of cognitive development. Sensorimotor structures provide the foundation necessary for the development of concrete operations which, in turn, enable the constitution of new syntheses in the

246

shape of formal operational structures. By contrast, little is known about the "oblique" relationships between concepts within the concrete operational period, particularly between the first notions of conservation of discontinuous quantities and those of continuous quantities (liquids, solid matter, and length), which are generally acquired between the ages of six and nine years.

Instead of supposing that chronological order of acquisition indicates a direct derivational relationship, we should hypothesize the existence of corresponding, or parallel, processes starting from a common base and developing as a function of the growing complexity of the reality a child tries to assimilate. However, we have little idea of the extent to which the relatively early acquisition of a conservation concept speeds up a child's grasp of more advanced concepts. In fact, the aim of the learning studies was to show what is and what is not transferable from a lower-level acquisition to one of a higher level.

Through observation of the progress in the child's reasoning in experimental training situations it should be possible to elucidate the epistemological nature of the concepts and the structural relationships between them. The problems of the transition between different substages and of links between concepts acquired at different ages are often indissociable and will be discussed together.

CONSERVATION OF MATTER

The acquisition of conservation of matter (liquids and modeling clay) was the object of three different learning studies. In the first (Chapter 1) the training sessions started off with continuous quantities; in the second (Chapter 2) training started with conservation of discontinuous quantities, with the collections being made up by means of repeated one-to-one correspondences; and in the third (Chapters 3 and 7) training consisted in using small, well-defined pieces or fragments to constitute continuous or semicontinuous quantities.

A detailed comparison of the effects of these three methods cannot be made, since the number of sessions and the initial levels of the subjects were not the same in each experiment. However, the method described in Chapter 8, which entailed six training sessions, proved the most enlightening as regards both the difficulties encountered and the ways they were overcome by children at the preconservation levels.

This training procedure called for repeated one-to-one correspondences using a variety of materials (progressing from discontinuous to continuous quantities). Those children who at the pre-test had little or no idea of conservation of continuous quantities, yet in the post-tests showed clear understanding of this notion, progressed as follows: they grasped that the one-to-one procedure allows an accurate, numerical comparison of the two collections, i.e., whether the collections are numerically equal can be determined simply by recalling whether or not the one-to-one procedure was strictly followed, regardless of the final arrangement of the collections. (Obviously, when one is working with separate elements, only whole units can be added or taken away.)

This "numerical equivalence" scheme derived from the one-to-one procedure then comes into conflict with a previously established scheme of "going beyond," which leads the child to judge, e.g., that the collection extending further contains the greater number of units. Inversely, a judgment of numerical inequality based on nonadherence to the one-to-one procedure may enter into conflict with one of equality based on frontier effects of the configurations of the elements. These conflicts may be overcome when the children begin to relate the spacing of units in a row to the distance between the first and the last, or (in the case of nonlinear lay-outs) to relate the spacing of units to the overall area occupied by the units, or (when the material consists of beads or seeds inside glasses of various dimensions) to relate the height and the levels of the contents of the glasses.

The training procedure was designed to lead to a similar conflict as regards continuous quantities: the two glasses of different diameters were filled by repeated one-to-one correspondences from small measures. The resulting conflict (between a judgment of inequality, based on the higher level of the liquid in the glass with the smaller diameter, and a judgment of equality, based on the one-to-one procedure) may be resolved in the same way, i.e., through the realization that the higher liquid level in one glass may be compensated for by the larger diameter of the other glass.

The important role played by such conflicts is shown directly by the behavior of some children who seemed to remain unaware of them. These children based their answers on the one-to-one method, apparently regarding any dimensional change as immaterial. They often gave correct answers at the first post-test, but failed in the second (especially with the shorter training method of Chapter 3). It seems that they have learned—for a while—simply to dismiss one part of the problem instead of integrating it into a solution. By contrast, when children have completely resolved the conflicts in one context—here, discontinuous quantities—they tend to apprehend an analogous situation, such as one involving continuous quantities, in the same way. What is transposed from the one context to the other is apparently an awareness of the similarity of the conflicts and contradictions.

The experiment described in the first chapter, in which the subjects receive no training in problems involving discontinuous quantities, provides negative evidence confirming the importance of conflicts between schemes for all progress in knowledge.

Very few of the children who had not yet reached an intermediate stage at the pre-tests made progress during the training sessions. They gave no sign of conflict between, e.g., the idea that it is necessary to let the total quantity of liquids from the top glasses flow through to the bottom glasses and the judgment that the higher liquid level in one of the glasses denotes greater quantity. Since these children had not received training in problems with discontinuous quantities, they had not encountered such conflicts in this easier situation; consequently, when faced with the more difficult task, they did not have a heuristic conflict model at their disposal and therefore did not question their judgments based on the height of the levels. When they found, e.g., contrary to their expectations, that the levels in glasses C and C′ turned out to be equal, they simply made ad hoc corrections, without modifying any of their previous judgments or attempting a new approach to subsequent problems. Their lack of awareness of contradictions was striking since the experimental situations provided a sort of illustration of the operations underlying conservation, i.e., identity and annulment or compensation. Such behavior provides further evidence for the general hypothesis that observable features become pertinent (i.e., actually help a child to develop his reasoning) only insofar as they can be integrated into inferential mechanisms.

By contrast, those children who had already given contradictory, conflict-provoking answers benefited from this type of training, and in the post-test they proved to have acquired the concept. Examining their reactions during the training sessions, we found that they constructed a series of inferences from their observations and noticed both contradictions and consistencies.

The experiment described in Chapter 3 dealt with the possible developmental links between numerical correspondence and conservation of matter. Its results gave insight into certain characteristics of young children's thinking which create obstacles for learning and which are only partially conquered during training.

This training procedure started with situations in which the children could check visually whether two collections contained the same or a different number of units (small cylinders of modeling clay, either two rows of the same number of identical cylinders or two rows each containing the same number of units of different sizes). These units could then be stuck together to form various shapes in order to illustrate the idea that a quantity of solid matter can be thought of as consisting of a number of small units. All the children who at the beginning of the experiment had already grasped the notion of quotity, but had not yet mastered that of numerical conservation, achieved the latter by the second post-test. Once again, however, the only children to make progress in the concept of conservation of matter were those who at the pre-test had already reached an intermediate level for at least one of the tasks (generally the liquids task). Observational data may appear completely clear to a subject who has already mastered the concept, and they may help those who are on their way to acquiring it, but they are of little or no use to those whose modes of reasoning cannot yet deal with any conservation task, not even that of elementary numerical conservation.

Which specific obstacles hinder the construction of conservation concepts? Two characteristics of preoperatory reasoning emerged clearly from the children's behavior during the training sessions: a lack of differentiation between intension and extension in logical quantification and a lack of differentiation between arithmetical and physical quantification.

At the lowest level, children may compare part of one of the two quantities to the whole of the other. Thus they may compare one of the fragments of modeling clay in the original row to the sausage made from all those in the other, and conclude that there is more clay in the latter. These children also often appear to attribute wrongly to the whole, properties of one of its parts: thus they may say that there is less modeling clay in the first row of "sweets," each made by joining two fragments, than in the second row, in which each "sweet" is made up of four fragments, basing their judgment on the fact that one "sweet" in the first row is smaller than one in the second. Apparently they attribute the quality "small" or "short" of one element to the whole row, through lack of differentiation between intensive and extensive properties.

That this is indeed a case of lack of differentiation and not of a one-way generalization is evidenced by the results of another experiment (Inhelder and Piaget, 1963) in which the child and the experimenter simultaneously take (one-to-one procedure) counters from two original piles, A containing more than B: some children think that the collection of counters taken from pile A is more numerous than the collection taken from B, as if each counter somehow shared the properties of the original pile. This situation is the converse of the one in the current experiment, but the principle is the same.

Lack of differentiation between arithmetical and physical quantification is closely linked to the so-called frontier effects was described in *L'image mentale chez l'enfant* (Piaget and Inhelder, 1966): this leads children to evaluate two quantities according to whether one extremity of an object or collection "goes beyond" that of the other. In the conservation tasks, which always have both a quantificatory and a spatial or physical aspect, the child who concludes that "there is more here because it goes further" may well refer both to the property of "going beyond" and to the change in the order of the extremities after modification of one collection or object. The two preconservation modes of evaluation (prelogical and spatial) reinforce one another and constitute a major obstacle to the development of true quantification.

The attribution of quantitative properties of the whole to its parts seems to disappear fairly quickly, whereas use of the spatial evaluation modes remains frequent. Those subjects who make considerable progress go through a period of trying to base their answers on the area covered by the collections, their frontiers, and the number of units in each. In order to resolve the contradictions they appear to make use of a newly constructed notion, i.e., an empirical return to the initial states. The realization that partition and reconstitution may be coordinated finally leads to the concept of conservation of continuous quantities.

CONSERVATION OF LENGTH

The learning experiment on the conservation of length (Chapter 6) yielded a number of details regarding the characteristics that are specific to this concept as well as the relationships that link it to other conservations.

The training procedure consisted of various construction tasks: the children were asked to use matchsticks to make "roads" of the same length as model roads constructed with matchsticks of a different size. Only subjects who had already acquired the concept of numerical equivalence were chosen for training so as to study the possible transposition of this knowledge (or its reconstruction) to the concept of conservation of length.

Number and measurement are based on isomorphic operatory structures: measurement is constructed from a synthesis of displacement and additive partitioning and number from a similar synthesis between seriation and inclusion. However, the first measurement concept (length) is achieved rather later than that of number. The objective of the learning experiment was to study the reasons for this chronology and to discover possible developmental links between the necessary preliminary structures that precede the concepts of number and measurement, i.e., the conservation of "countables" and that of "measurables."

Study of the results of the children who had made the most progress during the training sessions and at the post-tests provided further evidence of something that had already struck us during the conservation of matter experiment, namely, that these new acquisitions are not the result of a simple generalization of previously acquired knowledge to a new context, but of a true reconstruction on a new level. This reconstruction is analogous to that resulting in a child's grasp of conservation of numerical equivalences, and it takes place in a manner parallel to the acquisition of conservation of matter, although it is completed slightly later.

The analogy lies in the fact that in the acquisition process of the notion of length the children become aware of conflicts, and solutions to these conflicts, that are similar to those already encountered in numerical problems. In both types of problems, reasoning based on one-to-one correspondence schemes clashes with inferences drawn from frontier effects. When the children understand that correspondence judgments need not contradict configurational features, they start to attempt to solve other problems in a similar way. Indeed, when subjects at this stage were asked to place matches end to end to form a road of the same length as a model, a whole range of attempts to coordinate the two different methods of length evaluation was observed. In fact, before they discover that they need more matches in their road because theirs are smaller than those in the model and that "going beyond" does not necessarily mean "being longer," the children often try out a number of compromise solutions, which are very instructive as regards the regulatory mechanisms involved.

It is clear that in this experiment, as in the preceding ones, what is important for progress in knowledge and what is transposed from the solution of one problem to another is a strategy-model. The training situations are designed to present the child simultaneously with several possible approaches to a particular problem which, at his cognitive level, are incompatible. The material itself is only of secondary importance, as is shown by the fact that those children who were not intrigued by the contradictory results of the two methods of length evaluation made little or no progress.

The developmental link between the concept of numerical conservation and that of length thus has to be sought in a transposition of conflicts and strategies. However, the delay in the acquisition of conservation of length still has to be explained. It may well be due to the fact that a one-dimensional quantity such as length requires a far more complex process of differentiation than that needed for the very global concept of quantity of matter. "Length" is in fact an abstract notion whose meaning derives from its insertion into a system of measurement. Before a child can understand true measurement, and even before he can have any idea of quantification when faced with problems of conservation of dimensions involving the displacement or segmentation of units, he must already have an intuitive idea of "measurability," which corresponds to "countability" in the case of discontinuous elements.

The changes in the children's reasoning that take place between this first approximation and a complete understanding of conservation of length reveal most clearly the persistence of the frontier effects or of the "going beyond" scheme. This may perhaps be accounted for by the fact that conservation of the length of an object that is moved or bent is possible only inside a stable spatial framework. In fact, interfigural comparisons have to be made with reference to a system of implicit coordinates (as has already been shown in earlier research; Piaget and Inhelder, 1948). By contrast, a problem of conservation of matter can be solved by intrafigural comparisons and by a reference to the material itself (annulment of the transformation or compensations between different dimensions) without having to consider characteristics of space, left empty or filled by the material.

A second explanation, complementary to the first, concerns the initial lack of differentiation between the physical and the spatial properties of displacements of objects. The recent research on causality (Piaget, 1971) has shown that the child cannot differentiate between the displacement and elongation of an object so long as he continues to think that movement results from its own force (in other words, movement has, as Aristotle hypothesized, an "internal" as well as an external motor). It is only when movement is conceived of as the result of an external force (from about nine or ten years) that displacement and elongation are clearly differentiated. It is true that in our training situations this dynamic physical aspect has been deliberately minimized. However, in the pre-tests, the argument "it's longer because you pushed it" (or sometimes "shorter because you've squashed it, twisted it," etc.) might best be explained by a lingering of the early lack of differentiation between an object and its movement. In a way similar to what occurs during the sensorimotor period, conservation of the dimensions of a displaced object requires coordination of the displacements in a coherent spatial system that enables a child to differentiate between the physical and spatial properties of dimensions. The successive stages through which children pass before finally acquiring the concept of conservation of length reveal how they gradually master the system of spatial references that enables them to integrate ordinal and topological relations as special cases into a Euclidian system.

CONNECTIONS BETWEEN LOGICAL INCLUSION AND THE CONSERVATION OF MATTER

In any study of learning within a developmental and operatory framework, one must, of necessity, not only analyze how a previously acquired "piece" of knowledge contributes to the formation of a new piece of knowledge, but also how learning in one area of knowledge can help with problems pertaining to a neighboring one. Such links between knowledge in adjoining areas will be called "horizontal" connections in contrast to the "oblique" connections between formation processes that are parallel but occur at different points in the child's development.

An obvious first approach to this problem was a comparative study of the way in which children acquire the concepts of logical inclusion of classes and conservation of matter. The latter is of a quasi-physical nature in that it involves what could be called an "empty" scheme (Piaget and Inhelder, 1941) because such a conservation concept, unlike that of weight, is not concerned with specific physical properties. This comparison bears, therefore, on the acquisition of a system of operations on classes and their embeddings and a system ensuring the quantification of continuous quantities. In the experiments, care was taken to make the tasks involving these two key concepts equally difficult.

In the first experiment, concerning only the acquisition of logical quantification, a new technique was used whereby nothing was added or taken away from the total class and where, with $A + A' = B$, the child was asked to make up a second collection containing as much B but more (or less) of A. The experiment revealed the existence of several substages in class inclusion operations and yielded some preliminary indications of the connections and differences between the two methods of quantification.

When very young children consider classes and numerical collections, they do not differentiate between these and certain spatial relationships of contiguity. Children between three and four, when faced with sorting tasks, constitute what have been called figural collections, i.e., they arrange the objects into spatial forms—a type of behavior that could also be due to a lack of dissociation between intension and extension (Piaget and Inhelder, 1959). Similarly, in numerical problems, children of this age judge numerosity by the length of the row of objects. It is interesting to note that children can only begin to understand logical inclusion if they already possess the concept of quotity, which precedes a true grasp of number, but allows the individualization and composition of elements.

The training sessions for inclusion, based on a process of correspondences between the units of the two collections, seem to help the children rapidly overcome their preoccupation with the spatial appearance of the collections, while, when it comes to understanding number conservations and, a fortiori, conservation of continuous quantities, these same spatial estimations appear much more tenacious.

The sessions were also designed to help the children master the relationships linking the subclasses both to each other and to the total class. As with conservation problems, a system of compensations is necessary, this time between intension and extension, since the greater the number of criteria characterizing a subclass, the smaller the number of elements which make up its cardinal and vice versa. Such reasoning, bearing on the classifying operations themselves, seems to belong to a higher level of development than the type of reasoning necessary to understand the compensations between dimensions in conservation problems. The acquisition of logical quantification may well open up the possibility for new constructs, since it necessitates reflective abstraction (which draws its information not from the objects themselves, but from the coordination of the actions that one carries out on the objects); its favorable effects on the acquisition of conservation concepts might be explained in this way. However that may be, children at a more elementary level already display one aspect of compensatory activity during training that is comparable with, and yet different from, what we have observed in the case of the conservations: to maintain the cardinal of a class B constant while at the same time increasing the number of the units in one of the subclasses, A, the child must eliminate the equivalent number of units from the subclass A'. These compensatory mechanisms reveal a functional identity, despite the structural differences, in the ways that children attempt to master the conflicts and so make progress during the training sessions.

Both the subjects who received training in conservation and those who received training in inclusion made noticeable progress, not only in the post-test problems covered by the training procedure, but also in the problems of the adjacent field. This provides further confirmation that the acquisitions were truly operatory and that, during training, the children's mode of reasoning had altered in an essential way. Moreover, it reveals the dynamic character of such operatory acquisitions since they opened the way to new elaborations in another field of knowledge, which, although related to the first, has been shown to result from a different developmental process. Finally, the learning experiment provided better theoretical insight into the differences and similarities between these two key concepts. The essence of conservation concepts lies in the understanding that a certain quantitative property remains unchanged under transformations, while the most important aspect of logical inclusion is the composition of cognate relationships between classes. In fact, as Piaget has shown (Piaget and Garcia, 1971), at the level of the formation of the concrete operations, every action has two aspects: it has a particular, material result, which constitutes its causal part, and it requires very general coordinations, which constitute its logical part. As Piaget remarks (Piaget and Garcia, 1971, p. 115): "It seems difficult to dispute that the lack of reversibility of the prelogical structures is due to the primacy of causal actions over deductive operations." It is only with the dissociation of the causal and temporal aspects from the logical aspect of actions that an awareness of what is common to many different, specific actions leads to the establishment of operations. Considered in this light, the numerous successes obtained in the no-help problems (i.e., those not approached during training) become more explicable. The training procedures may have favored the differentiation between the two aspects of the subjects' actions and so helped them dissociate the properties of the particular, causal action from the logical or deductive operation. It is also possible that this differentiation elicited by our exercises is responsible for the dissymmetry of the children's results in the post-tests involving the concept not covered in their procedure: children who had been given training in logical inclusion made more progress in conservation than those given the conservation procedure made in logical inclusion. If children at the preoperational level generally focus on the causal aspect of the action, it is probable that a training procedure accentuating the logical and synchronous aspect of the actions, as is the case in our inclusion exercises, acts both more directly and more efficiently on the development of the concepts of conservation than vice versa. Furthermore, as the additive composition of classes was specifically stressed in the inclusion exercises, these could provide the children with a very general quantifying scheme which clearly facilitated the development of the concept of conservation of quantity. In the acquisition of conservation concepts, with their implicit part-whole relations, the subject focuses on the invariant property which is the resultant of a system of operations, while in the case of class inclusion, his focus is on the operations themselves.*

THE DYNAMIC PROCESSES OF PROGRESS

Study of the developmental relationships and connections between the acquisition processes of conservation and class inclusion concepts highlights the dynamic role played by the progressive coordinations between the various subsystems during their construction. These coordinations may lead to temporary disequilibria, which provide the impetus for new constructions, or they can lead to stable equilibria

---

* Focus on the object and its transformations (which are not pertinent to the problem) makes it impossible to carry out operations.

through mutual consolidation. The disequilibria are experienced by a child as conflicts or contradictions. His efforts to resolve such conflicts lead to interactions between schemes, and it is these interactions that often result in the compromise solutions or partial compensations invented by children just before they become able to give fully compensatory operatory solutions.

The frequent occurrence of such behavior in the learning experiments reinforces the conception of a regulation-based model for the functional continuity that links one level of cognitive development to the next, whereas it is the structural analysis of the operations which defines the separation between stages. We have already suggested a way in which the role of regulatory mechanisms in the transitions to higher-level stages or substages could be further defined, by proposing that at a certain moment children become able to apply their method of solving conflicts encountered in one problem situation of a given level of complexity to another similar, but more complex situation. This view of the acquisition process can be made more explicit.

The appearance of a succession of different attempts at solving conflicts is particularly frequent wherever various types of schemes are aroused. Spatial problems, in particular, and infralogical problems, in general, provide good examples. When faced with geometric concepts in problems where, e.g., the subject has to judge whether two objects of equal length remain so after their constituent elements have been displaced and/or bent, he cannot simply have recourse to the number schemes which proved adequate for the problem of conservation of discontinuous quantities; sooner or later he will coordinate these with schemes relative to the properties of continuous space, e.g., the spatial correspondence schemes. Since these schemes are not identical epistemologically with numerical schemes, nor contemporary in development, their coordination creates difficulties before a full understanding of a spatial metric system can be acquired. The way the children overcome these difficulties enlightens us as to how and why progress occurs during the training sessions.

In the learning experiment on the conservation of length it was possible to distinguish four steps in the progressive interaction of the relevant schemes.

In the earliest phase, the children keep the two modes of reasoning (based on spatial ordinal correspondence and on numerical correspondence) completely apart. Clear examples of such separation between schemes occur in the situation (see Fig. 6.5) where two roads each made up of seven matches of equal length, onto each of which was glued a model house, were presented; in front of the child, one of the straight roads was made into a zigzag. With no hesitation, the child judges that the number of houses remains the same, basing his opinion on the continued validity of the original one-to-one correspondence; immediately afterward, he judges the roads of unequal length, either referring verbally, or pointing, to the ends of the roads, which are not immediately one above the other, thus reasoning according to ordinal (and topological) correspondence. A rapid succession of questions on length and number, which incites the more advanced children to question their exclusive use of one scheme, has no effect whatsoever on children in this phase. The same type of one-track reasoning occurs when these children are asked to build roads of the same length as a model. In the situation where the straight road has to be constructed directly underneath the zigzag (see Fig. 6.5), they make this road stop at the same point without thinking of counting the matches; when they have to build a road away from the model, they immediately count the matches, and the experimenter's suggestions of comparison of the two situations have no effect. Each of the schemes is in fact satisfactory, in the child's view, for the solution of one particular problem.

The second phase, characterized by the juxtaposition of the schemes, is by contrast marked by the child's apparent urge to understand the discrepancy of his solutions. The situation where the children were asked to build a road parallel to the model but using shorter matches provides an example. After using counting to construct a road away from the model, they reapply this strategy, and noticing that use of the same number of matches makes their road stop short of the end point of the model, they become perplexed; one child exclaims: "It can't be done!" Others make the parallel road finish at the same point as the model, whereupon they realize that there are no longer the same number of matches in the two roads. Once the children become aware of the discrepancy in solutions resulting from two different strategies, they begin to try to reconcile them; the efforts employed in this direction characterize the next learning stage.

Compromise solutions are the main feature of the third phase, the most surprising and the most interesting as regards the dynamics of progress. For example, children find different ways of reconciling the ordinal correspondence of the ends of the roads with the numerical correspondence of the matches (or pieces of match) used: sometimes they break a match in two (see Fig. 6.22) to get the right number without going beyond the end point of the model; or they add a match, but put it perpendicular to their road (see Fig. 6.23); or they add a small fragment of a match to make the number right without making the protrusion too noticeable (see Fig. 6.24).

This phase seems to mark the beginning of an adjustment between two modes of reasoning in an effort to obviate contradictions resulting from their juxtaposition. Such compromise solutions may be said to be halfway between the juxtaposition of schemes, characteristic of preoperatory reasoning, and operatory coordinations. In fact, in this phase, the number scheme is applied despite the differences in the lengths of the individual elements and length is still estimated according to the position of the end points of the roads, despite the fact that one is straight and the other zigzags. These solutions are therefore obtained through incomplete, or partial, compensation.

Regulatory mechanisms begin to govern the interactions between schemes, but their reciprocal accommodation and assimilation are achieved only during the fourth phase, characterized by a complete compensation. Now the children seem to grasp the necessity of a double compensation, on the one hand between the number and length of the matches, and on the other between the extent to which the straight road goes beyond the other and the extent of the latter's zigzags. Such fully compensatory judgments require a grasp of an operatory system of logical transitivity. In the situation where two straight roads are parallel and directly underneath one another, the correct number of smaller elements required to make up the same length as the bigger elements of the model road can be determined. This discovery can then be used in the situation where the two roads are separate from each other and in that where the model is a zigzag.

It is only when operations of compensation bear both on the individual elements and on the total length which they constitute that conservation of length is truly acquired.

The nature of the transition mechanisms involved in the learning of the concept of conservation of continuous quantities and, more specifically, of length, thus appears to be closely linked to the relevant infralogical schemes. Does the coordination of the logical schemes which leads to a grasp of the quantification of class inclusion involve similar regulatory mechanisms? Since logical coordinations derive uniquely from the subject's action they can be neither favored nor hindered by physical properties of the objects acted upon. It is therefore unlikely that the same types of conflict-solving behavior would appear in logical problems.

On the other hand, operations of compensation are fundamental both in logical and in geometrical or physics problems. In fact, in order to solve a problem of logical quantification such as, e.g., whether or not there are more members in class B than in class A (if $A + A' = B$ and $A' > 0$), one has to understand that the logical addition is always matched by the subtraction, i.e., $B - A' = A$. Similarly, to keep the cardinal of class B constant while varying the respective cardinals of A and A', one must understand the reciprocal compensation of the additive and subtractive variations introduced in the complementary subclasses.

In the different behavior patterns observed during the training procedure, a first level was noted, at which the children have no idea of the possible compensation between addition and subtraction and simply reproduce the model given, e.g., four apples and two peaches, judging that A cannot be increased without changing B—in fact they sometimes say: "You can't do it." Alternatively, they increase the number of A without diminishing that of A', thereby increasing the number of elements in class B.

A subsequent, higher-level, behavior pattern is particularly interesting. To obviate the problem, the child tries to compensate by emptying or canceling out the complementary class A' so that he makes up a collection (B) consisting only of A elements. In most cases, this is not true compensation. This is obvious because immediately afterward the child may assert successively: "Both dolls have just as many fruits to eat" and then "One's got six and the other eight." He is amazed when asked to count the fruits. We even encountered arguments such as "both dolls have got more fruit," with the explanation: "This one, because he's got more apples (A) and the other one because he's got more peaches (A')." Such answers reveal the dominance of additive schemes over subtractive schemes. The child compares the cardinal increase of the subclass A_1 in the class B_1 with the cardinal increase of the complementary class A'_2 instead of adding and subtracting within the same class B_2.

Some children displayed only one of the above reactions, whereas, with others, both were encountered in rapid succession. As regards their functional significance, these reactions appear comparable with the compromise solutions encountered during the training sessions concerned with infralogical operations. Furthermore, they are often followed by a correct answer revealing genuine compensation, which appears generalizable to other situations.

A final level is reached when the child is clearly capable of genuine compensations and understands perfectly that, in order to keep the cardinal of the total class constant, each time the number of members in one subclass is increased, he must reduce by the same amount the number of members in the complementary subclass and vice versa.

A common factor in the logical inclusion and conservation of continuous quantities situations appears to be that the explicit juxtaposition of two or several schemes leads to a conflict and then to an attempt to relate the schemes. When this occurred in experiments on infralogical problems, it was actually possible to observe how, through retroactive and "pro-active" corrections, the regulations modified the interaction of the schemes and so prepared the complete coordinations from which new structures are derived. In the case of logic, the regulations became apparent when the children realized the contradictions in the succession of different answers that they had been giving to the various questions. There seems to be a fundamental difference between these reactions to the two different types of problems, although both show the dynamic features of an imminent transition to operatory structurations. The difference is due to the fact that in logic it is the subject himself who introduces an organization; this organization concerns the hierarchical relationships of the classes, which may be modified at will, provided that this does not entail modification of the logical system itself. By contrast, the subject cannot introduce or exclude at will a property of an object (e.g., weight in a problem of density), nor modify the dimensions of objects displaced in a problem of spatial conservation. To solve problems where the schemes are enriched and modified by the properties of the object, the subject plans actions whose result does not necessarily match his prediction; in the case of logic, there must of necessity be identity, whence the absence of contradiction and compromise in the solutions of logical problems.

The existence, and even the frequency, of the compromises in physical problems and their absence in that of the logico-arithmetic operations (apart from the modifications of schemes in the handling of the classes and subclasses referred to above) must be regarded in the light of the fact that in logical problems the contradictions lead either to regression or to rapid progress, while in physical questions conflicts between the resistances of reality and the subject's schemes, or between various, but still isolated schemes, are far more tenacious.

The interpretation given of the acquisition processes as observed in the learning experiments thus converges with Piaget's equilibration model (Piaget, forthcoming). In Piaget's words: "The subject does not intentionally seek incoherence and so always aims at certain forms of equilibrium, without, however, attaining them except perhaps momentarily." The problem is therefore to determine which psychological mechanism is responsible for the progressive improvements in the successive forms of equilibrium, improvements, and perfections that Piaget refers to today as *équilibration majorante*— "heightening equilibrium." The source of the progress is to be sought in the disequilibrium which incites the subject to go beyond his present state in search of new solutions. But as this motive cannot in itself be sufficient to explain the construction of novelties, we must try to analyze the actual formation process, which is revealed in the attempts the child makes to find a new equilibrium and which progressively lead him to go beyond the former limits of his knowledge.

The training procedures, more perhaps than other psychogenetic methods, can give insight into the functioning of the regulatory mechanisms in the quest for a new equilibrium. The so-called compromise solutions or the incomplete compensations, their psychological equivalent in the logico-arithmetical field, provide a convincing demonstration of the subject's own activity in the construction of new forms of knowledge.

The mechanisms bringing about improvements and progress in the various forms of equilibrium consist, first, in an application of existing schemes to an increasing variety of situations. Sooner or later, this generalization encounters resistance, mainly from the simultaneous application of another scheme; this results in two different answers to one problem and stimulates the subject seeking a certain coherence to adjust both schemes or to limit each to a particular application, thereby establishing their differences and likenesses. The situations most likely to elicit progress are those where the subject is encouraged to compare modes of reasoning which vary considerably both in nature and complexity, but which all, individually, are already familiar to him. Training procedures in which one type of reasoning is artificially isolated and exercised, as is often the case in certain programmed learning projects, are not, in our opinion, very useful, since they eliminate the element we consider necessary for progress, i.e., the dynamics of the conflict between schemes. Such systems or partial systems can be coordinated to form a larger, coherent entity only when their limits have been clearly defined in situations where they clash. Inferential processes, leading to predictions and adjustments, become involved when the subject has to account for sequences of observable features in physical events (see Chapter 1). Not only are disturbances or imbalances mentally compensated for, but new constructs are established through regulatory mechanisms, which themselves undergo further development during the acquisition process.

LEARNING AND THE EPIGENETIC SYSTEM

Finally, the general results of the learning experiments should be considered from the point of view of how they fit into a maturationist framework, an empiricist framework, or an epigenetic framework (a system that characterizes growth as a whole with interaction between the influences of environment and heredity).

The fact that many subjects progressed as a result of the training procedures and that in most cases this progress resulted in stable acquisitions is in itself sufficient to show that progress cannot stem from maturation alone: if it is possible, through adequate exercises, to shorten the intervals which "normally" (according to standards established through statistical studies) separate the successive cognitive stages, then development cannot be explained in terms of a genetically pre-established program with no modification resulting from the environment. Quite on the contrary, insofar as it is possible to compare learning achieved as a result of training procedures with that occurring over a greater time span in everyday life, the results demonstrate the importance of the interactions between a subject's tendency to assimilate reality and the reality with which he is brought into contact, and the importance of the general stimulation of his mental processes when opportunities for action and reflection are numerous.

The contributions of the environment must be stressed, since there appears to be a revival of the nativist view of cognitive development and since the psychogenetic view, as opposed to an empiricist position, is often confused with that of the maturationist.

Although the vital role of environmental forces in the construction of operatory behavior is easily demonstrated, it is far more difficult to determine their nature and the modes of interaction between the subject's activity and the contributions, or resistance, presented by reality.

Since the learning experiments concerned quantitative concepts of an elementary level, at which logico-arithmetical and infralogical aspects are still scarcely differentiated, the important part played by an awareness of what the experimentation is about and of what conclusions to draw from observations cannot be demonstrated. A study of the acquisition of concepts in physics would highlight this point. In the studies discussed here the constructive role of interaction with reality appears in two different forms: an awakening of the child's curiosity about new situations and his feelings of conflict when the outcome of an experimental event does not correspond to his predictions.

The children's amazement is often expressed in their exclamations:

"Oh! how come?—I don't get it." They appear astonished and intrigued. This "surprise" element can be introduced into training procedures in more varied situations and in a more rapid succession than the child is likely to encounter in his usual occupations. It induces the need to take account of all aspects of a problem, and to question first impressions and outward appearances. However, as was also demonstrated by the learning studies, the "surprise" element has no effect if the child does not yet possess the cognitive equipment which enables him to fit the unforeseen phenomena into a deductive or inferential framework. This was particularly apparent in the experiment described in Chapter 1, devised to demonstrate the relationship between liquid levels and quantity. The only children appearing to benefit from this training were those already capable of the following type of reasoning: when all the liquid has run out of the top glasses into the bottom ones, there must be the same relationship between their levels as there was between those in the top ones because the glasses are identical (see Fig. 1.2).

Conflict is introduced into the procedures by confronting the subjects with the discrepancy between their predictions and the experimental outcome, or, as in logical or logico-mathematical problems, between subsystems of the child's own reasoning. A typical example is that of the child who, in the number and length experiment, thinks he can make his road the same length as the model simply by using the same number of matchsticks, ignoring the fact that his matches are not of the same length. In the particularly clear situation where parallel roads are laid out one directly above the other, he realizes that this solution is wrong, and why, but this does not help him solve the problem in the other situations, unless a certain competence in the coordination of schemes (comparing different ideas and their respective results) is already present.

Experience, particularly experience of discrepancies between one's predictions and ideas and the actual outcome of their realization, is therefore an important factor in the acquisition of knowledge, but not in any empiricist or positivist sense. No simple empirical abstraction took place during the training procedures but, instead, pseudo-empirical abstractions—i.e., observations bearing on the properties of the object of which the subject has become aware through his action.

The subjects do not accept the observable sequence of events as ready-made knowledge; they assimilate their observations into the framework of their competence. The type of progress produced by the training situations—and by analogy, the developmental processes on which it is based—is therefore just as far removed from purely maturational evolution as from a simple accumulation of acceptances of empirical data.

Moreover, no empirical theory which places all importance for progress in knowledge on external contributions can account for the fact that whatever the content of the different training procedures the learning pattern always passes through the same stages, and encounters the same obstacles, that were observed in the earlier cross-sectional studies. Even though nothing was done to induce what might be called an "unnatural" course of development, the considerable modifications in the acquisition speeds were clearly the result of the training situations, and the absence of deviations from the known course of development cannot be explained away by assuming that the experiments simply provided the opportunity of once again observing the acquisition processes as they occur without training. The conjunction of these two phenomena—modification of acquisition speeds because of training and absence of modification of the main course of development—brings to mind a parallel in embryogenesis: the internal regulatory mechanisms called "homeorhesis" (the regulatory process compensating for disturbances resulting from interaction with the environment) in the epigenetic development of the embryo.

Another observation that fits into an epigenetic conception is the following: in the majority of cases, the results of the training procedures are directly linked with the subjects' initial level, so that in the post-test the original hierarchical classification of the subjects is preserved, while the differences in degree of development are accentuated. The more advanced a child is, the more he will gain from the exercises and the information they contain.

This last observation seems to confirm the existence of construction processes analogous to those that Piaget has called "assimilation norms" (by analogy with the reaction norms of the genome). In intellectual development the existence of such "norms" implies that the likelihood of new assimilations increases as a function of the possible combinations between already-existing assimilatory schemes. And indeed, it appears that as more possibilities for action on environment are opened up, each external contribution is assimilated more rapidly into the increasingly extensive and coherent networks of schemes.

In most of the experiments some extreme cases were encountered. Some children made very little or no progress and, in contrast, others very rapidly acquired a truly operatory structure. If progress were basically the result of specific stimuli or the product of sociocultural training, then these very different results in a group of children whose schooling, environment, and age were relatively homogeneous would indeed be incomprehensible. The concept of biological competence* is consonant with both such lack of sensitivity and such hypersensitivity to external information. The stability of complete acquisitions, in contrast with the fragility of incomplete solutions, seems to point to the fact that this "competence" does not concern isolated responses, but a system of new possibilities; to the biological competence of organized cellular tissue corresponds the psychological competence of cognitive structure. The delayed progress achieved well after completion of training by children who during the actual sessions managed to give only semioperatory solutions contrasts with the regressions displayed by other subjects and indicates the existence of mechanisms inherent to the organizing processes of the subject's own activity. How could external factors possibly be responsible for it? It seems likely that regulatory mechanisms activated during the actual training are, after its completion, again set into motion whenever the subject encounters a problem analogous to those presented during the sessions.

Recourse to biological concepts, which Piaget has always considered essential for an interpretation of psychological phenomena, is all the more necessary in the case of the learning studies, which allowed more direct observation of the functional continuity between the different stages and substages.

Although the part played by social factors in the formation of op-

---

* According to Waddington, there are periods in embryogenesis when the cellular tissue becomes sensitive to specific inductors, to which it was previously insensitive.

eratory structures was not of primary concern in this research, an experiment on the role of some verbal acquisitions and a study of certain cultural variations in the formation of conservation concepts have been reported. The results show that formation of the elementary structures of thought underlying these concepts is autonomous* and depends only indirectly on the contributions of sociocultural transmission. The investigation into expressions frequently used in conservation problems (Chapter 4), e.g., those describing quantitative comparison, revealed that verbal training, even when successful (at least in its lexico-semantic dimension), does not ipso facto lead to an understanding of the concept of conservation of quantities. On the contrary, it appears that it is the formation of the thought operations that leads to the use of appropriate terms.

The terms learned through training have a direct link with the logical and infralogical concepts of quantification. No such link exists for numerous other linguistic structures, and the results of this experiment cannot be generalized to different acquisitions. The relationship between the acquisition of various logical operations and of linguistic competence is extremely intricate, and it is likely that both are made possible as a result of more general cognitive and social development. This general development favors growth in several fields, of which some, depending on the social context, may be privileged (Ferreiro, 1971, preface by Piaget; Ferreiro and Sinclair, 1971).

The study of the role of the cultural environment (Chapter 5) demonstrated a certain universality as regards the processes of operatory development. For example, although subjects in the two populations achieved length conservation at different ages, their development followed the same course; in the case of conservation of matter, a temporary difference from the developmental course observed in Geneva was noted with the unschooled Algerian population.

Investigation in this field is only in its infancy, and much more research is needed. However, it seems plausible to conclude that, leading to the elementary concepts of conservation, there are necessary paths (reminiscent of the creodes invoked by Waddington, to which, after deviations caused by specific environmental circum-

---

* Reason, once it is formed, itself determines what is true and what is false, but this does not mean that its formation is not dependent upon multiple factors.

stances, the embryogenesis is compelled to return by the regulatory mechanisms). Within certain limits, variations in rate and direction of development are possible, but crucial steps cannot be omitted. This appears to be true of the acquisition of fundamental concepts, based on the most general types of interaction between the subject and his environment. Obviously, as regards more specific interaction patterns, there are important differences between individual members of one society and between different societies. That such specific interaction patterns may result in variations in systems of thought is indisputable, but the latter should be kept clearly separate from the basic thought operations that were the object of our research.

In sum, cognitive progress, as observed in our learning research, cannot be interpreted according to a maturationist model or according to an empiricist theory. Since neither external factors nor purely internal factors are sufficient by themselves to explain the dynamics of acquisition of knowledge, and since there is no absolute beginning, only a model that reflects the continuity between the biological genesis and the development of the cognitive functions is appropriate. Such a model is provided by the concept of an epigenetic system where each new stage incorporates the preceding ones, and where the influence of environment becomes progressively more important. Even at the embryological level a *system* is involved since there are no isolated but only connected phenomena, deriving from processes of reciprocal induction. In cognitive ontogenesis, there occur analogous phenomena of progressive integration and lateral connections of reciprocal assimilations between subsystems of knowledge.

Regulatory mechanisms play an essential part both in cognitive development and in organic life, since they participate in two processes fundamental to all living activity, which also constitute the two poles of learning: the preservation of existing structures, on the one hand, and their modification or enrichment in response to the needs of adaptation, on the other. Stimulus-response theories are mainly concerned with modifications that result in acquisitions, and nativist theories emphasize the conservation of structures; but it is the epigenetic system that assures the synthesis of these two processes, since it combines transformation and conservation. This is true

271

at the level of organic life, and even more so at the level of behavior. It is no less erroneous to assume that cognitive learning consists in the activation of already-existing structures than to suppose that it consists in a substitution of new modes of reasoning for old. Learning is a constantly renewed process of synthesis between continuity and novelty.

Appendix
Bibliography
Index

Appendix

ELEMENTARY NUMBER CONSERVATION
(SMALL COLLECTIONS)

See Piaget and Szeminska, 1941.

1. METHOD*

Materials: 10 red counters;
    10 blue counters.

Task Description

First situation. The experimenter lays out one row of about seven blue counters and asks the child to put out the same number of red counters: "Put out as many of your red counters . . . exactly the same number as I've put blue ones . . . just as many, no more, no less."

The child's response is recorded in his protocol and then, if necessary, the experimenter pairs off the red and blue counters (one-to-one correspondence) and makes sure that the child appreciates the numerical equivalence of the two rows.

The experimenter then modifies the lay-out by spacing out the counters in one of the rows, or by moving them together, so that they form either a longer or a shorter row: "Are there as many . . . the

---

* From the descriptions in this appendix, the interviews might appear rather standardized. In fact, each is adapted to the particular subject, especially with regard to the latter's understanding of the terms used in quantification.

same number . . . of blue ones as red ones or aren't there? Or are there more? How do you know?"

Counter-Arguments

If the child has given a correct conservation answer, the experimenter draws his attention to the lay-out: "Look how long this line is, aren't there more counters?" If the child's answer was wrong, the experimenter reminds him of the initial equivalence: "But don't you remember, before, we put one red counter in front of each blue one, and someone else said that there are the same number of red and blue ones now; what do you think?" In addition, the experimenter asks him a quotity question: "Count the blue ones (the experimenter hides the red ones). How many red ones are there, can you guess without counting them? How do you know?"

Second situation. Having collected all the counters, the experimenter takes about seven red ones and arranges them in a circle on the table, before proceeding as for the first situation. Having paired off the counters as before, the experimenter either makes one of the circles smaller by pushing the counters closer together or takes the counters from one of the circles and puts them into a heap before asking the same questions as in the first situation.

2. RESPONSES

Nonconservation (up to Four to Five Years) *

When they are asked to put out red counters on the table in the two situations, some children may try to count how many blue ones there are, some may just put some counters down in a haphazard way, while others roughly estimate the number required or pair off the blue and red counters.

In both situations, the conservation questions are answered incorrectly: "There are more red ones because the blue ones are all squashed together," etc.

Only some of the children give a correct answer to the quotity questions.

---

* Ages mentioned indicate approximately the start of the corresponding stage, but these may vary with the cultural and educational setting of the subjects.

Intermediate

The children determine the right number of counters to put on the table by pairing off the blue and red counters (one-to-one correspondence).

The following responses are noted when the experimenter asks these children the conservation questions:

a. Some children give correct answers in only one of the situations.

b. Other children hesitate and/or keep changing their minds in both situations: "There are more blue ones . . . no, red ones . . . they're both the same . . ." etc.

Even when these children give correct answers, they cannot explain and justify them adequately.

They give correct answers to the quotity problem, e.g.: "There are seven red ones . . . so I should think there are seven blue ones as well."

Conservation (from Five Years)

These children give correct answers to all the questions, are not swayed by anything the experimenter says to try to make them change their minds and give one or several of the following arguments:

"There are just as many blue ones as red ones because it was right before and we haven't taken anything away, they've just been squashed up" ("identity" argument).

"We could put the others in a heap as well, or put one by the other so there aren't more blue ones or red ones" ("reversibility" argument).

"Here the red ones are in a long row, but there's space in between the counters, so that makes it the same" ("compensation" argument).

CONSERVATION OF LIQUIDS

See Piaget and Szeminska, 1941.

1. METHOD

Materials: two identical glasses, A and A′ (about 5 cm in diameter and 8 cm tall);

one narrower and taller glass, N (about 3 cm in diameter and 12 cm tall);

one wider, shorter glass, W (about 7 cm in diameter and 4 cm tall);

four identical little glasses each about a fourth the volume of A, P_1, P_2, P_3, P_4;

two bottles containing different colored water (e.g., one red and one green).

Presentation. The experimenter first gets the child to agree that A and A′ are the same in both height and diameter. He then takes one of the bottles and pours water ("juice") into A. He asks the child to take the other bottle and to pour the same amount into A′: "Pour exactly the same amount, no more, no less." When the child has poured the liquid, the experimenter asks: "If you drink this juice (A) and I (or your friend) that juice (A′), will we both have the same amount to drink?"

Task Description

First situation. All the water is poured from A′ into N. "Have we both got the same amount or has one of us got more than the other . . . or has one of us got a lot and the other only a little . . . who? If we drank it . . .?" The experimenter tries to get the child to give an explanation: "How do you know? . . . How did you guess? . . . Could you show me?"

Counter-Arguments

If the child has given a correct answer, the experimenter draws his attention to the different levels of the liquids in the two glasses: "But here (N), it's higher . . . don't you think that makes more to drink in this one?" or "Someone else told me that there's more here because it's taller (in N) than there (A) . . . Do you think he's right or wrong?"

If the child has given a wrong answer, the experimenter reminds him of the initial equal quantities—"Do you remember how we put juice in both glasses (A and A′)?"—or draws his attention to the dimension he appears to be ignoring: "But there (N) it's narrow, while the other one (A) is wider, so perhaps there's more juice in here (A)?"

The experimenter once again asks the child for explanations and reasons. Then he asks him: "Now, if I put the juice back into this glass (A′), will there be the same to drink as in the other one (A)?" If the child does not correctly solve this "empirical return" problem, the experimenter actually pours the juice back into A′, whereupon the child sees that the quantities in A′ and A are equal and the same questions are asked as during the presentation phase.

Second situation. The water is poured from A′ into W and the same procedure is followed as in situation 1, ending with the "empirical return" problem.

Third situation. The water is poured from A′ into P_1, P_2, P_3, and P_4 and the same procedure is followed as in situations 1 and 2, with the experimenter emphasizing that the child must compare the four little glasses with the one glass A′.

The experimenter's counter-arguments are based on the number and size of the little glasses.

N.B. The various operations are sometimes carried out by the experimenter and sometimes by the child.

2. RESPONSES

Nonconservation (*up to Five to Six Years*)

In each situation, one of the quantities is deemed greater than the other: e.g., "That makes more (in glass N) because it's higher." When the experimenter draws the child's attention to the other dimension (e.g., the thinness of N), the child either sticks to his original answer or else changes his mind and judges the other quantity more. Reminding him of the initial equal quantities has no effect on the child's answers.

At this level, the "empirical return" problem is only sometimes correctly solved.

Intermediate

Three different kinds of response are noted at this stage:

Sometimes, when faced with the same situation, a child will change his mind as to whether the quantities are the same or different:

"There's more to drink in this glass . . . no, more in the other one . . . no, there's the same in both . . ." etc.

Sometimes a child will answer correctly for one situation and wrongly for another; e.g., the liquid in the narrow glass, N, is thought to equal that in the original glass, A, but that contained in the sum of the four little glasses (P) is thought to be different.

Sometimes a child is influenced by what the experimenter says: e.g., when the experimenter reminds him of the initial equal quantities, the child may correct his wrong answer, but if his attention is drawn to the different shapes of the glasses, then he may change a right answer into a wrong one. At this level, even when they manage to give correct answers, the children generally give unclear and incomplete reasons for them. However, they can solve the "empirical return" problem correctly.

Conservation (from Seven Years)

In each situation, the quantities are judged equal. The child is capable of giving one or several of the following explanations:

"There's the same to drink because we didn't take away or add any juice" ("identity" argument).

"There's always the same to drink because if you put it back into the other glass, it would be the same" ("reversibility" argument).

"Here (glass N) it's high, but it's thinner (than glass A), so there's the same to drink" ("compensation" argument).

Furthermore, these children stick to their correct answers even when the experimenter tries to make them change their minds.

LIQUID POURING PROBLEMS

1. METHOD

Materials: two glasses of the same height, but different diameter, one wide (W), the other narrow (N); one bottle of colored water.

Task Description

The experimenter checks that the child notices the different diameters of the glasses. He then half fills W (roughly) from the bottle before asking the child to put about the same amount of liquid into N: "You put in this glass (N) as much, the same amount as near as you can, of juice as I have in mine (W)."

Counter-Arguments

If the child has poured liquid into N such that it reaches the same level as the liquid in W, the experimenter draws his attention to the difference in the diameters of the two glasses: "Look, this glass (N) is much narrower than the other, is there really the same to drink in each? . . . Isn't there more in one than in the other?" If the child does not then correctly pour more liquid into N to raise the level, the experimenter does it for him and then asks him which is correct: that the levels are the same or that there is a higher level in N.

If the child has poured liquid to a higher level in N, the experimenter draws his attention to the difference in the levels: "But you made it higher in this glass (N) so isn't there more to drink? Wouldn't it be better to pour it so there's the same level as in glass W . . . ?" If the child does not agree, the experimenter removes enough liquid from N to make the levels in the two glasses the same, and then asks the child which of the two solutions he thinks is the right one.

2. RESPONSES

Incorrect Solution (up to Five to Six Years)

The child pours juice into glass N up to the same level as that in glass W. Even when his attention is drawn to the different diameters of the two glasses, he still sticks to his incorrect solution. When the experimenter adds enough liquid to N to make the level clearly higher than that in W, to compensate for the difference in the diameters, the child judges there to be more in N than in W.

Intermediate Responses

Two types of more advanced solutions are given by these children:

Having made the level in N the same as that in W, the child correctly judges that there is more liquid in the latter, but refuses to pour more liquid into N, since he thinks that there would then be more liquid in N; such children seem to feel that the problem is insoluble with the glasses N and W and sometimes ask for two identical glasses.

Other children, perhaps at a slightly more advanced developmental level, pour juice into N so that they get a slightly higher level than in W, but are hesitant about judging the quantities equal.

Correct Solution (from Seven Years)

The child immediately pours liquid into glass N such that the level is clearly higher than that in W. He is capable of explaining his solution by relating the height of the liquid to the diameter of the glass (compensation) and he sticks to this correct answer whatever the experimenter says to try to make him change his mind.

CONSERVATION OF QUANTITY OF MATTER

See Piaget and Inhelder, 1941.

1. METHOD

Materials: two balls of modeling clay (diameter approximately 4 cm) of different colors.

Presentation. The experimenter asks the child to make sure that the two balls are made of the same amount of modeling clay. "You see these two balls. I want there to be the same amount of modeling clay in each . . . Let's pretend they are made of pastry. Make it so that if we each ate one of them, we would both have the same amount to eat. Make sure that there's exactly the same amount of pastry in each (no more, no less)."

Task Description

First situation. The experimenter (or the child) molds one of the balls into the shape of a sausage (about 12 cm long). "Now, is there the same amount to eat in the ball and in the sausage, or is there more in the ball or, perhaps, more in the sausage (more to eat . . .) . . . How do you know? . . . Show me."

Counter-Arguments

If the child has given a correct conservation answer, the experimenter draws his attention to one particular aspect: e.g., "Look at this (sausage), it's very long, don't you think there's more to eat here than there (ball)?" or "Someone else told me . . ."

If the child has given a nonconservation answer (e.g., "More to eat in the sausage) based on one aspect, e.g., length, the experimenter reminds him of the initial equal quantities: "How did we make the balls before?" Or he draws his attention to the other aspect (e.g., the thinness): "But there (sausage) it's thin and the ball is fat, don't you think there's more pastry here (ball) than there (sausage)?" He encourages the child to explain his ideas before asking him: "If I now make the sausage back into a ball, will there be the same to eat or not?" If the child does not answer this "empirical return" question correctly, the experimenter remolds the sausage into a ball, if necessary, adjusting the size of the two balls until the child judges that they are exactly the same.

Second situation. The experimenter (or the child) flattens one of the balls into the shape of a biscuit (diameter about 7 cm) and then conducts the interview as above, including the "empirical return" question.

Third situation. The experimenter (or the child) breaks up one of the balls into about nine small bits and then conducts the interview as above, including the "empirical return" question.

2. RESPONSES

Nonconservation (up to Five to Six Years)

Each time one of the balls is remodeled, the child judges one of the amounts greater: e.g., "It's got more (in the sausage) because it's long." When the experimenter draws his attention to another dimension (e.g., the thinness of the sausage), the child either sticks to his incorrect answer, or else changes his mind and says that the other quantity (the ball) is greater. Being reminded of their initial equal quantities has no effect on the child.

At this developmental level, the "empirical return" problem is only sometimes correctly solved.

Intermediate

Three different main types of intermediate responses occur:

Faced with the same situation, the children change their minds as to whether the two quantities are equal: "There's more in the sausage . . . no, more in the ball . . . no, there's the same to eat in them both . . ." etc.

Sometimes the children answer correctly in the case of, for instance, the biscuit, but wrongly in that of the nine small bits.

Sometimes the children are influenced by what the experimenter says and, for instance, answer correctly when the latter reminds them of the equality of the initial quantities, or else change their minds after giving a correct answer, when, for instance, the latter stresses the difference in the shapes.

At this level, even when they manage to give correct answers, the children generally give unclear and incomplete reasons for them. However, they can solve the "empirical return" problem correctly.

Conservation (from about Seven Years)

In each situation, the quantities are judged equal. The child is capable of giving one or several of the following explanations:

"There's the same to eat, because we didn't take anything away or add anything" ("identity" argument).

"There's still the same, because if we made it back into a ball, it would be the same as before" ("reversibility" argument).

Here (biscuit) it's big, but it's thinner (than the ball), so there's the same to eat" ("compensation" argument).

Furthermore, these children stick to their correct answers even when the experimenter tries to make them change their minds.

CONSERVATION OF WEIGHT

See Piaget and Inhelder, 1941.

1. METHOD

Materials: two balls of modeling clay (diameter approximately 4 cm) of different colors;
scales with two pans.

Presentation. First of all, the experimenter checks that the child understands how to use the scales; then the child is asked to use them to help make the two balls of modeling clay weigh the same: "Here are two balls of modeling clay. I would like to have two balls weighing exactly the same . . . How are you going to get them to have the same weight?"

Task Description

First situation. One of the balls is squashed and pulled into the shape of a sausage (about 12 cm long) and the experimenter goes to put the ball in one pan and the sausage in the other (but does not actually do so): "Do you think that the sausage weighs the same as the ball, or does it weigh more, or perhaps less than the ball? How do you know? Can you tell me why?"

Counter-Arguments

If the child has given a correct conservation answer, the experimenter draws his attention to one of the dimensions: "Look, the sausage is very thin, don't you think it weighs less than the ball?" or "Someone else told me . . ."

If the child has answered incorrectly, the experimenter reminds him that the two balls initially weighed the same on the scales and draws his attention to the dimension he is ignoring. For example, if the child says that the sausage weighs more, the experimenter might say: "But the sausage is thin, and the ball is very fat, don't you think that the ball weighs more?" The experimenter then repeats the questions used in the presentation concerning the weight of the two balls.

He then asks the child: "If I now make the sausage back into a ball, will the two balls weigh the same?" If the child does not correctly answer this "empirical return" question, the experimenter remolds the sausage in the shape of a ball and then places the two balls on the scales to check their weights.

Second situation. One of the balls is flattened into the shape of a biscuit (diameter about 7 cm) and the experimenter conducts the interview as above, finishing with the "empirical return" question.

Third situation. One of the balls is broken up into about nine bits and the experimenter conducts the interview as above.

The experimenter's arguments concern the number and arrangement of the bits of modeling clay on the scales. For example, if the child says that the ball weighs more, the experimenter might say: "But look, there are lots of bits all over the pan, don't they weigh more than the ball?"

N.B. In all three situations, it is either the experimenter or the child himself who changes the shape of the ball.

2. RESPONSES

Nonconservation (up to Six or Seven Years)

Each time one of the balls is remodeled, the child judges one of the weights heavier than the other: e.g., "The sausage weighs more because it's long." When the experimenter draws his attention to the dimension he appears to be ignoring (e.g., the thinness of the sausage), the child either sticks to his wrong answer or else changes his mind and says that the ball is heavier. Even reminding him that the balls initially weighed the same makes no difference. At this developmental level, the "empirical return" problem is only sometimes correctly solved.

Intermediate

Three different kinds of intermediate response were noted:

Sometimes, when faced with the same situation, a child changes his mind as to whether the two shapes weigh the same: "The sausage weighs more . . . no, it's the ball that weighs more . . . no, they both weigh the same . . ." etc.

Sometimes a child answers correctly for one situation and wrongly for another: e.g., the biscuit and the ball weigh the same, but the bits and the ball do not.

Sometimes a child is influenced by what the experimenter says. For instance, when the experimenter reminds him of the initial equal weights, a child might give the right answer, but if his attention is drawn to the difference in the shapes, he might change his right answer to a wrong one.

At this level, even when they manage to give correct answers, the children generally give unclear and incomplete reasons for them. However, they can solve the "empirical return" problem correctly.

Conservation (from about Eight Years)

In each situation, the weights are judged equal. The child is capable of giving one or several of the following explanations:

"They're the same weight because we didn't take anything away or add anything" ("identity" argument).

"They weigh the same because if we made it (e.g., the sausage) back into a ball, they would be the same" ("reversibility" argument).

"Here (biscuit) it's big, but it's thinner (than the ball) so that makes the same weight" ("compensation" argument).

Furthermore, these children stick to their correct answers even when the experimenter tries to make them change their minds.

CONSERVATION OF LENGTH

See Piaget, Inhelder, and Szeminska, 1948.

1. METHOD (VARIATION OF THE ORIGINAL METHOD)

Materials: two flexible wires (e.g., electrical cables) of different lengths (approximately 15 and 10 cm), the longer one designated A, the shorter one, B.

Presentation. "Let us pretend that these two wires are roads. Now, on this road (A) is there just as far to walk as on this one (B) or is there perhaps farther to walk here (A) or there (B) . . . ?" "This road (A), is it the same length as that one (B), or longer, or not so long as this one (B)?"

The child thus notices the inequality and correctly judges A to be longer than B.

Task Description

First situation. The experimenter bends A so that its ends coincide with those of B: "And now, is there as far to walk on this road A as on this road B? . . . If two ants are walking, one on this road (A)

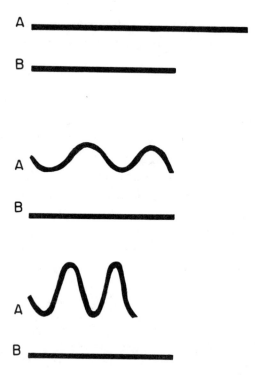

and the other on this road (B), would they both walk just as far?
. . . Would they both be just as tired or would one be more tired
than the other? . . . How do you know? . . . Show me how you can
find out . . ." etc.

Counter-Arguments

If the child has given a correct answer, the experimenter stresses
the fact that the end points of A and B coincide: "But look where
this road (A) stops, right where the other one does (B); perhaps
they're the same length, don't you think so? Tell me why you think
so."

If a child has answered incorrectly, the experimenter reminds him
of how A and B looked initially when they were both laid out
straight. "When this wire (A) was straight, how was it? Were they
both the same length, at the beginning?" Finally, the experimenter
draws his attention to the detours of A by running his finger along

them: "Look what this one's like (A) and that one (B) is quite straight."

The experimenter then straightens A as it had been originally.

Second situation. The experimenter twists A such that when the two wires are laid out one below the other A stops short of B.

The interview is conducted as for the first situation.

2. RESPONSES

Nonconservation (*below Six to Seven Years*)

These children give wrong answers to the conservation questions in both situations. In the first, they judge the two wires of equal length and in the second they think that A is shorter than B because it "doesn't go as far." Reminding them of the longer length of A, which they had observed in the presentation, does not lead them to change their answers.

Intermediate

Children at a first intermediate level give the correct answer in the first situation but not in the second. At a slightly higher level, children can give some correct answers in the second situation, but they are not convinced and cannot give a full explanation for any correct answers.

Conservation (*from Eight Years*)

These children give correct answers in both situations and give one or more of the following reasons:

"It's as far to walk, you've just bent the wire" ("identity" argument).

"If you put this road straight like it was before, it's longer than the other one, so now, even if it stops where the other one stops, it's longer" ("reversibility" argument).

"It's this wire (A) which is longer, it stops before the other one, but it's got bumps and zigzags" ("compensation" argument).

Furthermore, these children stick to their correct answers even when the experimenter tries to make them change their minds.

DIFFERENT CRITERIA SORTING TASK
(DICHOTOMY)

See Piaget and Inhelder, 1959.

1. METHOD

Materials: geometrical shapes cut out in cardboard:

five or six little round disks (diameter 25 mm), red ones
and blue ones;

five or six large round disks (diameter 50 mm), red ones
and blue ones;

five or six small squares (25 mm sides), red ones and
blue ones;

five or six large squares (50 mm sides), red ones and
blue ones;

two flat boxes.

Presentation. The experimenter puts all the shapes in a heap on
the table and asks the child to describe them: "Tell me what's there."

Task Description

Situation 1. Spontaneous sorting: "Can you put in a pile all the
ones that go together? . . . Put those that are very like each other
together."

When the child has finished, the experimenter asks him: "Why
did you put them like that?"

Situation 2a. Dichotomy: "Now could you put them all in just
two piles ('families') and put them into these two boxes?"

When the child has finished, the experimenter asks him: "Why
did you put all these together? And all those? What could you call
this pile? And that one?"

Situation 2b. First change of criterion: "Could you arrange them
any other way in two piles?" If the child has repeated his first solution, the experimenter says: "You've already done it like that. Can
you find a different way of putting them together in two piles?" If
necessary, the experimenter himself starts a new method of sorting
and asks the child to continue. The interview continues as for 2a.

Situation 2c. Second change of criterion: "Can you find yet another way of putting them in two piles? . . . Can you arrange them in a different way?" The interview continues as for 2a and 2b. Finally, the child is asked to recapitulate the first two ways of arranging the shapes: "The first time, how did you divide them? . . . And then?"

2. RESPONSES

Figural Collections (from Four to Five Years)

Some children put some roughly similar shapes together, but keep changing the criterion and do not use all the shapes.

Others arrange the shapes in a complicated way, explaining that the result represents, e.g., a train or a house.

First Attempts at Sorting (from Five to Six Years)

The children manage to make up small collections according to various criteria, but cannot link these small collections, e.g., "This is the pile of big red squares, this is the pile of little red circles and this is the pile of big red circles . . ." etc. The most advanced children at this level can, if helped, regroup the little collections into general classes, but cannot determine the main criteria before the collections have actually been established.

Sorting According to Several Criteria (from Six to Seven Years)

First of all, the children can announce the criteria, carry out the necessary action, and describe afterward two ways of dividing the shapes into two general classes. The third way has to be suggested by the experimenter. Subsequently, they spontaneously make use of all three criteria.

QUANTIFICATION OF CLASS INCLUSION (FLOWERS)

See Piaget and Inhelder, 1959.

1. METHOD

Materials: a bunch of ten yellow daisies and two or three red roses (artificial flowers).

Presentation. The experimenter asks the child to name the flowers and makes sure that he knows the generic term "flowers": "Are the daisies flowers? . . . Are the roses flowers? . . . Do you know the names of some other flowers? . . . Which ones?"

Task Description

Question 1. "Are there more daisies or more flowers in this bunch?" After the child's answer: "How do you know? . . . More . . . than what?" If the child answers, "More than roses," he is asked to repeat the question and if this is done incorrectly, the experimenter repeats it.

Question 2. "There are two little girls who would like to make up bunches. One of them makes up a bunch with the daisies. Then she gives the daisies back to me. The other little girl makes up her bunch with the flowers. Which bunch will be bigger?"

Question 3a. "If I give you the daisies, what will I have left in the bunch?"

Question 3b. "If I give you the flowers, what will I have left in the bunch?"

Question 4. "I'm going to make up a bunch with all the daisies, and you're going to make a bunch with all the flowers. Who will have the bigger bunch? . . . How do you know?"

2. RESPONSES

No Grasp of Inclusive Quantification (up to Five to Six Years)

The child is incapable of comparing the cardinality of a subclass to that of a more general class in which it is included; he systematically compares the two subclasses and so answers that there are more daisies than flowers; when he is asked, "More daisies than what?" he generally replies: "More daisies than roses." At this level, the child sometimes gives incorrect answers to questions 3a and 3b.

Intermediate Responses

There is no distinct intermediate category in this experiment. All that is observed is that some children hesitate when faced with the question "Are there more daisies or more flowers?" and answer, "It's the same thing," justifying this reply by the argument: "Daisies are flowers as well."

Grasp of Inclusive Quantification (from Seven to Eight Years)

These children give correct answers to all the questions, although some still hesitate and seem surprised by the first one.

INTERSECTION

See Piaget and Inhelder, 1959.

1. METHOD

Materials: three sorts of counters: five blue round ones, five red round ones, and five red square ones;

one sheet of paper on which two circles, one black and one yellow, are drawn; these circles intersect so that there is an area common to both original circles— hence three areas in all.

Presentation. The experimenter lays out the counters in the circles as follows: the round blue counters and the square red counters in the two outside bits and the round red counters in the intersection.

He asks the child to describe the counters and then says: "Why do you think I've put those (red round ones) in the middle?"

Task Description

The experimenter asks the following questions:

1. "Are there more blue counters or more red counters?"
2. "Are there more square counters or more round counters?"
3. "Are there as many, or more, or fewer round counters than red counters (intersection question)?"
4. "Are there as many, or more, or fewer square counters than red counters (inclusion question)?"

When the child has answered each question, the experimenter says: "How do you know? Can you show me?"

Supplementary questions, which the experimenter asks children who answer the above questions incorrectly, bear on the contents of the circles and their intersection: "What's in the black circle?" "Show me." "And in the yellow one?" etc.

2. RESPONSES

From four to five years, the questions bearing on the disjunct classes are correctly answered. By contrast, the questions on inclusion and intersection are not understood. Up to about six years, in fact, the supplementary questions reveal misunderstandings, e.g.: "What is there in the black circle?" Reply: "Red squares." Generally, the contents of the intersection are ignored.

From about six years of age, children generally give correct answers to the supplementary questions, but when it comes to those involving intersection and inclusion, they hesitate, change their minds, and only occasionally give a few correct answers.

From seven to eight years, all the questions are correctly answered straightaway.

SERIATION

See Piaget and Szeminska, 1941.

1. METHOD (VARIATION OF THE ORIGINAL METHOD)

Materials: ten little sticks ranging from 16 to 10.6 cm in length, each differing in length from the next by 0.6 cm.; a screen.

Presentation. The child is given the ten little sticks in a pile.

Task Description

a. *Seriation without a screen.* "You're going to make a pretty staircase with all these sticks by putting them in order, each one beside the next." The experimenter can, if necessary, demonstrate what he wants by arranging three sticks in the right order, or by putting down the smallest stick and asking the child to continue the series in ascending order. The experimenter notes how the child selects each little stick, the order in which he arranges them, and the shape of his "staircase." If necessary, he gives the child encouragement to finish his series or to correct a mistake.

b. *Seriation behind a screen.* If the child has successfully completed situation a, he is told to sit behind a screen and is given the pile of sticks. The experimenter tells him: "This time, I'm going to make the staircase; give me the sticks one by one . . . in the right order for me to make the staircase."

The experimenter notes how the child selects the sticks and the order in which he hands them to him.

2. RESPONSES

No Ordering (from Three to Four Years)

At a first level, the child does not understand the instruction; he arranges a few sticks more or less parallel to each other, horizontally or vertically, in no particular order .

Little Series and Groups of Sticks

a. The child puts the sticks in twos (one big and one small) or threes (e.g., one big, one medium, and one small stick). These groups are placed side by side with no link between them.

b. The child manages to make a more or less correct ascending line as regards the tops of the sticks, but he does not worry about their bases.

c. One of the more advanced responses is to make a complete series of four or five sticks without being able to fit in the remaining ones.

Success through Trial and Error (around Six Years)

By trial and error, the child manages to make up a correct seriation. However, at this level he cannot give the experimenter the sticks in the right order when he is behind the screen.

Correct Seriation (from Six to Seven Years)

The child uses a systematic method, first of all looking for the smallest (or biggest) stick, then the smallest (or biggest) of those remaining, and then putting them all upright or laying them all on a common base, which enables him to place them in the right order, without trial and error, in both situations.

Bibliography

(Presses Universitaires de France is abbreviated P.U.F.)

Apostel, L. 1959. Logique et apprentissage. In *Logique, apprentissage et probabilité* (vol. 8 of "Etudes d'épistémologie génétique") by L. Apostel, A. R. Jonckheere, and B. Matalon, pp. 1–138. Paris, P.U.F.

Apostel, L., and B. Mandelbrot. 1957. Logique et langage considérés du point de vue de la précorrection des erreurs. In *Logique, langage et théories de l'information* (vol. 3 of "Etudes d'épistémologie génétique") by L. Apostel, B. Mandelbrot, and A. Morf, pp. 79–172. Paris, P.U.F.

Apostel, L., W. Mays, A. Morf, and J. Piaget. 1957. *Les Liaisons analytiques et synthétiques dans les comportements du sujet* (vol. 4 of "Etudes d'épistémologie génétique"), pp. 1–138. Paris, P.U.F.

Bovet, M. 1967. Etudes interculturelles du développement intellectual et processus d'apprentissage. *R. suisse psychol. pure appl.*, 27, 3/4, 189–200.

———. 1971. Etude interculturelle des processus de raisonnement. Unpubl. diss., University of Geneva.

Braine, M. D. 1959. The ontogeny of certain logical operations. Piaget's formulation examined by non-verbal methods. *Psychol. monogr.*, 73, no. 5.

———. 1964. Development of a grasp of transitivity of length: a reply to Smedslund. *Child develop.*, 35, 799–810.

Bruner, J. S. 1964. The process of education. Cambridge, Mass., Harvard University Press.

———. 1964. The course of cognitive development. *Amer. psychol. 19*, 1, 1–15.

Bruner, J., R. R. Olver, and P. M. Greenfield. 1966. *Studies in cognitive growth*. New York, John Wiley.

Dasen, P. 1972. The development of conservation in Aboriginal children: a replication study. *J. int. psychol.*, 7, 75–85.

———. 1973. The influence of ecology, culture and European contact on cognitive development in Australian Aborigines. In *Culture and cognition: readings in cross-cultural psychology*, J. W. Berry and P. Dasen. London, Methuen.

297

De Lemos, M. M. 1966. The development of the concept of conservation in Australian Aboriginal children. Unpubl. diss., Australian National University, Canberra.

———. 1969. The development of conservation in aboriginal children. *Int. J. psychol.*, 4, 255–269.

Dobzhansky, T. 1937. *Genetics and the origin of species*. New York, Columbia University Press.

Donaldson, M., and R. Wales. 1970. On the acquisition of some relational terms. In J. Hayes, *Cognition and the development of language*. New York, John Wiley.

Ferreiro, E. 1971. *Les Relations temporelles dans le langage de l'enfant*. Geneva, Droz.

Ferreiro, E., and H. Sinclair. 1971. Temporal relationships in language. *Int. J. psychol.*, 6, 1, 39–47.

Galperine, P. J., and D. B. Elkonin. L'Analyse de la théorie de J. Piaget sur le développement de la pensée enfantine. Preface to the Russian translation of *The developmental psychology of Jean Piaget* by J. H. Flavell.

Goodnow, J. J. 1962. A test for milieu effects with some of Piaget's tasks. *Psychol. monogr. gen. appl.*, 76, 36.

Goustard, M., P. Gréco, B. Matalon, and J. Piaget. 1959. *La Logique des apprentissages* (vol. 10 of "Etudes épistémologie génétique"), Paris, P.U.F.

Gréco, P. 1959. L'Apprentissage dans une situation à structure aléatoire concrete: les inversions successives de l'ordre linéaire par des rotations de 180°. In *Apprentissage et connaissance* (vol. 7 of "Etudes d'épistémologie génétique") by P. Greco and J. Piaget. Paris, P.U.F.

———. 1962. Quantité et quotité. In *Structures numériques élémentaires* (vol. 13 of "Etudes d'épistémologie génétique") by P. Greco and A. Morf. Paris, P.U.F.

Greenfield, P. H. 1966. On culture and conservation. In *Studies in cognitive growth*, by J. S. Bruner, R. R. Olver, and P. M. Greenfield. New York, Wiley.

Grize, J.–B. 1963. Des groupements à l'algébre de Boole: essai de filiation des structures logiques. In *La Filiation des structures* (vol. 15 of "Etudes d'épistémologie génétique"), by L. Apostel, J.–B. Grize, S. Papert, and J. Piaget, pp. 25–63. Paris, P.U.F.

Inhelder, B. 1943. *Le Diagnostic du raisonnement chez les débiles mentaux*. Neufchâtel and Paris, Delachaux & Niestlé (2nd enlarged edition, 1963).

———. 1958. *The growth of logical thinking from childhood to adolescence. An essay on the construction of formal operational structures*. Trans. Anne Parsons et Stanley Milgram. New York, Basic Books, XXVI, 356 pp.; London, Routledge & Kegan Paul, 1958, XXVI, 356 pp.

———. 1966. Développement, régulations et apprentissage. In *Psychologie et épistémologie génétique: themes piagétiens*, pp. 177–188. Paris, Dunod.

———. 1968. Apprentissage et développement chez l'enfant. *Accademia nazionale dei lincei*, 365, 109, 283–291.

———. 1968. The diagnosis of reasoning in the mentally retarded. Trans. Will Beth Stephens et al. New York, John Day, p. 367.

Inhelder, B. 1972. Information processing tendencies in recent experiments in cognitive learning: empirical studies. In *Information processing in children*, ed. S. Farnham-Diggory, pp. 103–114. New York and London, Academic Press.

Inhelder, B., M. Bovet, and H. Sinclair. 1967. Développement et apprentissage. *R. suisse psychol. pure appl.*, 26, 1, 1–23.

Inhelder, B., and J. Piaget. 1955. *De la logique de l'enfant à la logique de l'adolescent*. Paris, P.U.F.

———. 1963. De l'itération des actions à la récurrence élémentaire. In *La Formation des raisonnements récurrentiels* (vol. 17 of "Etudes d'épistémologie génétique," pp. 47–120) by P. Gréco, B. Inhelder, B. Matalon, and J. Piaget. Paris, P.U.F.

Inhelder, B., and H. Sinclair. 1969. Learning cognitive structures. In *Trends and issues in developmental psychology*, ed. P. H. Mussen, J. Langer, and M. Covington, pp. 2–21. New York, Holt, Rinehart, and Winston.

Jonckheere, A., B. Mandelbrot, and J. Piaget. 1958. *La Lecture de l'expérience*. Vol. 5 of "Etudes d'ép stémologie génétique." Paris, P.U.F.

Kohnstamm, G. A. 1967. *Teaching children to solve a Piagetian problem of class inclusion*. The Hague, Mouton.

Lasry, J. C. 1965. Apprentissage empirico-didactique de la notion d'inclusion. Unpubl. diss., University of Montreal.

Le Ny, J. F. 1967. *Apprentissage et activités psychologiques*. Paris, P.U.F.

Matalon, B. 1959. Apprentissage en situations aléatoires et systématiques. In *La Logique des apprentissages* (vol. 10 of "Etudes d'épistémologie génétique"), by M. Goustard, P. Gréco, B. Matalon, and J. Piaget. Paris, P.U.F.

Mehler, J., T. G. Bever. 1967. Cognitive capacity of very young children, in *Science*, No. 3797, 158, pp. 141–142.

Morf, A. 1959. Apprentissage d'une structure logique concrète (inclusion): effets et limites. In *L'Apprentissage des structures logiques* (vol. 9 of "Etudes d'épistémologie génétique," pp. 15–83) by A. Morf, J. Smedslund, VinhBang, and J. F. Wohlwill. Paris, P.U.F.

Morf, A., J. Smedslund, Vinh Bang, and J. F. Wohlwill. 1959. *L'Apprentissage des structures logiques* (vol. 9 of "Etudes d'épistémologie génétique"). Paris, P.U.F.

Mosheni, N. 1966. La Comparaison des réactions aux épreuves d'intelligence en Iran et en Europe. Unpubl. diss., Paris, University of Paris.

Pascual-Leone, J., and M. Bovet. 1966. L'Apprentissage de la quantification de l'inclusion et la théorie opératoire. *Acta psychol.*, 25, 334–356.

———. 1967. L'Apprentissage de la quantification de l'inclusion et la théorie opératoire. Partie II: quelques résultats expérimentaux nouveaux. *Acta psychol.*, 26, 64–76.

Peluffo, N. 1962. Les Notions de conservation et de causalité chez les enfants provenant de différents milieux physiques et socioculturels. *Arch. psychol.*, 38, 151, 275–291.

Piaget, J. 1926. *La Représentation du monde chez l'enfant*. Paris, Alcan.

———. 1927. *La Causalité chez l'enfant*. Paris, Alcan.

Piaget, J. 1929. *The child's conception of the world.* Trans. Joan and Andrew Tomlinson. London, Kegan Paul, 1929; reprinted 1951, New York, Harcourt, 1929; reprinted 1951, 1960, 1964, 1967. Paperbound ed.: Patterson, Adams, 1960; reprinted 1963, 1965, 1967, 1969, 1972.

——. 1930. *The child's conception of physical causality.* Trans. Marjorie Gabain. London, Kegan Paul, 1930; reprinted 1951, 1966, 1970. New York, Harcourt, 1930, VIII, 309 pp.; reprinted 1960, 1965, 1966, 1969, 1972.

——. 1936. *La Naissance de l'intelligence chez l'enfant.* Neufchâtel and Paris, Delachaux & Niestlé.

——. 1937. *La Construction du réel chez l'enfant.* Neufchâtel and Paris, Delachaux & Niestlé.

——. 1949. *Traité de logique. Essai de logistique opératoire.* Paris, Colin. (New edition: *Essai de logique opératoire.* 2nd ed. of *Traité de logique. Essai de logistique operatoire,* ed. J. S. Grize, with an introduction by the author. Paris, Dunod, 1972).

——. 1950. *Introduction a l'épistémologie génétique:* vol. I, *La Pensée mathématique.* Paris, P.U.F.

——. 1952. *The origins of intelligence in children.* Trans. Margaret Cook. New York, International Universities Press, 1952; reprinted 1956, 1965, 1966, 1969.

——. 1953. *The origin of intelligence in the child.* London, Routledge & Kegan; reprinted 1966, 1970.

——. 1954. *The construction of reality in the child.* Trans. Margaret Cook. New York, Basic Books, 1954.

——. 1955. *The child's construction of reality.* London, Routledge & Kegan Paul; reprinted 1968 under the title: *The construction of reality in the child.*

——. 1958. Assimilation et connaissance. In *La Lecture de l'expérience* (vol. 5 of "Etudes d'épistémologie génétique") by J. Jonckheere, B. Mandelbrot, and J. Piaget. Paris, P.U.F.

——. 1959a. Apprentissage et connaissance (part one). In *Apprentissage et connaissance* (vol. 7 of "Etudes d'épistémologie génétique") by P. Gréco and J. Piaget, pp. 21–67. Paris, P.U.F.

——. 1959b. Apprentissage et connaissance (part two). In *La Logique des apprentissages* (vol. 10 of "Etudes d'épistémologie génétique") by M. Goustard, P. Gréco, B. Matalon, and J. Piaget, pp. 159–188. Paris, P.U.F.

——. 1959c. Introduction. In *Apprentissage et connaissance* (vol. 7 of "Etudes d'épistémologie génétique") by P. Gréco and J. Piaget, pp. 1–20. Paris, P.U.F.

——. 1961. *Les mécanismes perceptifs.* Paris, P.U.F.

——. 1963. Les Images mentales. In *Traité de psychologie expérimentale* by P. Fraisse and J. Piaget, vol. 7, pp. 71–116. Paris, P.U.F.

——. 1965. *Etudes sociologiques.* Geneva, Droz.

——. 1966. *L'Image mentale chez l'enfant.* Paris, P.U.F.

——. 1967. *Biologie et connaissance.* Paris, Gallimard.

Piaget, J. 1968a. Preface. In *Les Premières notions spatiales de l'enfant*, by Monique Laurendeau and Adrien Pinard. Neufchâtel and Paris, Delachaux & Niestlé.

———. 1968b. Quantification, conservation, and nativism. *Science*, 162, 976–979.

———. 1969. *The mechanisms of perceptions*. Trans. Gavin Nott Seagrim. London, Routledge & Kegan Paul.

———. 1970. *L'Epistémologie génétique*. Paris, P.U.F.

———. 1971a. Causalité et opérations. In *Les Explications causales* (vol. 26 of "Etudes d'épistémologie génétique") by J. Piaget with the collaboration of R. Garcia, pp. 11–140. Paris, P.U.F.

———. 1971b. Preface. In *Les Relations temporelles dans le langage de l'enfant*, by E. Ferreiro. Geneva, Droz.

———. 1971c. *Biology and knowledge. An essay on the relations between organic regulations and cognitive processes*. Trans. Beatrix Walsh. Chicago, Ill., University of Chicago Press; Edinburgh, Edinburgh University Press.

———. 1972. *The principles of genetic epistemology*. Trans. Wolfe Mays. London, Routledge & Kegan Paul.

Piaget, J., and R. Garcia. 1971. Explications physico-géometriques et réductionnisme. In *Les Explications causales* (vol. 26 of "Etudes d'épistémologie génétique") by J. Piaget with the collaboration of R. Garcia, pp. 141–186. Paris, P.U.F.

Piaget, J., J.-B. Grize, A. Szeminska, and Vinh Bang. 1968. *Epistémologie et psychologie de la function* (vol. 23 of "Etudes d'épistémologie génétique"), Paris, P.U.F.

Piaget, J., and B. Inhelder. 1941. *Le Developpement des quantités chez l'enfant*. Neufchâtel and Paris, Delachaux & Niestlé.

———. 1948. *La Représentation de l'espace chez l'enfant*. Paris, P.U.F.

———. 1956. *The child's conception of space*. Trans. F. J. Langdon and J. L. Lunzer. London, Routledge & Kegan Paul, reprinted 1963, 1967. New York, The Humanities Press, 1956, and Norton, 1967.

———. 1959. *La Genèse des structures logiques élémentaires*. Neufchâtel and Paris, Delachaux & Niestlé.

———. 1964. *The early growth of logic in the child. Classification and seriation*. Trans. Eric A. Lanzer and D. Papert. London, Routledge & Kegan Paul; reprinted 1970. New York, Harper & Row, 1964, and Norton, 1969.

———. 1968. (With the collaboration of H. Sinclair.) *Mémoire et intelligence*. Paris, P.U.F.

———. 1969. Mental images, in *Experimental psychology: its scope and method*. Ed. Paul Fraisse and Jean Piaget. Vol. 7, chap. 23, pp. 85–143. London, Routledge & Kegan Paul, 1969.

———. 1971. *Mental imagery in the child. A study of the development of imaginal representation*. Trans. P. A. Chilton. London, Routledge & Kegan Paul; New York, Basic Books.

———. 1973. *Memory and intelligence*. Trans. Arnold J. Pomerans. London, Routledge & Kegan Paul; New York, Basic Books.

Piaget, J., B. Inhelder, and A. Szeminska. 1948. *La Géométric spontanée de l'enfant.* Paris, P.U.F.

———. 1960. *The child's conception of geometry.* Trans. Eric A. Lunzer. London, Routledge & Kegan Paul. New York, Basic Books 1960, and Harper & Row, 1964.

Piaget, J., H. Sinclair, and Vinh-Bang. 1968. *Epistémologie et psychologie de l'identité.* Vol. 24 of "Etudes d'épistémologie génétique." Paris, P.U.F.

Piaget, J., and A. Szeminska. 1941. *La Genèse du nombre chez l'enfant.* Neufchâtel and Paris, Delachaux & Niestlé.

———. 1952. *The child's conception of number.* Trans. Caleb Gattegno and Frances Mary Hodgson. London, Routledge & Kegan Paul; reprinted 1961, 1965, 1969. New York, The Humanities Press, 1952, and Norton, 1965.

Sinclair, H. 1967. *Langage et operations.* Paris, Dunod.

Smedslund, J. 1959. Apprentissage des notions de la conservation et de la transitivité due poids. In *L'Apprentissage des structures logiques* (vol. 9 of "Etudes d'épistémologie génétique," pp. 85–124) by A. Morf, J. Smedslund, Vinh Bang, and J. F. Wohlwill. Paris, P.U.F.

———. 1961. The acquisition of conservation of substance and weight in children: III. Extinction of conservation of weight acquired "normally" and by means of empirical controls on a balance. *Scand. J. psychol., 2,* 85–87.

———. 1963a. Development of concrete transitivity of length in children. *Child develop. 34,* 389–405.

———. 1963b. Development of experience and the acquisition of conservation of length. *Scand. J. psychol., 4,* 257–264.

———. 1965. The development of transitivity of length: a comment on Braine's reply. *Child develop., 36,* 577–580.

Waddington, C. H. 1961. *The nature of life.* London, Allen & Unwin.

Wohlwill, J. F. 1959. Un essai d'apprentissage dans le domaine de la conversation du nombre. In *L'Apprentissage des structures logiques* (vol. 9 of "Etudes d'épistémologie génétique," pp. 125–135) by A. Morf, J. Smedslund, Vinh Bang, and J. F. Wohlwill. Paris, P.U.F.

———. 1968. Response to class-inclusion questions for verbally and pictorially presented items. *Child develop., 39,* 449–465.

Index

Abstraction: simple vs. reflective, 6–7; basic to logical operations, 13
Accommodation, 3, 23
Action schemes, 3
Additive identity, 31
Additive partitioning, 252
Additive relationships, 216; dominance of, 262–263
Additive-multiplicative relationships, 216, 236
Ages: of acquisition of concepts, 26; of subjects in cross-cultural studies, 120–121; of acquiring conservation of length, 125; of acquiring conservation of physical quantities, 125, 129–130. *See also* Developmental stages
Algeria, cross-cultural studies in, 117, 119–130, 270
Apostel, L., 11, 16
"Apprentissage et connaissance" (Piaget), 1
Aristotle, 254
Assimilation, 3, 4, 23; norms of, 268–269
Associations, mechanisms of, 18
Attention, changes in, and conservation, 128–129
Australia, 117
Autoregulation, 32

Behaviorists: organizational competence ignored by, 4; on knowledge, 8
Bever, T. G., 8
Biological approach to cognitive development, 2–6, 16
Biological competence, 269
Biologie et connaissance (Piaget), 5
Bovet, M., 117, 195

Braine, M. D., 132n
Bruner, J. S., 38, 39, 41, 59n, 80; on verbal training and cognitive structuring, 100, 116; cross-cultural studies of, 117, 128–130

Center for Cognitive Studies, 39
Center of Genetic Epistemology, 10. *See also* Genevan research
Chronology of conservation concepts, 246–255; vertical vs. oblique relationships, 246–247; conservation of matter, 247–252; conservation of length, 252–255
Class inclusion, 235; and conservation of matter, 171; logical nature of, 192; difficulties of, 192–198; role of language in, 195–197; role of memory in, 197–198. *See also* Inclusion, quantification of
Classes, logic of, 167, 192; and simultaneity, 192
Classification, training in, 168
Clinical method. *See* Critical exploration, method of
Cognitive constructions, 15; as hereditary, 8
Cognitive development: and experiments on learning, 1, 10–13; and competence, 5; stages of, 16; and total response, 128–130
Comparative terms, and conservation, 105–106, 112–113
Compensation of reciprocal relationships, 9, 31, 114, 133, 212, 246, 249; partial vs. complete, 261; between addition and subtraction, 262–263
Competence: stages of in development, 5; biological, 269

303